GAYLORD F

KATHERINE MANSFIELD

KATHERINE MANSFIELD

In from the Margin

Edited by ROGER ROBINSON

LOUISIANA STATE UNIVERSITY PRESS
Baton Rouge and London

Copyright © 1994 by Louisiana State University Press
All rights reserved
Manufactured in the United States of America
First printing
03 02 01 00 99 98 97 96 95 94   5 4 3 2 1

Designer: *Glynnis Phoebe*
Typeface: *Sabon*
Typesetter: *G & S Typesetters, Inc.*
Printer and binder: *Thomson-Shore, Inc.*

LIBRARY OF CONGRESS CATALOGING-IN-PUBLICATION DATA

Katherine Mansfield—in from the margin / edited by Roger Robinson
        p.   cm.
    Includes index.
    ISBN 0-8071-1865-6 (cloth)
        1. Mansfield, Katherine, 1888–1923—Criticism and interpretation.
    I. Robinson, Roger, date.
    PR9639.3.M258Z733   1994
    823'.912—dc20   93-25541
                                                            CIP

To Antony Alpers
in gratitude and admiration

Contents

Preface   *ix*

Abbreviations   *xi*

Introduction
In from the Margin   *1*
  Roger Robinson

"Finding the Pattern, Solving the Problem"
Katherine Mansfield the New Zealand European   *9*
  Vincent O'Sullivan

Katherine Mansfield and the Cult of Childhood   *25*
  Cherry Hankin

Katherine Mansfield Reading Other Women
The Personality of the Text   *36*
  Ruth Parkin-Gounelas

Katherine Mansfield and the Honourable Dorothy Brett
A Correspondence of Artists   *53*
  Gardner McFall

Contents

The Middle of the Note: Katherine Mansfield's "Glimpses" 70
SARAH SANDLEY

Reading "The Escape" 90
W. H. NEW

What the Reader Knows; or, The French One 112
PERRY MEISEL

My Katherine Mansfield 119
ALEX CALDER

The French Connection: Francis Carco 137
CHRISTIANE MORTELIER

The French Connection: Bandol 158
JACQUELINE BARDOLPH

"Finding the Treasure," Coming Home
Katherine Mansfield in 1921–1922 173
GILLIAN BODDY

Katherine Mansfield and Gurdjieff's Sacred Dance 189
JAMES MOORE

Contributors 201

Index 203

Preface

*These essays are based on a dozen of the more than sixty papers pre-*sented at two very successful centenary occasions in 1988: the Katherine Mansfield Centenary Symposium, "Life, Text, and Context," at the Newberry Library, in Chicago, and the Katherine Mansfield Centennial Conference, at Victoria University of Wellington, in New Zealand.

The convening of participants from Australia, Canada, China, France, Greece, Japan, the Netherlands, and other countries confirmed the international nature of Mansfield scholarship. The scholars who took part and the universities that made the participation possible are warmly thanked.

Many directions in Mansfield studies that aroused interest could not, regrettably, be represented here; attention to Mansfield's musical activities is an example of what had to be excluded. Some excellent imaginative work had its premiere at the time of the Centennial inspired—it is still the best word—by Mansfield: plays, dramatizations, films, poems, "remade" stories, many subsequently published. The opening of the impeccably restored Katherine Mansfield birthplace at 25 (formerly 75) Tinakori Road, in Wellington, was a significant part of the celebration.

The essays in this collection, like all work on Mansfield, owe an essential debt to the donors and custodians of her papers at the Newberry Library, in Chicago, to the Harry Ransom Humanities Research Center, at the University of Texas at Austin, and to the Alexander Turnbull Library, in Wellington. Permission to quote from papers held in these libraries is gratefully acknowledged. All previously unpublished material by Katherine Mansfield and John Middleton Murry is quoted also by generous permission of the Society of Authors, in London.

In addition to the generous hospitality all three libraries accorded, the Newberry granted Newberry Library Fellowships to several contributors, and the Turnbull mounted a major exhibit in conjunction with the Centennial.

Others in New Zealand, the United States, and Great Britain provided support of various kinds, most notably Bede Corry, Witi Ihimaera, Dr. Jock Phillips, and Willard White, as well as Dr. Michael Bassett, Sir David Beattie, Peter Boag, Gillian Boddy, Jim Collinge, Oroya Day, Helen Heazlewood, B. J. Kirkpatrick, James Moore, Vincent O'Sullivan, Kathrine Switzer, John M. Thomson, and Dr. Jim Traue. Assistance also came from Air New Zealand, the Bank of New Zealand, the Katherine Mansfield Birthplace Trust, the Katherine Mansfield Memorial Fellowship Trust, the Department of English at New York University, the Department of Internal Affairs of New Zealand, the Ministry of External Relations and Trade of New Zealand, and Victoria University of Wellington, especially its Department of English and Stout Research Centre.

Abbreviations

Alpers, *Life* Antony Alpers, *The Life of Katherine Mansfield* (London, 1980)

Collected Letters *The Collected Letters of Katherine Mansfield,* ed. Vincent O'Sullivan and Margaret Scott (4 vols. projected; Oxford, 1984–); letters herein are referenced by volume and page; letters dated after May, 1920, are referenced by date and best available published form (usually *Letters,* ed. Murry) or by date and MS location

Journal *Journal of Katherine Mansfield,* ed. J. Middleton Murry (Definitive ed.; London, 1954)

Letters, ed. Murry *The Letters of Katherine Mansfield,* ed. J. Middleton Murry (2 vols.; London, 1928)

Letters to Murry *Katherine Mansfield's Letters to John Middleton Murry, 1913–1922,* ed. John Middleton Murry (London, 1951)

Newberry Katherine Mansfield Papers, Newberry Library, Chicago

Novels and Novelists Katherine Mansfield, *Novels and Novelists,* ed. J. Middleton Murry (London, 1930)

Poems	*The Poems of Katherine Mansfield,* ed. Vincent O'Sullivan (Auckland, 1988)
Scrapbook	*The Scrapbook of Katherine Mansfield,* ed. J. M. M[urry] (London, 1939)
Stories	*The Stories of Katherine Mansfield,* ed. Antony Alpers (Definitive ed.; Oxford, 1984); references to the stories are by page number in the main text, for example, (505); all other references to the volume are in footnotes
Turnbull	Katherine Mansfield Collection, Alexander Turnbull Library, Wellington

Mansfield's punctuation in her private writings was idiosyncratic. Murry's transcription has been followed where it remains the best published version. With unpublished material, the original punctuation and spelling have been retained, without the use of *sic.*

KATHERINE MANSFIELD

Introduction
In from the Margin

ROGER ROBINSON

When Katherine Mansfield died at age thirty-four in 1923, it was seen as the sadly early end of an attractive but minor writer. When a small cult grew up, nourished by John Middleton Murry's careful husbanding of her unpublished papers, her following was still in a minor key. Hers was a small, sad legend of loss, romantic illness, and talent unfulfilled. Her story was better known than her stories.

Since then, despite some substantial biographical and editorial work, the general view of Mansfield has been the one D. H. Lawrence expressed: that she was a short-story writer who never quite graduated to the big league of the novel. Academically she has been praised for almost moving the short story up to poetry. But she has remained the literary colonial who was never quite accepted in Bloomsbury, the woman author publishing suspiciously popular stories on the fringes of a largely male Modernism. Her situation was on the margins, her roles subordinate—as the wife of John Middleton Murry (as her tombstone attests), as an imitator of Anton Chekhov, as the not-quite-friend of Virginia Woolf, as the model for a character in Lawrence, as a devotee of George Gurdjieff.

This collection of new essays, from our standpoint now, just over a century after her birth and seventy years after her death, affirms that Katherine Mansfield's stature is major and her place is at the center. Twelve essays, wide-ranging in their methodologies and philosophies, from scholars in Canada, England, France, New Zealand, and the United States, concur in finding Mansfield a substantial and crucial figure in twentieth-century culture. They show how, far from being merely imitative, she transformed the short story in English and contributed in essential ways to Modernism. The new biographical scholarship also reveals the interaction of her life and her texts to be more fruitful and more complex than was dreamt of in the old philosophy of mourning a supposedly secondary talent.

Katherine Mansfield was born on October 14, 1888, in Wellington, New Zealand, into a rising family that was relatively affluent by the standards of that small colonial town. Her childhood and adolescence there, which she thought to put behind by escaping in 1908 to the literary world of London, returned to her imagination later as the material for several of her best stories. Establishing herself as a short-story writer and reviewer, she was at all times a committed, assiduous, innovative, and deeply intelligent writer of fiction, and one of the most vital and engaging journal and letter writers in English.

She made many good friends, including significant literary and cultural figures, and was a quite frequent visitor to Lady Ottoline Morrell's artistic house parties at Garsington Manor, near Oxford. An unsettled personal life in her early years in England and Europe left her with two significant intimate relationships—with the critic and editor John Middleton Murry, with whom she lived intermittently from 1912 and whom she married in 1918, and with a Rhodesian friend of her schooldays, her devoted companion Ida Baker, most often called L.M. The death of her brother, Leslie, in the First World War in 1915 affected her deeply, at a time when she was also afflicted by tuberculosis and gonorrhea. Her last years became a quest for a home that might ease her increasing illness, and for the time and energy to write. Always nomadic, she lived with Murry or Baker in England, France, Italy, and Switzerland. Late in 1922, she sought spiritual consolation in Gurdjieff's Institute for the Harmonious Development of Man, at Fontainebleau-Avon, near Paris. She died there of hemorrhage of the lungs on January 9, 1923.

Four volumes of short stories were published during her lifetime, and a fifth shortly after her death, some 118 stories in all. Selections of her journals, scrapbooks, and letters, skillfully but partially edited by Murry, were published from the 1920s to the 1950s. The fully collected stories, edited by Antony Alpers, appeared only in 1984. Publication of the complete letters, edited by Vincent O'Sullivan and Margaret Scott, is now in progress, and that of the journals and scrapbooks is in preparation. Several pieces of fiction and much else even now remain unpublished.

A period during the First World War when Mansfield and Murry lived in Cornwall in close proximity with D. H. Lawrence and his wife, Frieda, provided Lawrence with material for the two main couples in *Women in Love*, Mansfield figuring in aspects of Gudrun. Murry's posthumous sentimentalizing of his wife is satirized in Burlap's cult of his dead child-wife Susan in Aldous Huxley's *Point Counter Point*. More recently, Mansfield's life has been dramatized and filmed, most notably in Brian Mc-Neill's *The Two Tigers*, in 1974, and Vincent O'Sullivan's *Jones and Jones*, in 1988.

Such a brief summary of a brief life gives little hint of the significance of the topics that Mansfield's work confronts or illuminates. The essays that follow examine several such concerns crucial to our century, including colonialism, migration, and exile; the First World War and the trauma it left in the international consciousness; the evolving situation and voice of women and the origins of modern feminism; marriage, sexual identity, and morality; class privilege and power; bodily illness and its literary rendering; the increasing internationalism of literature; and the interaction of literature with other art forms, among them cinema, in the Modernist movement.

These are big themes, but the texts sustain them, despite appearances. Some little girls getting a new toy now stands as one of the most potent of all the images of class encounter produced by the age of Shaw, Wells, and Lawrence. A businessman teasing a fly with ink has a place alongside "Strange Meeting" or *Goodbye to All That* in the imaginative literature of the First World War. Early dawn at an obscure colonial seaside suburb has been accruing resonance for over seventy years as an image of creation and earth's diurnal course. Mansfield's concerns were often substantial and central.

She often approached them obliquely, however, as those examples suggest. Habitually, she seemed most at ease when apparently at the edge, and her attention was drawn there, too. The social outcasts of her early stories set in New Zealand—the woman at the store, "old Underwood," the Maori who "kidnap" Pearl Button—live on the fringes of the farthest colony, the margins of the margin. Yet she published these stories in the intensely European *Rhythm* and *Blue Review* in a bid for a place in the London market and avant-garde literary world. Her three years' schooling in London and the heady taste of European culture they gave left her with an intense consciousness of the remoteness and insignificance of her place of origin, in an "undiscovered country," a "little land with no history." Those geographical constants continue a hundred years later to make New Zealand's culture an odd mix of diffidence and perverseness.

They made Mansfield's literary ways ambivalent, elusive, and perverse. Alpers, her best biographer, has written revealingly about her "uprootedness" and about the effects on a colonial of a lack of secure identity within the English class system: "The viewpoint had to be somewhere else, and somewhere insecure: it had to float."

The viewpoint floats indeed, geographically and in narrative location. Though Mansfield knew London and Paris, she rarely wrote of them. If she dealt with the pillars of the social establishment, it was at moments of dislocation and collapse, as in "Daughters of the Late Colonel," "Poison," or "The Stranger." The center fails to hold. Her people are ceaselessly on the move, traveling, wandering, often in foreign or threatening situations, as in "The Escape" or "The Little Governess." Her narration comes in very often from left field, from over the shoulder of the apparent protagonists, from Raoul Duquette or the Lady's Maid or the waiter into whose vindictive thoughts the ending of "The Little Governess" suddenly moves. The angles of vision are as unpredictable, as perverse, and as illuminating as they are in Manet or Conrad or the then newly familiar camera.

Mansfield wrote almost compulsively of outcasts, exiles, minorities, and fringe dwellers. There are the Maori ("Pearl Button") and Chinese, Old Tar and old Underwood, the lonely ("Miss Brill," "The Canary") and the dislocated (Miss Moss, in "Pictures"). Mansfield wrote of those in transition between homes ("Prelude," "The Voyage") or in frantic and fretful motion ("An Indiscreet Journey," "The Escape," "Six Years After"), of the lowest servant classes ("The Life of Ma Parker") and the poor ("The Garden Party," the untouchable little Kelveys, of "The Doll's House"), and of spinsters and rejected women (Miss Brill and Bertha and Mouse, the "elderly virgin, a pathetic creature," in "Psychology," and the doubly forlorn daughters of the late colonel).

Yet even as she touched such rejects into a central place in the imagination, Mansfield did so with an ironic agility that defies any simple conclusions about her attitudes. Her stories are no facile versions of disem-
powerment. By her mobility and multiplicity of vision, she disturbs
preconceptions and complacencies. The perspective can flip over discon-
certingly. In "Ole Underwood," a derelict's appalling act of cruelty is as
much a source of strength and release. "The Baron" presents a man as
shy and lonely as he is comically and patriarchally Teutonic. The boss in
"The Fly" reveals himself as emotionally inept and hapless while com-
mercially "stout, rosy, . . . still at the helm." Even the self-important
Stanley Burnell can suddenly be felt as a fringe dweller cast out by the
closed female ranks of his household. This is a valid though not fashionable reading of the third section of "At the Bay." As Stanley stomps off
to the office, he sees his wife "give a little skip," and the loss is like that
of the husband in "The Stranger": the one deprived of a kind parting, the
other of a joyful reunion. Mansfield's flickering cinema shifts camera, and
banishes both men to the margin of the frame, excluding them from the
light as pathetically as Miss Brill or the little Kelveys.

To read "The Stranger" as an outpouring of male marital love suddenly made to feel irrelevant is to be reminded of James Joyce's "The
Dead" and to realize that Mansfield too brought both a new fluidity and
a new intensity into the short story. Of all the accomplishments of Modernism, those in the short story have been least appreciated. Student
readers, for instance, who are fully attuned to *The Waste Land* or
Women in Love, still drift unsurely in *Dubliners* or "Prelude," which are
much less securely in the canon. Like Lawrence, readers aware of the
promise of Mansfield's stories have tended to ask, Yes, yes, but prelude
to what? But Mansfield did not need a novel to extend the boundaries of
fiction, she did not need comprehensiveness or bigness or resolution.
Rather, she worked in her own impressionist, and sometimes minimalist,
way toward obliqueness, open-endedness, discontinuous narrative, sub-
version of the concepts of wholeness and closure, and replacement of
significance by intensity.

With much less apparent labor than Virginia Woolf, Mansfield, too,
recorded the "myriad impressions" of human memory and emotions, the
moments of impulse and transition rather than the well-rounded narrative episode. Elizabeth Bowen acknowledged Mansfield's influence on the
short story and admired her skill at "isolating the moment," catching the

transient point of illumination or changed perception: Laura's in "The Garden Party," or Bertha's in "Bliss," or Our Else's in "The Doll's House" when there is the glimpse of the little lamp—and our own glimpse of the "rare smile" that that vision elicits.

Such moments of changed perception may be experiences of either growth or loss, and Mansfield is one of the century's best writers on both. Often she intertwines them, Linda Burnell's disillusionment with her pregnancy, a dead duck with a budding aloe. In "Her First Ball," Leila ends not only with the troubling question "Was this first ball only the beginning of her last ball after all?" but with radiance, lightness, and refreshed beauty. Even poor Bertha's sad discovery at the ending of "Bliss" brings new knowledge as well as new doubt, and in crying, "Oh, what is going to happen now?" she speaks truth about life for the first time and sees that "the pear tree was as lovely as ever and as full of flower and as still." These are not subversive shifts or ironies or volte-face endings but genuine dualities, equally true opposites. "The Voyage" is conducted through images of youth and growth as well as departure and loss, death brings "this miracle" to the lane behind the garden party, and the cloud covers and sails off the moon at the bay. Our Else does see the little lamp.

It is no coincidence that a volume of poems called *Moments of Vision* was published in 1917 by another writer whose centrality to Modernism is only belatedly being recognized. It is something of a platitude to say that Mansfield's prose is poetic. To compare her with Thomas Hardy, however, with his "seemings" and "discontinuous impressions," his "little ironies," "moments of vision," and "satires of circumstance," is to understand in what unlyric ways poetry and the short story were moving toward each other. "The Fly" could almost be a black-comic poem by Hardy, "The Shadow on the Stone" a wry-elusive story of lost love by Mansfield. No critic's phrase has yet fitted the boss better than Hardy's summary of the war impulse: "tickled mad by some demonic force." Perhaps it is—to anticipate where Vincent O'Sullivan's essay will begin this collection—that in the shadow of such a war, and all it implied for what Hardy called "this nonchalant universe," only such personal fragments of vision could seem worth making into literature.

Mansfield, then, is fragmentary, oblique, and "floating" habitually at the edge of human things, but in ways that can now be seen as crucial for her time, and for ours. Her "marginality" is scrutinized here largely because her own texts did so much to redefine marginality of many kinds. The redefinition the following essays seek takes them into many previously unexplored areas of her work and its contexts; yet in every case the effect is to show these to be central rather than peripheral.

O'Sullivan's overview defines and values Mansfield in relation to the First World War, and to the increasingly complex interconnection between Europe and the New World. Cherry Hankin and Ruth Parkin-Gounelas describe Mansfield's cultural contexts in other fresh ways, placing her against respectively the early-twentieth-century cult of childhood and the very different dynamic of modern women's writing, seen as making women, particularly Colette, Rachilde, and Woolf, part of the foreground of Modernism. The extensive manuscript research in Gardner McFall's study of the creative friendship between Mansfield and the painter Dorothy Brett amplifies this approach.

Examining Mansfield's "epiphanies" or "glimpses," in the light of her statements about painting, cinema, and music, Sarah Sandley shows Mansfield's responsiveness to the key developments in Modernism, and her innovativeness—slightly ahead of Joyce and Woolf in some respects, Sandley suggests—in translating them into lasting literature. Close textual reading is taken further in the contributions of W. H. New, Perry Meisel, and Alex Calder, which show how well Mansfield's stories respond to the most searching and contemporary scrutiny. That has radical implications for such familiar stories as "Je ne parle pas français," "Bliss," and "A Married Man's Story," and it moves a neglected one like "The Escape" unequivocally into the center of Modernist fictional texts.

Three of the studies relate text to biography. A "New Zealand mag writer," as Wyndham Lewis disparagingly called Mansfield—and, at that, one who was wandering sick and mostly miserable around Europe—may seem to have condemned herself to dismissal as culturally peripheral. But as her stories show, there are other ways of seeing. Christiane Mortelier and Jacqueline Bardolph float the viewpoint to France. Mortelier examines the French litterateur Francis Carco as something more than Mansfield's brief lover and satiric target. Quoted at some length, translated, and expertly discussed in detail for the first time in an English-language publication, he evinces personal and literary qualities that can be seen apart from Raoul Duquette's, and a new context is provided for "An Indiscreet Journey" and "Je ne parle pas français." Bardolph brings an equally inward eye to one of Mansfield's most important local habitations, Bandol, and shows how the writer transformed experience there into essential aspects of the story "Sun and Moon." Gillian Boddy, in the third study, adroitly tracks some of Mansfield's final peregrinations. Returning to where O'Sullivan began, to Mansfield the New Zealand European, she shows how the "pattern" may be found in Mansfield's last search for artistic and emotional home.

Last act of all, the final essay in this approximately chronological sequence considers Mansfield's dying weeks at the Institute for the Harmonious Development of Man. James Moore draws together the themes of Mansfield's womanhood, her relation to European culture, and her search for home and spirituality. To almost all her contemporaries, the choice she made to end her life among a fringe sect consigned her one last time to the margin. Moore considers her death from the point of view internal to the community among which she decided to die. Moore's conclusion is that center and fringe are not easily defined and that Mansfield's choice is not to be so lightly dismissed.

"Finding the Pattern, Solving the Problem"
Katherine Mansfield the New Zealand European

VINCENT O'SULLIVAN

At the very beginning of the Purgatorio, *Dante emerges on Easter morn-*ing from the "dead air" of the *Inferno,* and looks at the pure skies. Although he recognizes the planet Venus, what he sees is not the sky of his European readers as he turns "all' altro polo" and its "quattro stelle": "I turned to the other pole, and saw four stars never seen except by the first people." If Dante is drawing on reports by Marco Polo, the Southern Cross is inscribed in literature for the first time, and an alternative to Europe has been opened. For the Northern Hemisphere is now a "widowed place," denied the light of *quattro luci sante,* those four holy stars.[1] The south, the antipodes, becomes an ideal, somewhere closer to paradise: the *prima gente* who saw the stars would be inseparable in Dante's mind from the first parents. Some commentators, however, interpret the stars that have not been seen since Eden as the four cardinal virtues, which sometimes appear as statues in Renaissance paintings of the ideal city, the figures of Justice, Temperance, Prudence, and Mercy, with Love

1. Dante, *Purgatorio,* Canto I, 22–37.

at their center, binding the state together.[2] In any case, some of the classic conceptions in colonial discourse are apparent: opposition, reflection, difference, and the sense that there, where Europe is not, the primitive and the originary entice.

Well, we know how Europeans who read Rousseau reacted as they entered the Pacific—how the primitive and the original could cause Joseph Banks to raise his eyes from botanizing and commend the daughters of Eve, and how Herman Melville could experience another kind of frisson when he realized that the Marquesan girls decked in their fresh exotic flowers, so enticingly free of the sense of sin and time that the West waited to impose, must also have known that what were concealed in ceremonial parcels were human heads.[3] Thus the greatest writer to touch the Pacific during the nineteenth century perceived a central truth: that one cannot impose one's own expectations without fragmenting the unity of what one observes.

All New World experience impinges at some point on this bracketing between glamour and terror. It is a pattern already there before Dante looks at his stars, and it is still repeated in much "colonial" literature. I suggest that we might usefully read Euripides' *Medea* as the exemplary paradigm of New World transactions, of the exchange between the center and the borders of commerce. That drama of the foreign woman who helps her Greek husband to rise so spectacularly, who is then replaced by a younger woman and kills the new bride, her own sons, and the bride's father, is one of the theater's commanding texts on sexual revenge. One of its choruses has become celebrated for its feminist anticipations. Medea herself was depicted on Greek vase paintings as an oriental, her clothes and her skin different from those of the Greeks she lived among. It was implied that her exoticism, her not being one of us, was the key to those murders that destroy a state as much as a family. She is also a sorcerer, an expert in charms and potions. She can be neither defined nor contained by the civilized knowledge that surrounds her.

In the last decade, one of the most contentious texts in literary theory, and in a certain kind of philosophy, has been the examination by Jacques Derrida of Plato's *Phaedrus,* and that dialogue's claim that speech is ori-

2. Consider, for example, *Ideal City,* an anonymous painting from the late fifteenth century in the Walters Gallery, in Baltimore.
3. Herman Melville, *Typee* (1846), esp. Chap. XXXII.

ginary and pure, the source of true teaching and philosophical truth, whereas writing is derived, distancing, an occasion for distortion and falsehood. The crucial point is the ambivalence of the word *pharmakon,* which Plato uses of writing—a word that means poison but also cure and remedy.[4] These are meanings that on the face of it might seem mutually exclusive. But Derrida makes much of the lexical duality, of the need to have both meanings in mind in any single context. From there he elaborates his argument that our usual wish to establish particular consistent meanings will entangle us in textual problems we cannot foresee and cannot control. I mention this, which is a philosopher's business rather than mine, by way of suggesting that to look at the same word, *pharmakon,* and its cognates in Euripides' play involves us in a metaphoric pattern that is similarly ambivalent, and a potent trope for racial exchanges. It was the gift of Medea's foreignness, her exotic skill with drugs, that brought her husband Jason to eminence, made her an admirable wife and partner and a valuable member of society. As she benignly tells another Greek, "I can put an end to your childlessness, because I know such charms." But the gift the Greeks so valued is inverted as she sends a poisoned gown to the woman her husband leaves her for. "I will now anoint my gifts," she says, "with dreadful charms." What formerly served her husband will destroy him as she reverses Greek expectation and reverts to her own racial loyalties. The *pharmakon,* the gift that so contributed to the center as Jason would see it, now subverts it; a power that was thought contained and therefore usefully marginal takes over, replaces social order with anarchy. The chorus, as one would expect, sees this as deeply unnatural: "The sacred rivers are turning against themselves. Justice turns to injustice, the appointed order is confused."[5] For Medea, that reversal asserts the validity of her difference, her origins, as language as much as object is suddenly involved in undecidability. Medea's marriage vows now mean two things, just as *pharmakon* did all along.

If nothing else, literary theory has made us aware that texts are seldom univocal, and that language resists legal fixity. The Treaty of Waitangi, as we now know, was written in at least two ways at the same time. Accord-

4. Jacques Derrida, "Plato's Pharmacy," in *Dissemination,* trans. Barbara Johnson (Chicago, 1981), 61–171.

5. Euripides *Medea* 717–18, 410–11.

ing to Henry David Thoreau, in that first generation of American post-colonials, the trouble is that language is inherited, that it "executes nothing so faithfully as the will of the dead . . . *they* rule the world, and the living are but their executors."[6] When Hester Prynne, in Hawthorne's *The Scarlet Letter,* attempts to remove that defining letter *A* in the forest, it is not only the *A* of *Adultery,* and perhaps the *A* of *America,* she is anxious to be rid of. It is also the alphabet, the cage that language and inherited signs confine her to. Her attempt to claim that she can somehow become prior to expression, be free of language and definition, of course fails. Literature offers numerous examples not only of the outsider resisting imposed linguistic definitions but also of the *colonizing mind* turning on itself in spectacular ways once its categories are shaken: Joseph Conrad's Kurtz, finding Melville's frisson of terror within himself; Ernest Dowson's Englishman, returning from years of exile in Chile and jumping overboard as England comes into sight; Patrick White's Le Mesurier, cutting his throat in the desert as western metaphysics dehydrate.[7] Or for New Zealanders there is Charles Meryon as a French naval lieutenant at Akaroa for two years in 1840 who returned to work on those etchings of Paris that Baudelaire and Whistler thought the finest work of the century and who, as madness descended on him, placed whales and Maori canoes in the sky above the Ministry of Marine, and the southern Alps behind a panorama of Paris.[8] Time and again, the European mind is subverted by what expectation alone cannot prepare it for—as the New Zealand poet Allen Curnow puts it in "The Unhistoric Story," by that touching on "something different, something /Nobody counted on."[9]

The study of new or colonial literatures always compels us at some point to look at how the Medea Line, as one might call it, the moment when imposed or inherited values work against themselves, is approached skirted, erased, or redefined. Herman Melville, the year after *Moby Dick,* elaborated the image of a ship sailing down the Thames and

6. Henry Thoreau, *A Week on the Concord and Merrimack Rivers* (1849; rpr. New York, 1966), 158.

7. Joseph Conrad, *Heart of Darkness* (London, 1902); Ernest Dowson, "The Statute of Limitations," in *Dilemmas: Stories and Studies in Sentiment* (London, 1895); Patrick White, *Voss* (London, 1957).

8. For the best compendium of information on Meryon, see the illustrated catalog of the Charles Meryon Exhibition, published by the Musée de la Marine, Paris, in 1968.

9. Allen Curnow, *Selected Poems, 1940–1989* (London, 1990), 94.

setting its chronometer as it passes Greenwich.[10] As the ship sails across the globe, its crew can at any moment check the time they move farther from, an exactness they may require for certain calculations. But hour by hour, for the business on getting on with life, they watch the clock that keeps local time. Both are "true," both may be necessary, but we can live only by the second. That may be a way too of talking about a fundamental division in western thinking which colonialism lives out. For the colonial power, the person who lives by Greenwich time as it were, is inevitably a Platonist. His faith is in replication, imitations, fidelity to images that derive from a privileged source. The postcolonial just as inevitably is the example of what Aristotle speaks of in Book Six of the *Ethics,* the person who fulfills his moral being by the way he behaves in a social context at a particular historical moment. It is a notion that lies behind Hans-Georg Gadamer's assertion that we are all "thrown," as he says, into a historical context and subsequently work at modifying it; that we best understand the meaning of our being by attending to what is ready to hand.[11] That is the point I shall begin and eventually end with in my discussion of Katherine Mansfield, who started as a colonial and concluded as a Modernist, and who exemplified a third reaction to the Medea Line: rejection of the center, rejection of the borders as well, the sense of discomposure *everywhere,* the play of feeling present and absent at the same time in almost any place.

There is an entry in one of Mansfield's Wellington notebooks from December, 1907, where she imagines a story she would like to write. "About a girl in Wellington; the singular charm and barrenness of that place . . . And then to leave . . . and go to Europe. To live there a dual existence—to go back and be utterly disillusioned . . . to return (again) to London—to live there an existence so full and so strange that life itself seemed to greet her—and ill to the point of death return to W. and die there." She imagined the story would be called "Strife" and the woman would be—what else?—a half-caste. There may seem to be a certain prescience in that résumé. Only the end of the story does not square with

---

10. Herman Melville, "Chronometricals and Horologicals," in *Pierre; or, The Ambiguities* (1852), Book XIV.

11. See Hans-Georg Gadamer, "The Problem of Historical Consciousness," trans. J. L. Close, in *Interpretive Social Science: A Reader,* ed. P. Rabinow and W. M. Sullivan (Berkeley and Los Angeles, 1979).

Mansfield's own—until one remembers how she said of that collection of spiritual adventurers and Russian émigrés at Fontainebleau, "They are my own people, at last."[12] She had also called the characters in her stories "my people," as she called her own family. Antony Alpers is correct in supposing that Fontainebleau was the closest she could get to the Wellington of 1908 after all that had intervened.[13]

From any perspective, the most important public event in Mansfield's lifetime was the First World War. And it was her own perspective on that which so particularly marked her as a contemporary mind: the experience that took her from observing in her fin-de-siècle girl-in-Wellington mode that the charm of a situation "consists mainly in its instability" and that "I cannot—will not—build a house upon any damned rock," toward rephrasing the idea in a way that was central to Europe.[14]

In November, 1921, immediately after completing "The Doll's House," Mansfield began but did not finish a story called "Six Years After." It was written, as it happened, exactly six years after her brother had been killed in Belgium. Following as it did one of her most effective evocations of childhood, this new story took up a dead soldier's aging parents who are traveling at sea. In place of the burning presence of a child's lamp, one might say, there is the searing absence of the child himself. The mother is looking out from the ship's deck as she thinks "how lonely it will be when we have passed by. There will be nothing but the waves and those birds and the rain falling." That gulf, that emptiness, is what endorses the dead boy's presence in her mind. For "it seemed to her there was a presence far out there, between the sky and the water; someone very desolate and longing watched them pass and cried as if to stop them." The young man who is not there and is yet calling out then becomes the young boy telling her of a nightmare, telling her of lying in the woods covered in blackberry, calling out but unheard, "so I had to lie there forever" (508). How these details are presented exemplifies some of the devices Mansfield introduced to the English short story: the rapid transition of tenses and time levels, the future not simply anticipated but narratively held within the present, the present itself already contained in the past. It is a method Mansfield came to by hitting on the very simple

12. *Journal*, 37–38; October 24, 1922, in *Letters to Murry*, 679.
13. "[Mansfield] had been longing for years for the gregarious unthinking active life of her own extended family" (Alpers, *Life*, 378).
14. *Journal*, 15.

14

discovery that the technique of film could be applied to the short story. She was an enthusiast for the cinema, urging Dorothy Brett to join her at "the Fillums"; she acted in several movies; her letters frequently took up such images as the months that "stream by like a movie picture," and threw out such lines as "I am sorry we only saw each other for an inter-rupted moment; it was like a cinema!" One sees why the brevity of cine-matic images, their sense of transitory vividness, could appeal to a mind that habitually thought in similar terms: "How strange life is! One taps upon the counter and pays the waiter—pulls down one's veil—and goes." As she explained while writing "Prelude," she was trying "to catch that moment" which put her in mind of mornings at home, when "white milky mists rise and uncover some beauty, then smother it again and then disclose it." She went on, "I tried to lift that mist from my people and let them be seen and then to hide them again." [15]

Montage, one might even say, is the controlling method of that story, a series of discrete and disparate episodes where the emphasis is not so much on sequence as on relation—the short story, like the film, becoming as much about the way it is told as about any paraphrasable subject. It is a narrative method that particularly serves a temperament so strongly drawn to impressionism, to an insistence on the immediate at the expense of the linear, a "tremulous wisp constantly reforming itself on the stream," as her mentor Walter Pater had put it. [16] There was a Paterian note as well when the young woman in Wellington in 1908 spoke of the great wall of the town that cut her off from others. She extended that notion when she wrote to Ottoline Morrell in 1921, "How strange talk-ing is—what mists rise and fall—how one loses the other and then thinks to have found the other—then down comes another soft final curtain." [17] And so in the final brief section of the story of the bereaved parents on board ship, after the boy's last leave is told in the present continuous, there is a paragraph that begins with a row of dots, and a disruption to the narrative: ". . . But softly without a sound the dark curtain has rolled

15. To Dorothy Brett, August 11, 1922, in *Letters,* ed. Murry, II, 236; *Collected Letters,* I, 302, 320, 331. I have extended the discussion of Mansfield and the cinema in my intro-duction to *The Aloe,* ed. Vincent O'Sullivan (London, 1985). See also Sarah Sandley, "The Middle of the Note: Mansfield's 'Glimpses,'" in the present volume.

16. Walter Pater, *The Renaissance: Studies in Art and Poetry* (London, 1868), Conclusion.

17. To Ottoline Morrell, July 24, 1921, in *Letters,* ed. Murry, II, 122.

15

down. There is no more to come. That is the end of the play. But it can't end like that—so suddenly. There must be more. No, it's cold, it's still. There is nothing to be gained by waiting."

That sense of flow that Mansfield so admired in painting, the quick fluidity in what she called the "flowing shade and sunlight world," is also the flow that insists finally on isolation, on the nostalgia at the center of all impressionist art, reflecting the realization, as John Berger says in writing of Monet, that we know as we look at such pictures that what we look at can never happen again.[18] Heraclitus, at the head of Pater's famous conclusion to *Studies in the History of the Renaissance,* reminded us that we never step into the same river twice. A more rigorous accuracy could now insist that we never step into the *same* river once.

Mansfield was among the group of writers who understood early on how the First World War brought a permanent fragmentation of what living in Europe implied. Freud spoke to a Jewish discussion group in 1915 of the sense of collapse that threw one back primarily on oneself. He referred to the traditional appeal of Europe, to the advantages and attractions of civilized countries that form a reservoir of discourse and ideas, constituting a "museum," as he called it, that could offer individuals a "new and wider fatherland" than they were born to. But the Great War, on a vaster scale than might have been imagined, withdrew access to "the treasures . . . of civilised humanity."[19] Europe no longer meant what it had, and traditional values no longer held. That was why Mansfield, in reviewing Virginia Woolf's *Night and Day* in 1919, compared that novel to a great ocean liner—majestic but outmoded, no longer serviceable in a world no longer Edwardian. She spelled out her opinion of the book more clearly in a letter to John Middleton Murry: "My private opinion is that it is a lie in the soul. The war never has been, that is what its message is. . . . I feel in the *profoundest* sense that nothing can ever be the same that as artists, we are traitors if we feel otherwise."[20]

Mansfield's early reaction to her brother's death in 1915 had been a sonnet that inverted one of the most traditional of western images. "Six

18. To Dorothy Brett, December 26, 1921, in Newberry; John Berger, "The Eyes of Claude Monet," *New Society,* April 17, 1980, p. 113.

19. Sigmund Freud, "Thoughts for the Times on War and Death," in *Pelican Freud Library,* XII (Harmondsworth, Eng., 1985), 63.

20. "A Ship Comes into the Harbour" (Review of Virginia Woolf's *Night and Day*), *Athenaeum,* November 21, 1919; *Collected Letters,* III, 82–83.

Years After" has him lying under blackberry. In the poem, he offers her berries—poisoned berries she remembered from her childhood called dead-man's-bread. There is then a play on the Eucharist, the central Christian proposition on presence and absence. The bread of life for everyman, the assurance of salvation, becomes in her brother's hands instead the assuring comfort of oblivion, the young soldier coalescing with the dark Christ of death:

> By the remembered stream my brother stands
> Waiting for me with berries in his hands . . .
> "These are my body. Sister, take and eat."[21]

She wrote that poem in Bandol in early 1916, when for a time at least she considered death herself and then put her energies into finding an appropriate form for elegy, a new form, a "kind of *special prose*" as she called it: "No novels, no problem stories, nothing that is not simple, open."[22] A few days later she came on the year-old manuscript of *The Aloe*. In completing that, the longest of her fictions, then moving it into the twelve sequences of "Prelude," she hit on the narrative method V. I. Pudovkin, the early theorist of cinema, regarded as the essence of that medium—one that combines the effects of emphasis and elimination for dramatic effect. "The significance of editing," he wrote, "is of crucial importance."[23]

The method allowed her brief visits to what Freud called "this once lovely and congenial world,"[24] which the war had brought to an end. But those moments of privileged reentry had nothing to do with the massive certainties or assumptions of the novel by Virginia Woolf that Mansfield would so disbelieve in. Her scale was part of the recognition that a world had gone, and gone forever, as any postimpressionist knew. Anything like reality was no longer to be looked for in the larger social and religious structures the war had undermined, from a past that no longer related to oneself. "Do many people *really* read Dante?" she asked Virginia Woolf. "He does not write for men but for certain types of angels." Her own

---

21. "To L.H.B., 1894–1915," in *Poems*, 54.

22. *Journal*, 94.

23. V. I. Pudovkin, *Film Technique*, trans. Ivor Montago (New York, 1949), xviii. See also O'Sullivan, ed., *The Aloe*, xvii.

24. Freud, "Thoughts for the Times," 77.

world, she wrote to another friend, had contracted to a bed on which lie "a copy of Shakespeare, a copy of Chaucer, an automatic pistol, and a black muslin fan."[25] As her stories affirm over and over, reality is disclosed in how minds converge, drift apart, lose touch, come back—like the backgammon pegs as Beryl and Stanley play their game in "Prelude." It is found in images constantly on the point of becoming memory.[26] Like the poems T. S. Eliot was just beginning to write, "Prelude" offers its sense of order through the apparently random. As E. M. Forster said much later of Eliot's poems of the period, "For what, in that world of gigantic horror, was tolerable except the slighter gesture of dissent? He who measured himself against the war, who . . . said to Armadillo-Armageddon 'Avaunt' collapsed at once into a pinch of dust. But he who could turn aside to complain of ladies and drawing-rooms preserved a tiny drop of our self-respect, he carried on the human heritage."[27]

For a civilian, Mansfield saw a good deal of the war. She traveled in France frequently during it. She visited Francis Carco in the war zone, and was perhaps the first to record the effects of gassing, when she saw its victims only a few days after it had been introduced. In 1918, she was under direct bombardment for three weeks in Paris, where the German supercannon, called Big Bertha by both sides after Krupp's wife, shelled the city every eighteen minutes. Apart from her brother, several close friends died at the front. She was skeptical of the political arguments for prolonging the war, disliking David Lloyd George as much as she admired Woodrow Wilson. She saw through the Treaty of Versailles. And like Eliot and Freud, she noticed the collapse of Europe paralleled in individual lives. Although I do not wish to pursue energetically what has become the rather modish metaphor of the body as text, the text as body, it must be granted that Mansfield, in speaking of her own health, emphasized a sense of shared corruption between "the old battlefield," as she called her lungs, and a pillaged civilization.[28]

25. To Virginia Woolf [1920], *Adam International Review*, Nos. 370–75 (1972–73), 20; to Ottoline Morrell, June 23, 1921, in *Katherine Mansfield, Selected Letters*, ed. Vincent O'Sullivan (Oxford, 1989), 216.

26. This view is put more fully in the introduction to *The Aloe, with Prelude*, ed. Vincent O'Sullivan (Wellington, 1982), 9.

27. E. M. Forster, "T. S. Eliot," in *Abinger Harvest* (London, 1936), 88.

28. *Collected Letters*, II, 184. The image is taken up again in Mansfield's letter to Murry, February 4, 1922, in *Letters to Murry*, 649.

Anyone who has seen newsreels of modern war or newspaper maps with the movements of divisions reduced to dots, or for that matter has read *War and Peace* or Thomas Hardy's *The Dynasts,* must have felt how individuality is quite lost in the attendant diminution. George Steiner says, "It is that numerical scale, the daily inventory of death, which makes of 1915 the end of the European order."[29] In 1920, in "The Stranger," Mansfield presented a similar reduction when she wrote of shipboard life, "You could just see little couples parading—little flies walking up and down the dish on the grey crinkled tablecloth. Other flies clustered and swarmed at the edge" (364). If the individual appears in such reductive terms and the gigantic is credited with some kind of personal force, it is not too far to Hardy's President of the Immortals concluding his sport with Tess, or to Lear's wanton boys godlike killing flies for sport.[30] And we are also in the region of Mansfield's own great war story, "The Fly." She told a friend the story was about a bank manager, and the man in the story is called "the boss"—what she called her father. The patriarchal linkage is fairly obvious. That there are also a poem, a kind of semicomic Hardyesque fantasy, in which the "Great God" destroys the "tiny god," and another poem in which she imagines herself sitting on God's knee like a child on her father's, establishes a pattern we cannot miss: Father—Boss—God—Fate.[31] The fly itself was one of her consistent metaphors for bad luck and ill health. Alpers argues that a notebook entry for the last day of 1918 was written after her doctor told her that what she had for years thought was rheumatism was in fact gonorrhea: "4.45pm: Fly: Oh the times when she had walked upside down on the ceiling, run up glittering panes, floated on a lake of light, flashed through a shiny beam. And God looked upon the fly fallen into the jug of milk and saw it was good. And the smallest Cherubims and Seraphims of all who delight in misfortune struck their silver harps and shrilled, 'How is the fly fallen, fallen.'"[32]

There is also her remark, in 1918, that she saw a ship on the horizon,

29. George Steiner, *In Bluebeard's Castle* (London, 1971), 31.

30. "The President of the Immortals . . . had ended his sport with Tess" (Thomas Hardy, *Tess of the d'Urbervilles* [London, 1891], final paragraph); "As flies to wanton boys, are we to the gods,/They kill us for their sport" (*King Lear,* IV, i, 38–39).

31. "Waves" (written in 1916), in *Poems,* 48–49; "To God the Father" (written in 1912), *ibid.,* 37.

32. Alpers, *Life,* 289; *Journal,* 153.

"*inevitable . . . dead silent . . .* like the spot on a lung."[33] The war, as she said, was in all of us—a thought that may have been vivid enough in February, 1922, when she was writing "The Fly" in Paris while Dr. Manoukhin's treatment "bombarded," as they medically said, the spleen with X rays.

"The Fly" asserts the superiority of the strong over the weak, the healthy over the ill. The boss exults over a sick colleague, then, alone, watches the fly he picks from an inkwell. "The horrible danger was over; it had escaped; it was ready for life again" (533)—as Mansfield too would assure Murry during the treatment. But the boss has other plans, letting fall on "the newcleaned body another dark drop." The fly dies, the boss forgets the child he had been thinking about. The last sentence reads, "For the life of him, he could not remember." His presence has been confirmed by the absence he has engineered.

I am not pressing for a simple biographical reading of this story. But all biography is text, after all, as much as fiction is, and a reader may pass from one to the other without large claims of psychological uncovering. One is simply remarking on the continuity of pattern between text and text, the commerce of signs appropriate to both. That paradigm of wounding I've touched on is pervasive. It is dominant in Mansfield's last poem:

> Oh, waters—do not cover me!
> . . . .
> O my wings—lift me—lift me
> I am not so dreadfully hurt . . .[34]

That was written in Switzerland in July, 1922, within a few days of her last story, "The Canary," a deliberately sentimental narrative in which a caged bird gives "a flick, a shake," and then begins to sing what is both joyful and inexpressibly sad, suggesting a sadness not of external forces but of something intrinsic. "It is there," the story says, "deep down, deep down, part of one, like one's breathing" (541). Franz Kafka's story "The Penal Colony" comes to mind, where the bodies of criminals

33. *Collected Letters*, III, 36.
34. "The Wounded Bird," in *Poems*, 82.

are deeply tattooed with their crimes, so that the sentences of their lives are literally the discourse they die from.

In the same month that Mansfield wrote "The Fly," she reread *Antony and Cleopatra,* commenting on the image of a weed that "rots itself with motion" as it drifts upon the stream. "That is terrible," she wrote, "that '*rots* itself' . . . . And the idea of 'it' returning and returning. . . . You may think you have done with it for ever, but comes a change of tide and there is that dark streak reappeared. . . . I understand that better than I care to. I mean—alas!—I have proof of it in my own being."[35] She felt the war intrinsically in the same way. "It is never," she said, "out of my mind and everything is poisoned by it. It's *here in* me the whole time, eating me away."[36] There is not so much a logical sequence to this way of thinking as a focusing of reactions, a breaking of categories. If one was not also Europe and the war, one was not coughing, not ill, not wounded, not a living, dying, contemporary woman.

It seems to me that one might envisage Mansfield as living out in an exemplary way the thinking of her close contemporary Martin Heidegger. As he formulated the primary text of existentialism, the German philosopher asked whether there was any way to grasp at the wholeness of human being rather than at strayed and scattered bits. Was there any way, Mansfield continually put to herself in her last year or so, any way to reach beyond a life "*in glimpses* only," as she described her own?[37] How was one to be free of one's physical and moral limitations? As Heidegger argued, freedom is not a state we aspire to for some other time. Rather, it exists at this moment, in what we make of the tensions that variously define us—our history, family, and country, but also our body, our passing moods. Mansfield always sought the momentary, the adventitious, the historical drift, in her life. But what was she to make of things from 1920, when it became fairly clear that she was dying? Heidegger

---

35. To J. M. Murry, February 8, 1922, in *Letters to Murry,* 653. The lines from Shakespeare that Mansfield referred to:

> Like to a vagabond flag upon the stream,
> Goes to and back, lackeying the very tide,
> To rot itself with motion.
>
> (*Antony and Cleopatra,* I, vi, 45–47)

36. *Collected Letters,* II, 54.
37. To J. M. Murry, May 23, 1921, in *Letters to Murry,* 637.

would answer that to isolate the recognition of one's own death is itself
an assertion of freedom, the "freedom to death."[38] Only in that instant
of shedding, as it were, are we free of false selves, cherished illusions, the
absurdity of circumstance. It is a moment often enough achieved in the
letters of Mansfield's last years, as she faced and accepted the prospect of
dissolution: "I believe the greatest failing of all is *to be frightened*. . . .
Was that why I had to look on death? Would nothing less cure me? You
know, one can't help wondering, sometimes . . . No, not a personal God
or any such nonsense. Much more likely—the soul's desperate choice."[39]

Mansfield was never happier than in her last two months at Fontainebleau. But that had little to do with George Gurdjieff. He was kind to
her, and she respected him, but he was not her guru. True to form, she
referred to him in passing as the "rug merchant." But at Fontainebleau
she arrived at her own conception of time, which had always obsessed
her. She came to an acceptance of the existential point that A. J. Ayer has
said was made in a general way by the war of 1914–1918: that man no
longer moves *meaningfully* within history or even place, that there are no
sustaining or metaphysical frameworks, and that true responsibility is
grounded, rather, in the structure of personal time.[40] She had sailed close
to this recognition years before, but from an aesthetic tack, when Henri
Bergson's claim for the artist's subverting mechanistic time had shaped
the editorial views of Murry's *Rhythm*, as well as providing his magazine
with its name. That, in existentialism's insistent word, was authenticity.
Mansfield's last months offer vividly enough an applied instance of that,
even as Heidegger's great theoretical text was being written. As Mansfield
turned from Europe (How small a part of our minds we use in the West,
she said), as she turned from English intellectualism (Dig the garden, she
told Murry, play less chess), as she learned her few phrases of Russian
for the things that mattered materially, she wrote in one of her last letters
to Murry of a hope that had nothing to do with happiness or health or

38. Martin Heidegger, *Being and Time*, trans. J. Macquarrie and E. S. Robinson (London, 1962), Sec. 2. See also the discussion of death by Magda King in *Heidegger's Philosophy* (Oxford, 1964), and by James M. Demske in *Being, Man, and Death: A Key to Heidegger* (Lexington, Ky., 1970).

39. To J. M. Murry, October 18, 1920, in *Letters to Murry*, 567.

40. A. J. Ayer, "Some Aspects of Existentialism," quoted by Alasdair MacIntyre in "Existentialism," in *The Encyclopedia of Philosophy* (8 vols.; New York, 1967), III, 153.

love or success as a writer but had a great deal to do with what existentialism was to call being "properly historical" and adopting the role that gives meaning to time, that prevents the fear of time's overwhelming her, as it did in one of her letters, where "my little watch raced round and round, and the watch was like a symbol of imbecile existence." But now she said, "If I were allowed one single cry to God, that cry would be: *I want to be* REAL." Here is both Mansfield's final text and the direction of existential thought, that insistence on the real and the authentic, the act of mind that transforms necessity into resolution. It is the awareness with which Nikos Kazantzakis would write his monumental epitaph: "I hope for nothing. I fear nothing. I am free." Mansfield put it in different words two weeks before she died: "This place . . . has taken from me one thing after another (the things never were mine) until at this present moment all I know really, really is that I am not annihilated."[41]

When Mansfield wrote, "finding the pattern, solving the problem"—the words I have taken as my title—it was as a twenty-one-year-old New Zealander confronting European history in framing a poem to Stanislaw Wyspiansky, the Polish writer, artist, and patriot. She was "from a little land with no history," as she saw it,

> Making its own history, slowly and clumsily
> Piecing together this and that, finding the pattern,
>   solving the problem,
> Like a child with a box of bricks.[42]

The existential hint is already there, the emphasis on what one does rather than what one inherits—on facticity, as Heidegger will call it, the fact that we live in a world pragmatically defined but whose meaning we make as we go along. There is something overtly dramatic in this, just as there is something that isolates one in a continual performance to oneself. The role refutes expected lines and simple categories: Medea knows that nowhere is as it was, that anywhere is as one makes it, that boundaries are in the way one says it. To read Mansfield's body of stories, letters, poems, and notebooks in order to question her technical inventiveness,

41. J. M. Murry, December 26, 1922, in *Letters to Murry*, 698.
42. "To Stanislaw Wyspianski," in *Poems*, 30.

her deft shifts in thought and presentation, for what is New Zealand in them, what European, is limited and parochial. What seems to me of far more interest is to hear a modern, extremely clear, extremely tested twentieth-century voice.[43]

43. This paper, in slightly different form, was delivered in conjunction with the Katherine Mansfield Centennial Conference, at Victoria University of Wellington, on October 11, 1988, and was published in 1989 as No. 7 of Victoria University of Wellington Inaugural Addresses, New Series.

Katherine Mansfield and the Cult of Childhood

Cherry Hankin

Time and again over the years, detractors of John Middleton Murry have pointed to Aldous Huxley's satiric portrait of him as Burlap in *Point Counter Point,* suggesting that it contains, in the way of any good caricature, more than a germ of truth. Less commented upon is whether there is justice in Huxley's representation of Katherine Mansfield as Burlap's childlike dead wife, Susan. "Thank you, thank you for your memories of what I have always felt to be the *realest* Susan," Burlap writes to a well-wisher after her death, "the little girl who survived so beautifully and purely in the woman, to the very end; the lovely child that in spite of chronology she always was, underneath and parallel with the physical Susan living in time. In her heart of hearts, I am sure, she never quite believed in her chronological adult self; she could never quite get it out of her head that she was a little girl playing at being grown up." Huxley added, "And so it went on—pages of a rather hysterical lyricism about the dead child-woman."[1]

Mansfield's admirers in the decade following her death would hardly

---

1. Aldous Huxley, *Point Counter Point* (1928; rpr. Harmondsworth, Eng., 1975), 170.

have noticed the malice behind Huxley's view of her as little more than a grown-up child, for what the sardonic Huxley and his literary friends perceived as a serious weakness in Mansfield's personality they found positively enchanting. Writing in the *Dalhousie Review* in 1930, for example, C. W. Stanley noted with satisfaction that Mansfield's directness was that of a child, "wondering about some of the mysteries of life; the child curious, disgusted and thrilled—but not wicked or abnormal—just a child, hurt at the wickedness and selfishness of this world, and deeply wounded by the cruelty of life."[2] His views were more than shared by George Harper, who observed about the same time in the *Quarterly Review* that "little girls up to the age of eight or nine are surely the sweetest and most winsome creatures in the world. Imagine such a little girl, bright and curious, clearsighted and honest, and keeping all her laughing, childish ways, but also enriched with the experience of a grown woman who has read and travelled and conversed with interesting people, and suffered deeply; give her also a genius for the use of language; and you have Katherine Mansfield."[3]

The problem for Mansfield's image was that when the tide turned against Edwardian romanticism, the adulatory responses of people like Stanley and Harper gave way to much sharper critical assessments. Taking a cold, hard look at her in the light of modern psychology, other readers found, as Huxley had done, that the cult of childhood was ultimately unprofitable. By 1940, Louise Bogan was writing in the *New Republic,* "It was not only childishness, but the neurotic love of childishness which gave poignance to many of [Mansfield's] effects. . . . It was this purity which makes her finest stories what they are. But childhood prolonged cannot remain a fairyland. It becomes a hell."[4] In 1951, even Sylvia Berkman admitted, "The world Miss Mansfield has created is constructed by a woman's intellect out of the emotional apprehension of a child."[5] In 1963, Frank Swinnerton, who had known—and not disliked—Mansfield in the days of *Rhythm* and the *Blue Review,* was still more forthright: "Nobody knew what passed in Katherine's mind. It was egocentric; and it had two chief preoccupations, Art and her own un-

2. C. W. Stanley, "The Art of Katherine Mansfield," *Dalhousie Review,* X (1930), 37.
3. George Harper, "Katherine Mansfield," *Quarterly Review,* CCLIII (1929), 385.
4. Louise Bogan, "Katherine Mansfield," *New Republic,* CII (1940), 415.
5. Sylvia Berkman, *Katherine Mansfield: A Critical Study* (New Haven, 1951), 195–96.

matured childishness. . . . Katherine's mind remained unaffected by her experience. She never grew up."[6]

Whatever behavior Mansfield displayed as a younger woman, she finally repudiated the self that, like Beryl's in "Prelude," sought childlike refuge in playacting. "I'm always acting a part. I'm never my real self for a moment," the fictional Beryl reproached herself (258). In 1922, Beryl's creator similarly faced up to her failings. "Let me take the case of K.M.," she wrote in her journal. "She has led, ever since she can remember, a very typically false life."[7] Mansfield's self-scrutiny toward the end of her life was searching. It is all the more important, therefore, to try to put into perspective the cult of childhood that, for better or worse, has dogged critical opinion about both her personality and her writing.

Although Mansfield came to be known as a modernist writer whose intellectual links were with the avant-garde, she grew up in the late Victorian and Edwardian periods. The child of conventional middle-class parents who—unlike those of Virginia Woolf and Huxley—were not intellectuals, she received as part of her literary inheritance a rather romantic, sentimental ideal of childhood. The comments of Stanley and Harper reveal that the Edwardian idealization of children persisted until well after her death, even among educated people. The reasons were both literary and social. Charles Dickens' influence remained powerful in the first decades of the twentieth century. Dickens' fiction championed all the children in the world, as it were, who were mistreated or misunderstood by adults. Part of the appeal of Dickens' children, to Mansfield's generation as well as her parents', was that in spite of, or perhaps because of, being neglected or abused by adults, they somehow seemed morally and spiritually superior to them. Mansfield titled a schoolgirl story about an abandoned but musically gifted child "Misunderstood." When the elderly Lord Hunter hears the little girl singing "Ave Maria" in the hospital, "the same sense of awe and wonder filled him as . . . before."[8] Mansfield's juvenilia and her letters and notebooks reveal that her addiction to Dickens, especially to the semiautobiographical *David Copperfield*, extended through most of her life. Given Huxley's portrayal of her as Bur-

6. Frank Swinnerton, *Figures in the Foreground: Literary Reminiscences, 1917–1940* (London, 1963), 60.
7. *Journal*, 330.
8. In Turnbull.

lap's dead child-wife, it is interesting that she was especially attracted to David Copperfield's child-wife, Dora. In *The Aloe,* written in 1915, the character of Doady Trout makes up melodramatic stories in which, with the aid of Dickens, she plays the part of Dora. Doady fantasizes, "'your child lives *but*'—and here the nurse pointed one finger upwards like the illustration of Agnes in *David Copperfield*—'your wife is no more.'" Mansfield frequently asked in her letters to Murry that he send copies of Dickens' novels, and more than once in 1918 she described herself to Lady Ottoline Morrell as "feeling rather like David Copperfield's Dora."[9]

Dickens' preoccupation with children, however, was merely one strand in the romantic revival at the turn of the century. Nostalgia for lost childhood, for time past and for a rapidly vanishing age of innocence all coalesced in Edwardian England. During that period people felt—rather desperately—the need to play. To think of themselves as still children was to give themselves permission to do so—and to push into the background the troubles of adulthood, the intimations of looming war, and the knowledge of mortality. Childhood became the fashionable focus of an escapist looking-back toward a more carefree time. Safely penned up in the nursery, the child seemed to writers and readers alike to possess a simplicity, innocence, and vision of life untainted by adult experience. In an almost Wordsworthian sense, children were seen to enjoy closer contact with the natural world than adults. Because their minds were intellectually undeveloped, moreover, they had the advantage of responding, through a kind of natural instinct, or Bergsonian intuition, to unseen forces in their environment, whether mystical or supernatural.

It was no accident, therefore, that a good many books written ostensibly for children found favor with adults. Among the great successes in the genre were *Alice in Wonderland, Treasure Island, Puck of Pook's Hill, Rewards and Fairies,* and later, *The Young Visiters.* But by far the most successful and influential literary work about children to appear in the Edwardian period was J. M. Barrie's play *Peter Pan,* which was staged almost every Christmastime for some thirty years after its opening in 1904. The great appeal of the play to Mansfield's generation was its central fantasy: that of remaining a child forever, of never growing up and, hence, of never dying. "One does not criticise this play, one renews one's

9. *Collected Letters,* II, 24.

youth in it," wrote a contemporary reviewer. Another epitomized the Edwardian romanticizing of children when he said, "The secret of the charm of *Peter Pan* [is] the beautiful child's world of the fairy, so far removed from the cold, commercial and bitter world that has long lost fairyland because it has long lost its childhood innocence."[10] Such was the attraction of the play with its cast of children and fairies that other writing of the early twentieth century came to abound with references to fairies—and to *Peter Pan*. Some intellectuals ridiculed the cult. Huxley has Mark Rampion say of Walter Bidlake in *Point Counter Point,* "The man's a sort of Peter Pan—much worse even than Barrie's disgusting little abortion."[11] But others, including Swinnerton, mentioned fairies quite seriously.

Mansfield, as a young, impressionable writer, was no exception. A notebook entry for 1906 refers to the "fairy tales that she devoured voraciously during her childhood,"[12] and in 1910 she entitled a fantasy story, which Murry later turned down for *Rhythm,* simply "A Fairy Story." But though some of her early pieces do contain uncanny echoes of children's fairy stories, it is in her focus upon children as literary material that the Edwardian influence chiefly manifests itself. As an adolescent in 1903, Mansfield was conforming to the spirit of the age when, on her way to school in England, she wrote "Little Fern Fronds." The subject matter of these singsong, sentimental verses about children who are unhappy or on the verge of death had the complete approval of ordinary middle-class Edwardians. Riding the fashion, Mansfield during the next year contributed two conventional little child stories to the school magazine: "The Pine Tree, the Sparrow, and You and I," and "Your Birthday." Even after her return to New Zealand in 1907, she—perhaps inspired by Robert Louis Stevenson's *A Child's Garden of Verses*—was still writing child verses that she admitted to herself were artificial in their inspiration. A journal entry for June 1907 reads, "And I have written a book of child-verse. How *absurd!* But I am very glad; it is too exquisitely unreal." A little later she noted, "I do not think I shall ever be able to write any child-verse again. The faculty has gone, I *think.*"[13] Mansfield then made

10. Patrick Braybrooke, *J. M. Barrie: A Study in Fairies and Mortals* (London, 1924), 122.

11. Huxley, *Point Counter Point*, 137.

12. "Juliet," *Turnbull Library Record*, III (March, 1970), 25.

13. *Journal*, 15, 17.

the momentous decision to become "ultra-modern." Although that did not prevent her from writing about children again, it did turn her away from the facile Edwardian idealization of children in fiction toward a far more profound and "modern" psychological investigation of the workings of a child's mind.

In her subsequent writing, Mansfield, like Woolf, broke decisively from Edwardian convention and in so doing assured herself a permanent place in English literature. Nevertheless, hers was a complex personality, and it sometimes suited her, in what she called her "public rooms," to pander to the typical romantic view of children. It especially suited her, on occasion, to play—to her own advantage—the role of the winsome if demanding little girl. As a vulnerable young woman adrift in London, interested in the theater, certainly aware of Barrie's popular play, she often did act the part of a female Peter Pan, of an adult who retains all the innocence and charm of the child who has never grown up. What the role conveniently masked from her admirers, as pieces like "Brave Love" demonstrate, was a certain ruthlessness, a willingness to use other people for her own ends. Indeed, the deception worked so well that it became almost a part of her personality. William Orton says of his meeting with her in 1910 that a sort of instant recognition passed between them when she suddenly asked, "Do you believe in Pan?" Orton makes the telling observation in his autobiography that although she often perceived inanimate objects as possessing human qualities, just as a child might perceive its toys, "she was not really fond of [children]."[14] If Mansfield affected, rather than felt, a fondness for them, that was as much as anything because, like Linda Burnell, the immature mother in "Prelude," she was emotionally in competition with them. Nowhere is her real attitude to children more evident than in an early fictional fragment she wrote about an ambitious singer, Elena, and her young son, Peter. Elena's sole interest in Peter is in the attention he draws to her. She admits to herself that "there is always something wonderfully touching in the sight of a young mother with a delicate child—and when the mother is beautiful and radiant . . . then the sight is enough to melt the most frozen heart."[15]

Observers like Swinnerton saw through her behavior, but acting on

14. William Orton, *The Last Romantic* (New York, 1937), 271.
15. *Turnbull Library Record*, V (May, 1972), 22.

occasion in a childlike manner did win the adult Mansfield sympathy. Lady Ottoline Morrell wrote in her memoirs, "Hidden away behind her mask there was a passionate desire for sympathy, a desire which she would not allow herself to indulge in. If it was offered to her it was as a gift is offered to a lonely child, who couldn't quite believe in it, and would hide it away, to keep it for herself alone, to take out and look at when alone, and perhaps to break it to see if it was real." [16] Playing the child also became, as Mansfield grew older, a way of burying the sins of her past, of privately disowning the side of her personality that as a precocious young woman had committed sexual indiscretions she preferred to forget. She wrote in Orton's notebooks, "I am become a little child again. I know not the world, the flesh and the devil. . . . It is not that I wish so much to renounce the world—it has gone. I have left it." [17] She joined in the fantasy of the child upon whom is somehow conferred an innocence and grace that are denied to grown-ups.

To quite some extent, Mansfield's early relationship with John Middleton Murry was built upon a sharing of that fantasy. The game of being each other's playfellows, of being children together, enabled them to avoid feeling trapped by the traditional roles and responsibilities of husband and wife; it also united them against the rest of the world in a childish secret society of two. Their correspondence from 1913 onward is full of references to their perception of each other as children. As their lives became more troubled, the game became, if anything, more important. In 1915, after Mansfield's brother's death, Murry consoled her in Bandol, "For you and I are not of the world, darling; we belong to our own kingdom, which truly is when we stand hand in hand, even when we are cross together like two little boys. Somehow we were born again in each other, tiny children, pure and shining, with large sad eyes and shocked hair, each to be the other's doll." [18] She responded happily, "How I love you—we are two little boys walking with our arms (which won't quite reach) round each others shoulders & telling each other secrets & stopping to look at things." [19] And as if she and Murry were Peter

16. *Ottoline at Garsington: The Early Memoirs of Lady Ottoline Morrell, 1915–1918,* ed. Robert Gathorne-Hardy (London, 1974), 166–67.

17. Quoted in *Journal,* 48.

18. Cherry A. Hankin, ed., *Letters Between Katherine Mansfield and John Middleton Murry* (New York, 1991), 66.

19. *Collected Letters,* I, 220.

Pan and Wendy on the island in Barrie's Never-Never Land, she in the same letter proposes that they should "keep very close together . . . and make ourselves, on our island, a palace and gardens and arbours and boats for you." Playing Peter Pan to his harmless pirate, she wrote a few days later, "A *third* ship is coming in & you are walking on the deck in your corduroy trousers & spanish boots—an Awful Knife in your sash."[20] She also declared, "We are still quite babies enough to play with dolls."

After 1918, as Mansfield became more ill, the pattern changed. The couple played a little more desperately, using the Japanese dolls, Ribni and O'Hara San, as symbols of their continuing childlike love. It is ironic that when Mansfield's health made it physically impossible for her to bear children, she embarked with Murry on a significantly different version of their fantasy game. Instead of playing the role of childlike playmates, they took to acting out, in their correspondence, the game of father and mother. She told Murry in December, 1917, "You will have to have two homes & we shall have to have all our babies in pairs, so that we possess a complete 'set' in either place."[21] Their children—and their go-betweens when relations became strained—were the dolls, later joined by their cat, Wingley, and his companion, Athy.

By December, 1919, however, Mansfield was too ill and unhappy to maintain any longer the pretense that she and Murry were two independent children who had chosen each other as playfellows in the game of life. After a serious quarrel, she grimly faced in her private journal the recognition that she could no longer act the role of the whimsical child. She had become a dependent woman who needed to lean both emotionally and financially, as a wife, upon the man she had married: "We'd been *children* to each other, openly confessed children, telling each other everything, each depending equally upon the other. . . . Then this illness—getting worse and worse, and turning me into a woman and asking him to put himself away and to *bear* things for me. He stood it marvellously. It helped very much because it was a romantic disease (his love of a "romantic appearance" is *immensely* real) and also being "children" together gave us a practically unlimited chance to play at life, not to live. It was child love."[22]

20. *Ibid.*, 224.
21. *Ibid.*, 357.
22. *Journal*, 183–84.

In a sense, Mansfield was being absolutely truthful when she later described the withering of romantic love between her and Murry as the killing of a child: "I'd say we had a child—a love-child, and it's dead. We may have other children, but this child can't be made to live again. J. says: Forget that letter! How can I? It killed the child—*killed* it *really* and *truly* for ever as far as I am concerned. Oh, I don't doubt that, if I live, there will be other children, but there won't be that child." [23] In her subsequent letters, the child imagery cropped up from time to time, but it is significant that it was no longer herself she represented as a child, it was Murry. Addressing him, "My silly little Trot," and "Darling little fellow," and "My precious little Paper Boy," she told him on one occasion, "I always rejoice when you buy clothes. When I am rich you will have such lovely clothes all real lace and silk velvet . . . just wait." [24]

Because Mansfield was an intensely autobiographical writer, her personal attitudes to life are echoed in her fiction. For instance, her 1914 story "Something Childish but Very Natural" prefigures remarkably the change that took place in her relationship with Murry in 1920. The idyllic—because childlike—companionship of a young couple, Henry and Edna, is ruined by Henry's desire for a more normal, adult relationship. "The Little Governess," written in 1915, is the harshest of several stories that Mansfield wrote on the subject of women who through willfulness or circumstances continue to see themselves as and act like children rather than adults. There runs through "Bliss" and "Marriage à la Mode," with their pitiless focus on female protagonists who persist in behaving like children rather than as wives and mothers, a vein of satire worthy of Huxley himself. And although Mouse, the child-woman in "Je ne parle pas français," and the aging sisters who have never grown up in "Daughters of the Late Colonel" are presented sympathetically, nothing mitigates the hopelessness of their situations.

Understanding only too well the psychology of the child-woman, Mansfield presented it brilliantly in fiction with a somber message the very antithesis of Barrie's. One of her greatest gifts as a writer was in thinking herself unsentimentally into the mental processes of actual children. What is so ironic is that even as she played at being a grown-up

23. *Ibid.*, 187.
24. *Collected Letters*, III, 218. "My silly little Trot" is another allusion to *David Copperfield*—to David's childhood nickname, Trotwood.

child with Murry, she was writing stories that broke away, in the main, from the stereotyped portrayal of children in Edwardian literature. In a range of works, from "New Dresses" and "The Little Girl," of 1912, to "Prelude" and such later New Zealand stories as "At the Bay," "The Voyage," and "The Doll's House," Mansfield extended the boundaries of adult fiction by representing children realistically, from the perspective of their own psychology.

It can be fairly concluded that Huxley's lightly sketched caricature of Mansfield in *Point Counter Point* bears some resemblance to the reality. She, like other Edwardians, indulged in a romantic longing for the lost innocence of childhood—especially her own childhood. The trouble is that Huxley seized on only half the truth. While recognizing the Edwardian side of her personality, he completely ignored the modern. To Mansfield's credit, it was the tough-minded Modernist who finally prevailed, both in her writing and ultimately in her relations with Murry.

Katherine Mansfield's famous phrase "the defeat of the personal" probably refers to the symbolic killing of the "dream child" she had shared with Murry. After the fantasy they had shared became no longer sustainable, she turned away from playing a child to re-creating, in fictionalized form, the child she imagined herself to have been. What her journal entries reveal is that she displaced the intensity of the emotions she had once bestowed upon her husband to the life she had known as a young girl. Free now to recollect in tranquillity the people and places of her childhood, she also wondered aloud about her lifelong preoccupation with childhood: "Is it not possible that the rage for confession, autobiography, especially for memories of earliest childhood, is explained by our persistent yet mysterious belief in a self which is continuous and permanent. . . . This is the moment which, after all, we live for, —the moment of direct feeling when we are most ourselves and least personal."[25]

Toward the end of her life, as she engaged in a bout of intense self-examination, honesty became her credo. "O those that come after me, will you believe it?" she wrote. "At the end *truth* is the only thing *worth having*."[26] The truth that admirers and critics alike of Mansfield must accept is that her life was marked by a complex pattern of personal and

25. *Journal,* 205.
26. *Ibid.,* 185.

artistic development. In an age when adults looked back sentimentally to their own lost childhood—epitomized by *Peter Pan*—she fantasized along with the best of them. But the remarkable thing is that while in real life she was playing the game of let's-pretend-we're-children, she was mastering in her stories the art of depicting fictional children as if they were actual living beings. Katherine Mansfield's achievement is that in giving such children in her stories as Kezia, Lottie, and Isabel Burnell their own distinctive inner life, as well as recognizably childlike speech and behavior, she transformed utterly the representation of children in adult English fiction.

Katherine Mansfield Reading Other Women
The Personality of the Text

RUTH PARKIN-GOUNELAS

Katherine Mansfield and other women: the alignment does not on the face of it seem very promising. We know all about the backbiting and the disloyalties. And apart from a passing gesture of teenage support for the suffragette movement (*"excellent* for our sex—kicked policemen or not kicked policemen"),[1] Mansfield made no overt commitment either to female solidarity or to a tradition of women's writing, in the way, for example, Virginia Woolf did. Not unnaturally, literary models for her work have been looked for in a predominantly male tradition: Theocritus (Antony Alpers), Anton Chekhov (Mansfield herself, and numerous others), A. R. Orage (Claire Tomalin), and the confessional tradition from Jean Jacques Rousseau to Marcel Proust (Cherry Hankin).[2]

When Mansfield insisted in later years that she was "a writer first and a woman after,"[3] she was expressing not so much the priorities of her life

---

1. *Collected Letters,* I, 47.
2. Mansfield referred to herself, in a doggerel verse on the flyleaf of a volume of Chekhov's stories, as the "English Anton T." See Gillian Boddy, *Katherine Mansfield: The Woman and the Writer* (Ringwood, Austl., 1988), 174.
3. Alpers, *Life,* 323.

choices as the sense, shared by most women writers, of the unhappy fellowship of femaleness and artistic endeavor. It was all very well to espouse radical feminism as a young woman needing to shock parochial Wellington. But as a mere colonial and outsider in London, Mansfield had a vested interest in channeling her energies toward her acceptance as an artist first and foremost, without taking on the whole question of the eligibility of women in the pantheon of Art. Her ridicule of a suffragette meeting to Garnet Trowell in 1908, within a month of arriving in London, is characteristic of the insecurity of marginalization seeking applause for disloyalty.[4]

But if Mansfield denied women her waking allegiance, her dreams and daydreams, narrated in letters and the journal, allowed them a different kind of hearing. Of the women writers who figure in these narrations, each appears to have stimulated a different aspect of her conscience. George Sand evoked a language of vague mystical sisterhood: "Had a strange dream. 'She is one with the moonlight.' George Sand—ma soeur."[5] With the Brontë sisters, she seems to have shared a sense of the rigor, isolation, and bleakness of the female literary condition: "I dreamed that I went to stay with the sisters Bronte who kept a boarding house called the Bronte Institut—*pain*fully far from the railway station and all the way there through heather. It was a sober place with linoleum on the stairs. Charlotte met me at the door & said 'Emily is lying down.'"[6] There was also Colette, who conjured up one particular daydream in the arch, fey mood Mansfield cultivated on certain occasions:

> I should like to be at a large circus tonight, in a box—very luxurious, you know, very warm, very gay with a smell of sawdust & elephants. A superb clown called Pistachio—white poneys, little blue monkeys drinking tea out of Chinese cups—I should like to be dressed beautifully, beautifully, down [to] the last fragment of my chemise, & I should like Colette Willy to be dressed just exactly like me and to be in the same box. And during the entr'actes while the orchestra blared Pot Pourri from The Toreador we

4. *Collected Letters*, I, 60.

5. *Journal*, 198. Mansfield seems to have regarded Sand as a type of the endurance of female creativity, telling Murry in 1918 that a young doctor "made me feel like an old writing woman—a sort of old George Sand tossed up by the tide last night" (*Collected Letters*, II, 176).

6. *Collected Letters*, I, 178.

would eat tiny little jujubes out of a much too big bag & tell each other all about our childhood.[7]

In 1902, a play adapted by Colette's husband, Willy, from one of her schoolgirl novels, *Claudine à Paris,* appeared at the Théâtre des Bouffes-Parisiens with the young actress Polaire as the lead. It was an enormous success, and Willy, a publicist of the first order, took to appearing in public with Colette and Polaire dressed as identical twins.[8] For Mansfield to imagine herself as Colette's identical twin under such circumstances clearly made an appeal to her theatricality, too.

Colette's attraction for Mansfield, however, was more than just a question of style. In 1915, at the very time references to Colette occurred in the journal and letters, Mansfield was reunited with her brother in London and was on the lookout for a discursive model to apply to the childhood experiences Chummie had helped her recall. Colette's novels provided just such a model. On the face of it, the childhoods of the two women seem to have had little in common aside from the rural setting: Colette had been pampered by an adoring mother in an old village in Burgundy, whereas Mansfield suffered from a sense of parental neglect in new Wellington. But the identity lay in what their childhoods had come to stand for in their adult consciousness. Like the French woman, Mansfield had chosen independence over security and left home at an early age for a large cultural capital. Both women, symbolically identical in Mansfield's perception, were attempting the same kind of reenactment of female childhood across adulthood. It is hardly surprising, then, that Mansfield chose Colette, at this vital point in the development of her writing, as her auditor and mentor.

The price both paid for their independence is reflected in the sometimes nostalgic, compensatory tone of their backward looking, and in this both writers were conforming to a turn-of-the-century tradition that sentimentalized childhood as redemptive.[9] They alike stressed, in particular,

7. *Ibid.,* 212–13.
8. Margaret Crosland, *Colette: The Difficulty of Loving* (1973; rpr. New York, 1975), 77–78.
9. For discussion of turn-of-the-century treatments of childhood, see Marcia Jacobson's analysis of *What Maisie Knew* in *Henry James and the Mass Market* (University, Ala., 1983), esp. 100–108. See also Cherry Hankin, "Katherine Mansfield and the Cult of Childhood," in the present volume.

the importance of the qualities of watchfulness and responsiveness to nature which are fostered in childhood. Colette wrote of learning to "regarde" (a favorite word) from her mother, whom she immortalized as Sido and who was unable to pay a long-awaited visit to her daughter because she had to watch the pink cactus about to burst into rare bloom. This incident, described at the opening of *La Naissance du jour,* of 1928, is a curious echo of the scene in "Prelude," of ten years earlier, in which both Kezia and her mother are similarly transfixed by the aloe cactus. The child, trained by the mother in creative observation, acquires the habit of formulating such verbal icons from nature's reserves and of resurrecting them to last through the deserts of urban adulthood. For Mansfield, as much as for Colette, the famous words from the French writer's *Les Vrilles de la vigne* could stand as a motto to most of what she wrote: "I belong to a land that I have abandoned." [10]

But Colette offered something new, as well, in the depiction of childhood: a postlapsarian, incipiently sexual young girl, a wayward dreamer whom she called the "innocent libertine." Claudine, Minne, and their type roam the fields in a state of drowsy intoxication, devouring cigarette papers and lime buds. Kezia moves with something of the same half-conscious stealth as she "thieves" away from company in "The Doll's House" or retreats, "far too quickly and airily," from Beryl's dressing table at the end of "Prelude." [11]

Mansfield's references to Colette began in late 1914, when she wrote in the journal for November that "Colette Willy is in my thoughts tonight." Twelve days later she wrote, "I've re-read *L'Entrave.* I suppose Colette is the only woman in France who does just this. I don't care a fig at present for anyone I know except her." [12] The terms of personal acquaintance were to characterize her references to Colette throughout. I want to argue later that it was the particular nature of Mansfield's response as a reader, as it has been of other women readers, to construe the text not as an object but as a manifestation of the subjectivity of the absent author. *L'Entrave* (The shackle) had much for her to identify with, even though it was, like its companion piece, *La Vagabonde,* a very different kind of book from those of the *Claudine* series. It engages with

10. Quoted by Margaret Davies in *Colette* (Edinburgh, 1961), 1.
11. *Stories,* 503, 259.
12. *Journal,* 61, 62.

that more immediate pressure point in both authors' lives, their predicament as bourgeois women attempting to reconstruct themselves in relation to a new urban bohemia. Their frames of reference in the new environment were remarkably similar, in spite of their national difference. Both had husbands who were literary editors, and both had experimented or would experiment with a variety of homo- and heterosexual relationships, Colette rather more scandalously than Mansfield, although the young New Zealander is known to have performed at a lesbian club, as Colette did. In their attraction to emasculated men, they even shared a friend in Francis Carco, who turned out to be more loyal to Colette than to Mansfield. (His *Les Innocents,* of 1916, which contains a brutal assassination of a female character thought to be based on Mansfield, was dedicated to Rachilde, a close friend of Colette's and an author Mansfield admired greatly.) In addition, both Mansfield and Colette performed in music halls and brought to their writing a quality mentioned by Brigid Brophy in 1962 in relation to Mansfield: "the obvious—indeed, dazzling—talent . . . for multiple impersonation, through sketches whose form must be derived partly from her music-hall turns." [13]

L'Entrave, like *La Vagabonde,* which Mansfield had almost certainly read, is about a woman conditioned only to love but driven by an irresistible need for solitude and independence. That need is constructed out of an actress' compulsive travel from one city to another in a permanent state of vagabondage, like several other *femmes seules* around but apart from her. The phrase *femme seule* is Colette's in *La Vagabonde,* of 1911, but Mansfield appropriated and assimilated it so naturally as a frame to her own discourse, both fictional and nonfictional, that it has come to seem her own. Throughout 1915, the words *femme seule*—or, alternatively, *dame seule*—occurred frequently in Mansfield's letters, journal, and stories, most conspicuously, perhaps, in "The Little Governess," of May of that year. At the same time, John Middleton Murry played his part in endorsing Mansfield's self-image in Colettean terms—as in a letter of March, 1915: "You are . . . the eternal woman . . . (You is a type—the wonderful type from Aspasia to B.B. Colette Vagabonde, and you above all moderns)." [14] That bombast was deflated by Mansfield on

13. Brigid Brophy, *Don't Never Forget: Collected Views and Reviews* (London, 1967), 257. On Colette, Rachilde, and especially Carco, see Christiane Mortelier, "The French Connection: Francis Carco," in the present volume.

14. C. A. Hankin, ed., *The Letters of John Middleton Murry to Katherine Mansfield* (London, 1983), 53–54.

a later occasion, however, when she wrote Murry from Cornwall, in May, 1918, "I feel extraordinarily better and stronger with no pain at all, but I cant write you the letters I should like to because my 'vagrant self' is uppermost—& you dont really know her or want to know her."[15] Her self-definition as "femme seule," the vagrant-vagabond who could never be satisfied with the alternatives of cabaret artist and bourgeois wife, between which she vacillated, was one that persisted for her till the end but left Murry increasingly behind.

The nature of Colette's attraction for Katherine Mansfield had as much to do with the reader response the French woman aroused as it did with the two writers' similarity of preoccupation. Mansfield described that response in a letter of October 1916 to Mary Hutchinson: "For me she is more real than any woman Ive ever known."[16] Knowing, as an intimacy of reader and text, was more meaningful than anything that might occur in the contingencies of personal friendship.

When we talk about friendship in Mansfield's life, we think of the precariousness of her contact with others as much as of the rapport, even with her most intimate companions, Murry and L.M. (Ida Baker). Much had undoubtedly to do with the strain of maintaining the fixity of the different persona she presented to each acquaintance: from the "brassy little shopgirl of literature" (Frank O'Connor) or the "foul-mouthed, virulent, brazen-faced broomstick of a creature" (Lytton Strachey) to Murry's "sensitive . . . frail . . . delicate" dream child.[17] Her society's construction of behavioral models for woman, or rather for women writers, offered a series of alternatives that bewildered her into an intensive search for a "real" self, a postulate others also tried to abstract from her. Virginia Woolf, for example, thought she could see beneath, as she put it, the "hard composure" of Mansfield's facade.[18] Mansfield was skeptical of Polonius' advice to Laertes: "To thine own self be true." "True to oneself!" she exclaimed in a journal entry of 1920, "which self? Which of my many . . . ?" But the multiplicity seemed deceitful, to her as it did

15. *Collected Letters,* II, 188.

16. *Ibid.,* I, 282.

17. C. K. Stead, *In the Glass Case: Essays on New Zealand Fiction* (Auckland, 1981), 34; Margaret Drabble, "The New Woman of the Twenties: Fifty Years On," *Harpers and Queen,* June, 1973, p. 135; Hankin, ed., *Letters of Murry to Mansfield,* 196.

18. Anne O. Bell, ed., *The Diary of Virginia Woolf* (5 vols.; London, 1977–84), I, 265 (entry of April, 1919).

to others, and she attempted to make a distinction between the "personal," which she defined as that which is made and unmade as a result of "all we acquire and all we shed," and the "self," that which is "continuous and permanent" within each individual and which "flowers" at the peak of our existence. It is in the light of this distinction that we need to understand what she called, in the same year, "my philosophy—the defeat of the personal." [19]

Her "personalities" formed an imprisoning mesh of other people's constructions of her, and with an impersonator like Mansfield, the more public the occasion, the greater the temptation to perform. The private moment, as when writing to herself in her journal, suited her best, as it has done many women. Reading, too, invited a different kind of personal contact, for here, instead of being the object of another's construction, *she* was in the subject position.

In reading, Mansfield looked for signs of what she thought of as authorial presence, that shape or figure of a personality she put together from the text, often in the attempt at self-recognition. Some authors made themselves accessible in this respect, and others did not. Virginia Woolf, for example, was a closed book for Mansfield and seemed to have no textual personality. That was because, in Mansfield's words, she was not "of" her subject—unlike Mansfield, who felt she could "become" a duck, or an apple—but, rather, above it, like a bird who hovers, dips, and skims from on high.[20] Rachilde, on the other hand, was a "fascinating creature"—or at least her textual presence was, for of course Mansfield never met this woman known in France as the Queen of the Decadents. But she read her, through her own preoccupations, into the introspective, erotic narrative of *L'Heure sexuelle,* of 1898, and would have agreed with Maurice Barrès, another of Rachilde's admirers, that "in all her work . . . Rachilde does little but write the self."[21] Other writers, too, had authentic selves as well as made-up personalities, and Mansfield, in her attempt to distinguish the one from the other, privileged reading as an act of the most personal intimacy. The experience of reading the poem by Emily Brontë "I know not how it falls on me" illustrates the effect of the process on her. The poem, with two personal

19. *Journal,* 205, 195.
20. *Collected Letters,* II, 333–34.
21. M. Barrès, Introduction to Rachilde's *Monsieur Venus* (1884; rpr. Paris, 1977), 13. My translation.

pronouns in the first line, seemed to invite a particular kind of closeness. Mansfield wrote, "The first line—why is it so moving? And then the exquisite simplicity of 'Forgive me' . . . I think the Beauty of it is contained in one's certainty that it is not Emily disguised—who writes—it is Emily. Nowadays one of the chief reasons for ones dissatisfaction with modern poetry is one can't be sure that it really does belong to the man who writes it. It *is* so tiring—isn't it—never to leave the Masked Ball—never—never—"[22]

She could not be sure that a poem of her day really belonged to the man who wrote it; the word *man* here, I think, needs to be read in a gender-specific way. Mansfield was finding her literary voice at the very time that Modernist poets—an all-male battalion headed by Ezra Pound, T. S. Eliot, and William Butler Yeats and accompanied by novelists like James Joyce and D. H. Lawrence—were formulating a poetics based on what Maud Ellmann, in a recent book on the subject, calls "scriptive self-occlusion."[23] While Mansfield wanted to *leave* the Masked Ball, her male contemporaries were in the thick of the revels. Yeats, following Oscar Wilde, had made his well-known statement ten years before that "all happiness depends on the energy to assume the mask of some other self . . . all joyous or creative life is a re-birth as something not oneself."[24] Related statements by his contemporaries are equally well known; Eliot wrote in 1919, the same year as Mansfield's letter about Brontë's poem, "Poetry is not a turning loose of an emotion, but an escape from emotion; it is not the expression of personality, but an escape from personality," and "The more perfect the artist, the more completely separate in him will be the man who suffers and the mind which creates."[25] There was also Stephen Dedalus, the refined, impersonalized mask of his creator, James Joyce: "The personality of the artist, at first a cry or a cadence or a mood and then a fluid and lambent narrative, finally refines itself out of existence, impersonalizes itself, so to speak."[26]

22. *Collected Letters*, II, 334.

23. Maud Ellmann, *The Poetics of Impersonality: T. S. Eliot and Ezra Pound* (Brighton, Eng., 1987), ix.

24. Richard Ellman, *Yeats: The Man and the Masks* (1949; rpr. London, 1973), 177.

25. T. S. Eliot, "Tradition and the Individual Talent," *Selected Essays* (London, 1976), 21, 18.

26. James Joyce, *A Portrait of the Artist as a Young Man* (1916; rpr. Harmondsworth, Eng., 1974), 214.

Mansfield, as much as these men, was a product of the 1890s, a decade of extravagant poseurs like Lionel Johnson and Aubrey Beardsley, who spent a lifetime trying on different masks. But although Mansfield's stint as a Wildean impersonator may have suited her in her late teens and early twenties, the process of multiple self-invention, of fabricating images to fit the occasion, became an increasing strain.[27] Privately—and Mansfield became an increasingly private person after 1916—the dissatisfaction with "personalities" and the obsession with "selfhood" grew, accompanied by a mounting interest in models of self-inscription in the work of other writers, particularly women.

Is there, then, any connection between Mansfield's interest in detecting methods of self-inscription in the work of others, and her own fiction, which is in one sense perversely "unknowable," dispensing as it does with a narrative voice and exploiting a series of evasions of a stable subject position? Her ability to assume the voice of a wide range of characters in a series of gliding shifts in stories like "At the Bay" is usually recognized as her most outstanding contribution to the short story, even if it has laid her open to the charge of "promiscuity," as Orage put it.[28] Such a writer would seem to have little need to invest in a memorable textual presence. The voice of the journal is intensely familiar, exhorting itself to authenticity at the very moment it watches itself perform. Is it necessary to carry our awareness of Mansfield the rigorous self-analyst over from the journal and letters into the stories in order to respond to something other than a ventriloquistic mastery in her fiction?

In some cases, yes, I think it is. The journal and letters are so enormously instructive because they display an effort, concentrated to breaking point toward the end, expended on groping for discursive forms true to Mansfield's experience as a woman writer. And that required an iron-willed resistance to the voices she acquired with such facility from a predominantly masculine literary discourse, voices she could succumb to with alarming ease in the stories. She soon learned that there were no rewards to be gained from the fulminating resistance she had learned

27. For discussion of Wilde's influence on Mansfield from 1906 "for at least four years," see Vincent O'Sullivan, "The Magnetic Chain: Notes and Approaches to K.M.," *Landfall* (New Zealand), No. 114 (1975), 95–131.

28. A. R. Orage wrote of her "promiscuity of reflection, taste, judgment, character and intelligence" in "A Fourth Tale for Men Only," by R. H. Congreve (Orage), Part III, *New Age*, XI (May 16, 1912), 62.

from Marie Bashkirtseff in her youth and practiced in the journal ("Damn my family!").[29] Mansfield never did find a story mode that completely matched her best letters of the "look here" kind, written to L.M. in particular, or the angry—not the conciliatory—ones to Murry.

Recent feminist critics, following Julia Kristeva, have written about the discourse of the hysteric as characteristic of a great deal of women's writing. By this they mean a simultaneous refusal of, yet submission to, femininity as it is constructed under patriarchy, woman's enactment of herself as a lesser male.[30] Mansfield's writing illustrates that process in several of its forms. The *German Pension* stories represent, on one level, a major attempt to conform to rigorous masculine standards. The stories in the first person are narrated by a voice that we initially feel tempted to hear as "Katherine." She does, after all, call herself that in "Being a Truthful Adventure," a story not in the volume but close to it in time and manner. This "Katherine," however, is probably the least accessible of all her guises in that it refuses allegiance to anything but its own gibes. The narrator is problematically evasive rather than simply anonymous.[31] She constructs what we think will be the world of her observation, only to raze it to the ground with a cavalier wave of the hand—in asides like one in "Epilogue II: Violet": "I thought how true it was that the world was a delightful place if it were not for the people" (143). Mansfield had been a quick pupil in the Oragean school and could outdo the master himself in what Tomalin summarizes as the Oragean style: "the sharp observation, the puncturing aside . . . understatement, and an eye for absurdity."[32] Yet there is something in these stories that makes them subversive of their own practices. Mansfield may well, as one character says at the beginning of "Violet," have "put [the] collective foot down upon the female attempt to embroider everything" (142). But the first-person narrator's iconoclastic astringency turns out to be not quite so victorious over her preconceptions of female sentiment and embellishment as she would have us believe. The story in fact performs a subtle act of realignment whereby Violet's naïve sentimentality and ability to "sympathise" serve to expose the narrative detachment, rather than vice versa.

29. *Journal,* 21.

30. See especially, Juliet Mitchell, *Women: The Longest Revolution* (London, 1982).

31. This description was offered by Pamela Dunbar in her paper at the Katherine Mansfield Centenary Symposium, at the Newberry Library, in Chicago, September 8–10, 1988.

32. Claire Tomalin, *Katherine Mansfield: A Secret Life* (London, 1987), 81.

Another form of the hysteric appears in the reviews she wrote for the *Athenaeum* in 1919–1920. Like the *New Age* contracts, this writing made a particularly public demand on her. What resulted was a series of attempts at an experienced, armchair manner of the sort mastered by Virginia Woolf, who added her own inflections to the acquired paternal voice of Leslie Stephen, editor of the *Dictionary of National Biography*. Mansfield was less adapted to the Olympian manner, and her language registered her discomfort. There were evasions and euphemisms. She expressed her dissatisfaction with two books, Jane Mander's *The Story of a New Zealand River* and Margaret Symonds' *A Child of the Alps,* for what she considered their faintheartedness: "What is extremely impressive to the novel reviewer is the modesty of the writers—their diffidence in declaring themselves what they are." Given that she was attacking a failure in personal accountability, as the rest of the review makes clear, the word *impressive* is positively disingenuous. The sheltering reference to herself as the "novel reviewer" (more common was the bland, avuncular *we*), as well as the euphemism *modesty* when she clearly meant *vapidity,* illustrate the very faults she found in the authors she was reviewing. In a review of a novel by the woman writer W. Bryher, she attacked, from an elevated height, the writer's "female" disposition. But she again became an illicit accomplice with her victim: "What could be more 'female' than her passion for rummaging in, tumbling over, eyeing this great basket of coloured words? That she can find no use for them; that, lovely as they are, she has nothing to pin them on to, nothing to deck out in them; that *la bonne Littérature* in fine, has not bid her bind her hair, is no great marvel. She has been to a feast of languages ever since she was old enough to beat a spoon on the table."[33] If Bryher's basket of words was full, it could be no more so than Mansfield's, which had at least five mixed metaphors into the bargain. If it were not for the fact that such extended metaphors are one of Mansfield's favorite devices throughout the reviews, we might be tempted to read ironically this exploitation of the very devices she would abjure. The contorted syntax and repeated double negatives, the verbosity and the royal *we* all add up to an evasiveness barely comparable to the spareness, mobility, and directness of Mansfield's more private voice. Virginia Woolf thought that Mansfield's reviews showed that she was not interested in novels.[34] She

33. *Novels and Novelists*, 220, 231–32.
34. Hankin, ed., *Letters of Murry to Mansfield,* 221.

was, but never succeeded in finding a public discourse suited to her interest.

The novelist Frank Sargeson complained in "The Feminine Tradition," written for the *New Zealand Listener* over forty years ago, that Mansfield's writing was limited because she lived in "a state of suspension" where "you have to depend on yourself too much—and what you find *in* yourself."[35] Today, a feminist, poststructuralist age invites us to read her stories as being about what she could not find in herself because of all that she was "acquiring" and all that she was "shedding," to use her own words. Her "feminine" acquisitions were the most tenacious and long-lived of all. They were everything that a woman writer was as condescended to for being as condemned for not being: bright, effusive, self-deprecatory, petulant, wheedling, infantile. Many readers from Mansfield's time to the 1960s heard that tone in the stories and called it cheap, as Virginia Woolf did at one stage, though she admitted later that she had been too deafened by jealousy to hear anything else.[36] We read Mansfield differently now because we perceive the counterpoint of the driving intellectual, Mansfield as the most ruthless critic of her own collusion with femininity. Her writing is thus a brilliant enactment but also deconstruction of the feminine code of practice.

That is most noticeable in her correspondence with Murry, the last to want to know her vagrant solitary self. Here she is in a letter to him in late 1920:

My [mental] landscape is terribly exciting at present. I never knew it contained such features or such fauna (they are animals various, aren't they?). But I do want a gentleman prepared to pay his own exes, to join me in my expedition. Oh, won't YOU come? No one else will do. But when you do it's a bit sickening—all my wild beasts get a bit funny-looking—they don't look such serious monsters any more. Instead of lions and tigers it's apt to turn into an affair of:

35. Frank Sargeson, "The Feminine Tradition: A Talk About Katherine Mansfield," *New Zealand Listener*, XXIX (August 6, 1948), 10–12.

36. "I thought her cheap, and she thought me priggish . . . then she came out with a swarm of little stories, and I was jealous, no doubt; because they were so praised; but gave up reading them not on that account, but because of their cheap sharp sentimentality, which was all the worse, I thought, because . . . she could permeate one with her quality, and if one felt this cheap scent in it, it reeked in ones nostrils" (Virginia Woolf to Vita Sackville-West, August 8, 1931, in *Katherine Mansfield,* by Tomalin, 204).

> The Turkey ran pas' with a flag in his mas'
> An' cried out: "What's the mattah?"

Not that I think for one minute that you don't treat me au GRAND sér-ieux or would dare to question my intelligence, of course not. All the same—there you are—Alone, I'm no end of a fillaseafer but once you join me in the middle of my seriousness—my deadly seriousness—I see the piece of pink wool I have put on your hair (and that you don't know is there).

Queer, isn't it? Now explain that for me.[37]

The games are apparent: the piece reads like a model of the feminine style as analyzed by a linguist such as Robin Lakoff.[38] There are the insecurity of the tag questions and repeated emphases, the juvenile vocabulary ("a bit sickening," "a bit funny-looking," "queer") alternating with the slightly pretentious (mental "landscapes" and "fauna" and French phrases). Yet she makes her complaint against Murry's trivialization of her with such gaiety and grace that she wins a very feminine forgiveness for the seriousness of her charge, at the same time that she apes his expectations of her.

A hypothetical Murry seems to be the assumed auditor of a number of the stories. Like her cousin Elizabeth von Arnim, whose shadow as successful literary Antipodean, a female one at that, hung over Mansfield for much of her life, she found it easy at times to earn praise for a style described as feminine for its high-strung sensitivity and animation. Both would write of objects like books or tables looking as if they might begin dancing.[39] When Mansfield told her cousin at the end of her life that most of what she had produced seemed "little stories like birds bred in cages,"

37. November 8, 1920, in *Letters to Murry*, 590.
38. Robin Lakoff, *Language and Women's Place* (New York, 1975).
39. "With so much colour and such a big fire and such floods of sunshine [the library] has anything but a sombre air, in spite of the volumes filling the shelves. Indeed, I should never be surprised if they skipped down from their places, and, picking up their leaves, began to dance" (Elizabeth von Arnim, *Elizabeth and Her German Garden* [1898; rpr. London, 1904], 73–74). Compare Mansfield, at the end of the unfinished story "Father and the Girls": "All gay, all glittering, the long French windows open on to the green and gold garden, the *salle à manger* stretched before them. And the fifty little tables with the fifty pots of dahlias looked as if they might begin dancing" (*Collected Stories of Katherine Mansfield* [London, 1953], 482).

she was acknowledging her own, and perhaps also her cousin's, complicity in breeding the feminine consciousness.[40] Ellen Moers has analyzed the prevalence of bird imagery in women's writing. Mansfield turned the image against itself in a conscious gesture of self-exposure.

If feminization is accentuated by the inevitably patriarchal pressures of public situations, what happens when women are alone or in solely female company? That question lies behind a number of Mansfield's stories. Much of the energy of her women characters is expended in seeking solitude, even if the solitude, when found, is as torturous as or more torturous than its alternative. The women are like Linda Burnell, in "Prelude," who constantly dreams of escaping—of driving away from everybody in a small buggy "and not even waving" (233), or of being rowed faster and faster away in the thorny aloe ship, warding off pursuers. Or they are the "femmes seules," fleeing potential violation, gusts of wind tugging threateningly at their hats and skirts. Or they are like Jinnie Salesby, in "The Man Without a Temperament," who has a querulous excitability and an enforced dependence and for whom there is little left but to attempt to penetrate the reserve of her husband. With the odd exception, like Reggie, in "Mr and Mrs Dove," or Dick Harmon, in "Je ne parle pas français, "the men exude confidence—confidence in their bodies (like Stanley Burnell), in their talents (like Reginald Peacock), in their sexual prowess (like Herr Brechenmacher), and in their power (like the Late Colonel, or like the boss, in "The Fly"). Against this, the women suffer from their nerves, like the woman in "The Escape," or retreat to their chaise longues to become, like Mrs Trout, in *The Aloe,* a "perfect martyr to headaches."[41] These "femmes seules" have far less nerve than Colette's and are as much preyed upon by their imaginative projection of fearful possibilities as by any experienced threat.

In the moments when women are together with women in Mansfield's stories, the text often quiets to a brief moment of composure as reserves are lowered. There are the scenes with Con and Jug, in "The Daughters of the Late Colonel," the Fairfield women sewing, in *The Aloe,* Bertha and Pearl Fulton at the pear tree, in "Bliss," and most memorably, the relief of the women in the Burnell household after Stanley's departure, in

---

40. December 31, 1992, in *Letters,* ed. Murry, II, 268.
41. Vincent O'Sullivan, ed., *The Aloe, with Prelude* (Wellington, 1982), 129.

"At the Bay." The story most conspicuously "female" is "Prelude," which builds the female life cycle, from youth to old age, into its structure. The three and a half generations of Fairfield women are presented in subtle nuances of interrelatedness whereby each is present in the others in echo. In the earlier story "A Birthday," the grandmother had been from the paternal side. This time, Mansfield chose a direct female line.

The echoes may arise from shared preoccupations. For example, both Kezia and Linda fear the thrusting forces in the environment around them, whether the dogs, parrots, or camels that rush at Kezia's imagination, "their heads swell[ing] e-enormous" (228), or the very real Stanley who jumps up and barks at Linda. Linda "had always hated things that rush at her, from a child" (254). Both mother and daughter, too, are haunted by the "coming alive of things" (235), things that seem to demand something of them, or call for submission. Kezia, alone in the empty house, calls them "IT" (226); for Linda, "THEY were there" (235). Dream or daydream preoccupations are also shared by the sisters Beryl and Linda, for all their waking differences. They dream of birds, and of escape, of "waiting for someone to come who just did not come, watching for something to happen that just did not happen" (235), as Linda puts it. The only form of escape available to Beryl's imagination is that of ravishment by a dark lover. Together, Linda and Beryl embody the fate of women of their class: passive, unfulfilled, temperamental, idle.

Just as there are projections backward—Kezia reacting as Linda had done as a child—so there are conjectural leaps forward. At the end of the story, after Beryl has powdered her nose and gone down to meet a male visitor, Kezia takes her place at the dressing table to play with the makeup, thus offering herself up as a potential victim of feminization. Beryl's guilty acquiescence in the process is a major concern of the story. Kezia, with intuitive insight into the acquiescence and the inevitability of her own future complicity, creeps guiltily away. Similarly, Linda's future as Fairfield grandmother is foretold in the penultimate scene with her mother, when all the tensions and frustrations of her bourgeois life-style as wife and mother are resolved into a version of Mrs Fairfield's resignation and serenity, with yet more children and proliferating gardens.

This identity between the women, from one generation to another, extends also to a telepathic communication, as when Linda, in mock indifference to her children's welfare, speculates that "Kezia has been tossed by a bull hours ago" (238), when Kezia *has* in fact just had a confrontation with a bull. Or, one step farther, the text may exploit an ambiguity of the pronoun *she,* referable to either one or the other of the females between whose consciousness it is constantly fluctuating. An example of this occurs when the narrative shifts from Linda, still in bed, to Kezia, playing outdoors with her sisters:

> "Where are you going to, Kezia?" asked Isabel, who longed to find some light and menial duty that Kezia might perform and so be roped in under her government.
>
> "Oh, just away," said Kezia . . .
>
> Then she did not hear them any more. What a glare there was in the room. She hated blinds pulled up to the top. (234–35)

Is the "she" at the end here Linda, who did not hear the three girls anymore, or Kezia, who did not hear her two sisters as she wandered off? That is clarified only by the context of the next sentence.

All four women are united under the moon, when the aggression of daytime, patriarchal activities, symbolized by the daytime aloe, that "fat swelling plant with its cruel leaves and fleshy stem" which cuts blindly into the air (240), is replaced by the nighttime aloe, cool and watery, promising escape. Linda is "discovered" by the moon (243), the same moon, we are told, "that Lottie and Kezia had seen from the storeman's wagon" (253). Under its influence, Linda speaks to her mother "with the special voice that women use at night to each other as though they spoke in their sleep or from some hollow cave" (253–54).

Recent work in object-relations theory by feminists like Nancy Chodorow and Jane Flax has suggested that there may be important sociopsychological reasons why women are less liable than men to set up a firm distinction between subject and object, self and other, and why identification or merging with others may be an early-implanted female characteristic. As long as women continue to "mother," to be the primary caretakers of infants, they argue, baby boys will be conditioned to differentiate from this primary object in order to establish separate ego boundaries, while girls will be free of this necessity. Mansfield seems, fleetingly, to capture such moments of female relatedness and to grope toward the kind of specifically female discourse that feminists like Hélène Cixous have recently celebrated. Cixous refers, incidentally, to Colette's

51

writing as a prominent twentieth-century example of the inscription of the female.[42]

The essence, however, is the ephemerality of such moments in Mansfield's writing. Mrs Fairfield's mind wanders away from her daughter to the traditional feminine activities of jam making; Pearl Fulton switches from female ally to rival over the man; Con creeps away from Jug to lie in lonely communion with the full moon; the Fairfield women quarrel. Mansfield's writing seems to me to be important as an inscription not of the female but of its corruptibility, and of the exploitation of *feminine* discourse as defensive option.

But whereas writers like George Eliot succumbed with apparent ease to a version of the female hysteric, as Elizabeth von Arnim did to a feminine discourse, Mansfield's submission, like Colette's, was Modernist in its self-consciousness. Her work offers an extraordinary record of the encoding of both submission and resistance to the feminine by a woman as exceptional as mimic as she was discerning as critic of that mimicry. It is for this reason, I think, that her writing is as "knowable" (in her sense) today as it has ever been.

42. Elaine Marks and Isabelle de Courtivron, eds., *New French Feminisms: An Anthology* (Brighton, Eng., 1980), 249*n*.

Katherine Mansfield and the Honourable Dorothy Brett: A Correspondence of Artists

Gardner McFall

The Newberry Library's collection of the Katherine Mansfield Papers contains what to our knowledge is the first surviving letter of Katherine Mansfield to the painter Dorothy Brett, whose works' primitive style aimed at combining the real and the spiritual. From 1915, when they first met, Brett was one of Mansfield's most devoted friends. This letter is the beginning of an intense correspondence, of which the Newberry has ninety-eight items, not all of which have been published. This one is addressed to Brett at Lady Ottoline Morrell's Garsington Manor, near Oxford. It was at Garsington that they became close. Subsequently they shared a residence in London at 3 Gower Street.

The elder daughter of the second viscount Esher, the Honourable Brett, known as Doll to her family, was by birth and upbringing a privileged London debutante. As a child, she took dancing lessons at Windsor Castle, often under Victoria's eye; she had her appendix removed by King Edward VII's personal physician; she was presented at court in 1903 and was urged, though unsuccessfully, to marry early and well.[1] But Brett's

---

1. The biographical information concerning Dorothy Brett is taken from Sean Hignett's *Brett* (New York, 1983).

self-image as a painter, acquired at the respected Slade School, which she attended from 1910 to 1916, and sustained through years of work at the cost of alienation from her family, supplanted any she might have had as a titled British woman.

She emerged from the Slade no longer a debutante but all boots and breeches, with short-cropped hair, known in the Slade School fashion by her surname Brett. She was, as her sister aptly described her, a "bravely independent girl in her boyish attire and short haircut who was incapable of doing anything, in the eyes of our mother, that was either dutiful or right."[2] Unlike Lady Ottoline Morrell, who capitalized on her social position to attract the company of leading writers and artists, Brett eschewed hers. In this respect, she resembled Mansfield, who fled her comfortable upper-middle-class existence in Wellington in 1908 for the literary world of London.

Vincent O'Sullivan has perceptively noted in his introduction to the first volume of *The Collected Letters of Katherine Mansfield* that during Mansfield's life "almost every close friendship made with a woman . . . was to be with one who was not, in any usual sense, English."[3] That point suggests—what in Mansfield and Brett's case was true—that exiles, whatever the character and cause of their exile, have an affinity with each other.

Mansfield considered herself the "little Colonial walking in the London garden patch—allowed to look perhaps, but not to linger. . . . She is a stranger—an alien."[4] And though Brett's privileged upbringing might have made her feel at home in London in a way Mansfield's did not, her self-imposed exile from the upper social registers made her a suspicious character in the artistic circles she longed to enter. The label *dilettante*, which dogged her during her first years at the Slade, lingered on in the form of Brett's intellectual insecurity vis à vis the Garsington crowd that at various times included John Middleton Murry, the Stracheys, Vanessa and Clive Bell, Bertrand Russell, T. S. Eliot, Mansfield, and others. Brett came from a background that, according to O'Sullivan, "had not much to do with ordinary English life."[5] That she abandoned it to embrace the world of art suggests a personality and temperament Mansfield could only have sympathized with.

2. Hignett, *Brett*, 41.
3. *Collected Letters*, I, xi.
4. *Journal*, 157.
5. *Collected Letters*, I, xi.

The condition of exile that both women suffered was further compounded by illness and handicap. From the time Mansfield met her, Brett was deaf, and her impairment, though it did not equal the magnitude of Mansfield's illness, formed a point of contact between them. As Mansfield wrote to her on August 29, 1920, "I am simply a woman with a craving to work. . . . My one regret is—health—and that doesn't *remind* me—but gives me the chance to say to you how much, how deeply I feel for you in your deafness. Perhaps you think people 'accept' it—forget it. I never do and I never could."[6]

Both women were acutely aware of the exile that illness imposed. Mansfield expressed this as "that shadowy country that we exiles from health inhabit."[7] Brett also felt severed from the rest of the world, writing to Russell in 1918, then imprisoned as a conscientious objector, "I feel prison must in some ways be curiously like the life I lead."[8]

Given their respective exiles, Brett and Mansfield sought consolation, affirmation, and selfhood in their work. Brett wrote in her letter to Russell, "I think if it were not for my painting I would end it all. . . . You can realize what devastating attacks of depression I get—and what touch and go it is when my painting goes wrong."[9] In a similar vein, Mansfield declared in her journal in 1919, "Life without *work*—I would commit suicide. Therefore work is more important than life."[10]

If Brett's and Mansfield's work drew them together, it was the difference in their work, Brett a painter and Mansfield a writer, that may have permitted a kind of closeness that was not possible, for example, between Mansfield and Virginia Woolf. Brett, when Mansfield knew her, was exploring portraiture and still life. That struck a chord with Mansfield, who wrote her on October 11, 1917, "It seems to me so extraordinarily right that you should be painting Still Lives just now. What can one do, faced with this wonderful tumble of round bright fruits, but gather them and play with them—and *become them,* as it were."[11] There was no artistic competition between the two as there was between Woolf and Mansfield, only mutual support. As Mansfield wrote Brett on March 26, 1920, "We have our gesture to make which has its place in the scheme of things. We

---

6. To Dorothy Brett, August 29, 1920, in Newberry.
7. October 4, 1920, in *Letters to Murry,* 549.
8. Hignett, *Brett,* 51.
9. *Ibid.,* 51.
10. *Journal,* 166.
11. *Collected Letters,* I, 330.

must find what it is and make it—offer up ourselves as a sacrifice. You as a painter and me as a writer."[12]

The nature of their friendship, between painter and writer, is suggested in the prose passage "Pic-Nic," contained in Mansfield's journal. Although Mansfield probably had another friend in mind, the painter Anne Estelle Rice, it serves to document the difference and similarity that attracted her to Brett as well:

> When the two women in white came down to the lonely beach—*She* threw away her paintbox—and *She* threw away her notebook. Down they sat on the sand. The tide was low. Before them the weedy rocks were like some herd of shaggy beasts huddled at the pool to drink and staying there in a kind of stupor.
>
> Then *She* went off and dabbled her legs in a pool thinking about the colour of flesh under water. And *She* crawled into a dark cave and sat there thinking about her childhood. Then they came back to the beach and flung themselves down on their bellies, hiding their heads in their arms. They looked like two swans.[13]

Here, the rapport is clearly symbolized in terms of difference ("paintbox" and "notebook"; "thinking about the colour of flesh under water" and "thinking about her childhood") and similarity (both women wear white; both resemble swans). The text demonstrates the correspondence and union of painter and writer in the verbal picture it ends with, that of two women lying on the beach, swanlike, in an air of harmony and peace.

Of course, the friendship of Mansfield and Brett was not all harmony and peace. The serenity was shattered when Mansfield learned that Brett was having an affair with her husband. On one level, Mansfield felt deeply betrayed by Brett's dalliance with Murry, but when Murry went on to other flirtations, she could hardly hold Brett alone responsible for their indiscretion. She was able to rise above the personal grievances she harbored, for the sake of addressing and perfecting her work. Brett and Mansfield's friendship brooked the agitation of a competing love interest, because both were committed to the idea and experience of female bonds, and to the importance of art, and both needed the written correspondence they pursued.

12. *Collected Letters*, III, 262.
13. *Journal*, 140.

Mansfield was a profuse letter writer. In her separations from Murry and her ceaseless travel to find a climate that might cure her illness, letters were a main lifeline out of her exile and despair. Brett employed letters as a way of transcending her deafness and overcoming her inhibitions of verbal self-expression.[14] She had, as Mansfield told her, a "very rare gift for writing letters."[15] Unfortunately, there is only one, incomplete, surviving letter from Brett to Mansfield, written January 29, 1922, when Mansfield was in Paris for radiation treatments, but its energy, immediacy, and expressed concern are enough to reveal why Mansfield, especially in the last years of her life, valued Brett's correspondence. It begins,

> Tig dearest,
>   I can hardly sit still. I fidget & fidget & am in such a temper all because of your trip to Paris. I can't do anything but think of you, follow you into the train, to your hotel in Paris & leave you on the doorstep of Manhoukin & walk up & down outside until I know—the exact day he begins the cure.[16]

Exile from normal English life, eschewal of family background, illness, commitment to art, need for women friends, and penchant for letter writing marked the lives of Mansfield and Brett, and drew them together. Even Murry was, however ironically, a linkage between them, and it is of no small interest that the letters Mansfield wrote to Brett some time after Brett's liaison with Murry are lusher and more admiring than earlier ones.

Yet the friendship was not simple, nor simply marked by these similarities. It was, at least on Mansfield's side, fraught with contradiction, in keeping with her whole life. She was contradictory in that she was smart but disavowed the intellectual; she loved life but, disappointed by much of it, created it anew in her fiction; she had scandalous personal relations but increasingly came to see herself as a moralist, not a modern woman at all; she left her provincial home in New Zealand only to return to it in her fiction; she was distant from her father yet even at the end of her life craved his approval; she was intensely serious about her work but

---

14. Hignett, *Brett,* 82.
15. To Dorothy Brett, October 16, 1922, in Newberry.
16. In Turnbull.

spoke of it in terms of play ("I remember everything . . . the great joy of life to me is in playing just that game");[17] she turned away from her biological family but adopted a literary one; her life and her work—constituting and refiguring her life—came both to differ and to be indistinguishable. Paradox marked Mansfield's life and work. It is not surprising that it also marked her relationship with Brett.

Mansfield's almost one hundred letters to Brett provide a window on their friendship, as well as on Mansfield's character and work. They contain memorable descriptions, theoretical explorations concerning art and writing, and details to delight the biographer: Mansfield's favorite party game was musical chairs; she applied rose water to her hair to make it grow. It is important, however, to read her letters in the context of her other correspondence. Although the letters to Brett tell us much about Mansfield, the course of their friendship must be outlined from various sources. Her tenderness toward Brett in the letters to her, which frequently begin with "Brettushka," "my little lamb," "my little golden bee," and "my precious little artist," and the occasional critical remarks about her in letters to other friends bespeak not hypocrisy but Mansfield's complexity, competing needs, and highest goals as an artist and human being.

Mansfield and Brett first met at a party Brett gave for D. H. Lawrence and Frieda Lawrence on November 5, 1915. Brett had met Lawrence the month before through Mark Gertler, a painter and friend from the Slade. Mansfield and Murry, who had met Lawrence at Christmas in 1914, were invited. Brett described the meeting:

> Katherine Mansfield and Murry appear . . . Katherine small, her sleek dark hair brushed close to her head, her fringe sleeked down over her white forehead; she is dressed in black. Her movements are quaintly restricted; controlled, small, reserved gestures. The dark eyes glance about much like a bird's, the pale face is a quiet mask, full of hidden laughter, wit and gaiety. But she is cautious, a bit suspicious and on her guard. Middleton Murry rolls in with the gait of a sailor, his curly dark hair is getting a bit thin on top. He is nervous, shy, a small man. The eyes are large and hazel, with a strange unseeing look; the nose is curved one side and perfectly straight the

17. To her sister Jeanne, October 14, 1921, in Turnbull.

other, due to its having been broken. His lips are finely cut, the mouth sensitive, the chin determined.[18]

The party was a failure, because of gate-crashers that included Lytton Strachey, but it was successfully restaged a few nights later.

Mansfield and Brett became close through their visits to Garsington in the spring of 1916. Late in life, Brett remembered the time as being filled with anxiety and pleasure with regard to Mansfield: "Her reputation of brilliancy, of a sort of ironic ruthlessness toward the small minds and less agile brains, simply terrified me."[19] She described Mansfield as playing a guitar and singing folk songs after dinner but abruptly stopping when she sensed criticism in the air. Later that night, she went to Brett's room and "asked me to be her friend. We made a secret pact of friendship that was never broken for the rest of her life. . . . She gave me the encouragement I needed badly. Katherine really started me doing serious painting in England."[20]

Brett was working on a portrait entitled *Umbrellas,* featuring Ottoline's weekenders Strachey, Murry, Mansfield, Gertler, Aldous Huxley, Julian Morrell, and Brett. It favorably impressed both Murry and Mansfield. Mansfield wrote to her, "I must tell you how excited I am that Murry is so enthusiastic about your picture—and I cant help delighting in the thought of you listening to all Clive's bubble blowing with this [quiet] trump card up your monastic sleeve. Do tell me how it goes on & what you decide about the 'background.' Murry was especially impressed with the middle figure in the bonnet: with your easy, beautiful handling of it. . . . Thinking about you Ive got such a picture in my mind to entreat you to paint—that I long to describe it. But Ill wait till we meet."[21]

At the end of September, 1916, Brett became a tenant of Maynard Keynes's house in Gower Street with Mansfield, Murry, and the painter Dora Carrington. The house, nicknamed The Ark, became a kind of

18. Dorothy Brett, "Reminiscences of Katherine," *Adam International Review,* Nos. 370–75 (1972–73), 84.

19. *Ibid.,* 85.

20. *Ibid.,* 86–87.

21. *Collected Letters,* I, 320. Brett and Mansfield shared an ambivalence toward the "Bloomsburies," as Mansfield called them. Brett's studio at Garsington was called "the monastery." See Brett, "Reminiscences," 86.

roundabout for the traffic of their friends, most of whom were detoured and detained by Mansfield and Murry living on the ground floor. Brett and Carrington resented this, but soon enough Mansfield recognized her own need for privacy. She moved out in February, 1917, but not before enjoying a flirtation with Bertrand Russell, Ottoline's erstwhile lover, at the same time Murry was writing provocative letters to Ottoline. Attempting to explain Mansfield's curious behavior to Ottoline, and ignorant of the ironies, Brett wrote her, "*I think she is in Love, some man has risen like the dawn on her horizon like they all will all her life—the Call of the Wild is in her and she can no more resist the call when it comes than any other wild animal. Poor Katherine she is torn in two I believe—Pity for the shy gentle clinging man she lives with and the passionate desire for freedom.*"[22]

On May 3, 1918, Brett and the painter J. D. Fergusson were witnesses at Mansfield and Murry's marriage. Brett's attendance at the long-awaited ceremony was obviously significant to Mansfield, whose letters two months afterward reflect embracive warmth:

> Dearest Brett,
>
> Your long absorbing interesting letter came yesterday. You are as Kot[eliansky] would say a 'wonderful being'—and if ever in a dark hour you feel that nobody loves you—deny the feeling on the spot. For I do. I love you dearly. So does Johnny [Murry]. You seem to me to have the most *exquisite* virtues. I only hope that one day you will become a part of our life for a time and we'll share a gorgeous existence somewhere painting and writing and looking out of the window on to the sea perhaps—[23]

Mansfield would have appreciated the painful irony in her wish.

In August, Mansfield and Murry moved into 2 Portland Villas, in Hampstead, not far from Brett's house in Thurlow Road. The proximity Mansfield insisted upon did not bear up under reality's test. In December, she responded to Ottoline's complaints of Brett's cloying frequency at Garsington: "Brett, too, really is a problem. I so understand your feeling. She is too birdlike altogether. She wants your life to be her tree—where she can sun herself and sing and hide and never have to fly."[24]

22. Alpers, *Life,* 221.
23. *Collected Letters,* II, 259.
24. *Ibid.,* 294.

For Mansfield, the disparity between wish and reality regarding Brett would be a recurring motif in their relationship. She seemed to value her more at a distance than up close—much in the way she as a writer valued the past and the distance that time cast on a subject. In June, 1919, she reported to Ottoline, "I went one day to see poor Brett. Poor little creature! Like a flea on a ladder in her Victorian jungle. She will never be straight. . . . I felt wretched for her. She is so *helpless*."[25] When Brett suggested to Mansfield that they live together in the Victorian jungle and create another Ark, Mansfield dismissed the idea, writing to her, "I have to keep solitary as I can—to have nobody *depending* and to *depend* as little as I can."[26] On the same day, she wrote cruelly to Ottoline of Brett's disorderly life and bad hygiene.[27]

Perhaps Mansfield's doubts about Murry's constancy and her instinct—albeit repressed—about his and Brett's attraction made her lash out. If she had suspicions, no doubt heightened by her impending departure for the Italian Riviera and, later, Menton, they were justified. In the early months of 1920, while Mansfield was in Menton on her doctor's orders, Murry and Brett's liaison began. Brett's name occurred frequently in Murry's letters to Mansfield during that period. He often described trips into the country with her. At the end of February, Mansfield wrote him,

> My own Bogey,
> . . . I am so glad you love Brett so much. I used to feel in Italy that if I died you'd marry Brett very soon after—I nearly wrote to you about it. Shes wonderfully suited to you in a thousand ways.[28]

Brett was writing Mansfield, too, telling of "orgies" and "drink" at Ottoline's, which prompted Mansfield to entreat Murry to reform: "I do feel so very deeply the need for dignity in this present Life. Its the only protest one can make—to be dignified and sincere and to—somehow keep *love* of human beings in ones heart."[29] On March 25, she was sterner: "What is our love worth if it hasn't taught us *pride* if we don't

25. *Ibid.*, 323.
26. *Ibid.*, 328.
27. *Ibid.*, 326.
28. *Ibid.*, III, 236.
29. *Ibid.*, 248.

defend each other and keep the shield bright for each other. Your honour is my honour."[30] Curiously enough, "Your honour is my honour" is a line she edited out of a 1908 narrative, "The Unexpected Must Happen," in which the husband reprimands his wife for her indiscretions.[31] It shows how Mansfield dramatized the self in both her life and her work, and suggests how amid life's imperfections—it is, after all, a bourgeois cliché she crossed out of her fiction—she came to prize work over personal relations.

Mansfield went home to 2 Portland Villas at the end of April, having described a letter from Brett as "pathetic."[32] She also pronounced Brett "a dear creature . . . but much more a friend of yours than mine."[33] Brett eased her anxiety and guilt by sending Mansfield a stove and a bunch of yellow roses to welcome her home. Brett was living close by, and they were all thrown together more than Mansfield would have liked.

At the end of August, as Mansfield was preparing to go away for the winter, she found a letter from Brett to Murry that suggested the extent of their intimacy. That prompted nasty confrontations, with Murry and Brett denying Mansfield's accusations, and bitter entries in Mansfield's journal. Mansfield arrived at the assessment "The truth is she flattered him and got him!"[34] She wrote Brett asking her to return all the letters she had sent her:

> If you really *do* feel any friendship for me—it is a rare feeling, terribly rare—will you send me any letters you have of mine to you . . . There were one or two or even three times when I committed to paper what I ought never to have let out of my heart. Grant my prayer for the sake of any good moments we may have had. . . . I felt (very queerly) that you were in a specially confidential "position" because you had been a witness at the Registry Office—But that was great nonsense. Such ceremonies are no more binding than tea parties. Please send the letters.[35]

Brett, obviously, did not return them, and Mansfield went off to Menton. There, she received letters from Brett and Murry indicating that they

30. *Ibid.*, 258.
31. Mansfield Notebook 2, in Turnbull.
32. *Collected Letters*, III, 277.
33. *Ibid.*, 290.
34. Mansfield Notebook 25, in Turnbull.
35. To Dorothy Brett, August 19, 1920, in Newberry.

were continuing to see each other, their visits taking the form of tennis games, and Mansfield continued to plead with him, "Don't let her come near . . . Don't let her touch you."[36]

In December, Mansfield wrote Brett, "Don't worry about telling me everything. We shall know each other by our work."[37] She was clearly eager to lose and find herself in her writing, not in her personal relations. Mansfield's side of the correspondence suggests that Brett felt a need to continue talking about the events of the spring and summer in an effort to exonerate herself and regain standing in Mansfield's eyes. Mansfield told her, "The day won't come when I shall say I was wrong. Why should it? How have I been *wrong?* . . . I don't want to protest about it. It makes me feel uncomfortable and inclined to hang my head. It's undignified. What is in the past had a great deal better be buried—bury the good even to get the bad safely under—and begin again."[38]

Murry's head was soon turned by another woman, Princess Elizabeth Bibesco, and to the extent that Mansfield directed her anger at her, she was able to move forward in her friendship with Brett. Their rift did become a thing of the past. The reason was simply that Mansfield's investment no longer lay in people but in her work, and in her race to complete as much as possible before the approaching end. She prided herself on dignity, on being able to rise above the corrupt disappointments and betrayals of life. As she wrote Murry in December, 1920, in response to his confession of an encounter with Princess Bibesco, "What happens in your personal life does *not* affect me. I have of you what I want . . . I do not in any way *depend* on you, neither can you shake me. Nobody can. I do not know how it is but I live *withdrawn* from my personal life. . . . I am a writer first. . . . You are dearer than anyone in the world to me—but more than anything else—more even than talking or laughing or being happy I want to write. This sounds so ugly. I wish I didn't have to say it."[39]

In May, 1921, Mansfield went to Sierre, and in June, Murry joined her. Her time there was extremely productive. During the summer and autumn she wrote "At the Bay," "The Voyage," "A Married Man's Story," "The Garden Party," and "The Doll's House." It is no coincidence that her letters to Brett were highly descriptive, engaging, and warm.

36. To J. M. Murry, October 10, 1920, in Turnbull.
37. To Dorothy Brett, December 9, 1920, in Newberry.
38. To Dorothy Brett, January 9, 1921, in Newberry.
39. To J. M. Murry, December, 1920, in Turnbull.

With work going well, the energy and excitement naturally spilled over into her letters.

Mansfield eagerly awaited a visit from Brett in the summer of 1922. She had kept abreast of Brett's work through photographs Brett sent her, and their exchange of letters about art and writing, with Mansfield often adopting a directive, maternal tone, made Mansfield eager to talk with her:

> I, too, feel we are only at the beginning. But I already have *such* memories of you to think over—moments, glances, and words spoken and left unsaid. I feel I am with you. You are dear to me. I look forward—to a real friendship. But a close tender friendship—no less. We shall have a marvellous time, darling. Don't you feel that, too?
>
> with love, my precious little artist,
>
> Tig[40]

But almost as soon as Brett arrived, reality trespassed on the dream created and sustained in the letters. Mansfield sent a card to Murry saying, "Brett is very very chastening. God has sent her to me as a trial. I shall fail. It serves him right."[41] And the day before Brett's departure, after her stay through the month of July, Mansfield wrote to S. S. Koteliansky saying that Brett was frightening evidence for the damage that background and upbringing could cause.[42]

Brett's visit could not have been a complete failure, however, for before Brett left, Mansfield finished "The Canary," her last story, a gift she had promised Brett in exchange for a painting of cyclamen. When Mansfield went to London before traveling to Paris and entering Gurdjieff's institute, she did not hesitate to stay with "my good friend, Miss Brett," as she called her in a letter to her father.[43]

That was the last time Mansfield and Brett saw each other, though they continued to write. From the Select Hôtel, in Paris, Mansfield wrote, "Oh—Brett! I have not really left your little house. It is there, just round

---

40. To Dorothy Brett, June 14, 1922, in Newberry.
41. To J. M. Murry, July 5, 1922, in Turnbull.
42. Hignett, *Brett*, 43.
43. To Sir Harold Beauchamp, August 10, 1922, in Turnbull.

the corner. . . . I wish you could walk into my funny little room for tea, you will at Christmas, perhaps." [44]

Brett attended Mansfield's funeral, at Avon, outside Fontainebleau, the site of Gurdjieff's institute, on January 12, 1923. Soon after, unable to accept Mansfield's death, she began a series of letters to her that she kept in her diary. In one dated February 23, 1923, she remembered their days at Sierre: "I see you again flitting round the garden at Sierre perching here and there, while I, with one eye on you pretend to be busy with my painting—you sit for a little while on the chair facing the Aloe Tree . . . with its gray green leaves like swords and its trembling silver bells. You are wearing a little dark brick red hat—and the blue jersey I bought you—what a lovely colour it was—" [45] The letters she wrote after Mansfield's death show the great loss she suffered. She had, after all, lost a friend who, by her own admission, gave singular impetus to her work. Brett no doubt felt a psychological dependence on Mansfield in that regard.

What, however, did Mansfield have in Brett? What particularly does her written correspondence with her tell about Mansfield's personality and work? She was clearly both attracted to and repelled by Brett. The disjunction between her expectations for their friendship revealed in the letters and the reality of that friendship when they were together is not unlike the gap between Mansfield's lived past and the transformation of it afforded by time and distance in her fiction. In fact, one can argue that she needed the gap in order to produce the work as well as the letters.

In the correspondence with Brett, Mansfield could sustain a perfect pitch of attention and closeness. And more crucially, while idealizing her, she could project herself on Brett. She could draw from her what was analogous to and important for her own writing without being bothered or impeded by the reality of Brett's presence. There was more than a little truth in Mansfield's jocular plea to Brett in 1921 that she send her a photograph of herself. "I'd *like* one," she wrote. "I should very much like to have you on a wall." [46]

From an imaginative point of view, which came to be the all-consuming if not only one for Mansfield, there was every reason to main-

44. To Dorothy Brett, October 3, 1922, in Newberry.
45. Brett, "Reminiscences," 92.
46. To Dorothy Brett, October, 1921, in Newberry.

tain her relationship with Brett, because there was something of the painter in Mansfield, and something about the nature of painting meaningful to her work. She occasionally supplemented her letters with amusing ink drawings, and once described herself in a letter to Brett as a "kind of Royal Academy picture *Waiting for Pa* in a velvet dress, lace collar, curls, tartan sash, with one foot on a five barred gate, an almost lifeless puppy under one arm."[47] She told Ottoline, "There is always something fascinating, captivating, about the *names* of pictures: 'Woman Drying Herself; Woman in a Hammock; Lady on a Terrace.' One seems to dip into a luminous life."[48]

The luminous life and the arrested moment were long-standing preoccupations of Mansfield's. As early as 1917, she wrote Brett describing her intentions in "Prelude": "Well, in the early morning there I always remember feeling that this little island has dipped back into the dark blue sea during the night only to rise again at beam of day, all hung with bright spangles and glittering drops—(When you ran over the dewy grass you positively felt that your feet tasted salt.) I tried to catch that moment—with something of its sparkle and its flavour."[49] In 1921, from the vantage point of a writer with similar aesthetic concerns, she responded to one of Brett's pictures, "I seem to see what you're getting at . . . the sudden arrest, poise, *moment, capture* of the figure in a flowing shade and sunlight world."[50]

Although Mansfield claimed to be "ignorant about painting," she had very definite responses to painters, admiring Manet and van Gogh, and dismissing Renoir: "His feeling for flesh is a kind of super-intense feeling about a lovely little cut of lamb. I am always fascinated by lovely bosoms but not without heads and hands as well. . . . [I]t is the spirit which fascinates me in flesh."[51] Her own painter's eye is evident in the stories, and no less in her letters to Brett, where in a matter of a few sentences she could capture a scene: "The way to Paris was lovely. . . . All the country just brushed over with light gold, and white oxen ploughing and

47. To Dorothy Brett, July 29, 1919, in Newberry. The full version is not yet included in *Collected Letters.*

48. *Collected Letters,* II, 346.

49. *Ibid.,* I, 331.

50. To Dorothy Brett, December 26, 1921, in Newberry.

51. Mansfield Papers, V, 17, in Newberry; to Dorothy Brett, August 29, 1921, in *Letters,* ed. Murry, 131.

a man riding a horse into a big dark pond. Paris, too, very warm and shadowy with wide spaces and lamps a kind of glowworm red—not yellow at all."[52]

In another letter, she wrote Brett a characteristic description of herself within the landscape. The need to fix herself in the physical world through verbal description marked her letters and stories alike: "I am on the wide balcony which leads out of my dressing room. It's early morning. All the treetops are burnished gold, a light wind rocks in the branches. The mountains across the wide valley are still in sunlight: on the remote drowsy peaks there are small cloud drifts—silvery. What I love to watch, what seems to become part of one's vision, though, are the deep sharp shadows in the ravines and stretching across the slopes."[53] When Mansfield wrote this letter, she was beginning "At the Bay." Note the similarity of mood in the story: "Very early morning. The sun was not yet risen, and the whole of Crescent Bay was hidden under a white sea-mist. The big bush-covered hills at the back were smothered. You could not see where they ended and the paddocks and bungalows began. The sandy road was gone and the paddocks and bungalows the other side of it; there were no white dunes covered with reddish grass beyond them; there was nothing to mark which was beach and where was the sea. A heavy dew had fallen. The grass was blue" (441). In both passages, Mansfield depicted early morning. The landscapes differ, but the time of day is quiet and private. Stillness and remoteness are evoked in the letter, absence in the story. In both she used color and contrast to create atmosphere.

It becomes quickly apparent that Mansfield's letters to Brett functioned as a kind of elaboration on and continuation of her work. In August, 1921, she observed to Brett that the channel stood between people living in England and adventure: "And by Adventure I mean—yes—The wonderful feeling that one can lean out of heaven knows what window tonight—one can wander under heaven knows what flowery trees. Strange songs sound at the windows. The wine bottle is a new shape—a perfectly new moon shines outside."[54] That is very much the mood in the twelfth section of "At the Bay," where Beryl waits expectantly at the win-

52. To Brett, October 3, 1922, in Newberry.
53. To Dorothy Brett, August 8, 1921, in *Letters*, ed. Murry, II, 125.
54. To Brett, August 29, 1921, *ibid.*, 131.

dow, regarding the scene where "the beautiful night, the garden, every bush, every leaf, even the white palings, even the stars, were conspirators, too" (467). It is well known that Mansfield worked quickly when writing a story. She did minimal revisions. It is likely that this was possible not only because, as she said, she held an idea in her head until its completion but because she could use her letters as oblique exercises for them.

It is not my intention to suggest that Brett contributed nothing distinctive to the friendship, or that Mansfield could have written these letters to anybody and achieved the same opportunity for elaboration. At the start of October, 1921, after Brett had sent Mansfield a photograph of one of her paintings, Mansfield responded, "I am very interested in your doll still life. I've always wondered why nobody really saw the beauty of dolls. The *dollishness* of them. People make them look like cricket-bats with eyes as a rule. But there is a kind of smugness and rakishness combined in dolls and heaven knows how much else that's exquisite, and the only word I can think of is *precious*. What a life one leads with them! How complete! Their hats—how perfect—and their shoes, or even minute boots."[55] Here, Brett's still life evoked a response that reads like an exercise for "The Doll's House," a story Mansfield finished on October 30. The portion of the story describing the dollhouse from Kezia's point of view is a verbal still life, with all the attention and care that Mansfield could characteristically lavish on the miniature. One cannot help wondering how much Brett's picture had to do with prompting this story, since there is no evidence that Mansfield was working on it prior to October, 1921.

Perhaps of all Mansfield's stories, "The Canary" is the one Brett has been most frequently identified with, since Mansfield wrote it as a gift for her. Because of the circumstances surrounding its creation, many have taken it as being about Brett, the interpretation fostered after Mansfield's death, no doubt, by Brett's recollections: "Katherine would come up to my room on the top floor to feed and clean my canary. She did it twice. The stairs were too much for her. She would sit and gasp for ten minutes before she could clean the canary."[56] Yet it seems impossible to read "The Canary" without first and above all reading it as Mansfield's elegy for herself. In February, 1922, Mansfield wrote Brett from Paris, "I think my story for you will be about Canaries. The large cage opposite has fasci-

---

55. To Dorothy Brett, October 1, 1921, *ibid.*, 140.
56. Brett, "Reminiscences," 89.

nated me completely. I think & think about them—their feelings, their *dreams*, the life they led *before* they were caught, the difference between the two little pale fluffy ones who were born in captivity and the grand-father and grandmother who knew the South American forests and have seen the immense perfumed sea . . . Words cannot express the beauty of that high shrill little song rising out of the very stones."[57] The loss and longing in this passage, as in the story itself, propelled some of Mans-field's finest fiction. They were characteristic modes, because they char-acterized her life experience. To the extent that she and Brett shared the imprisonment of illness, she could "give" this story to Brett, and possibly have held her in some compartment of mind when composing it. If Brett on any level brought the story to the surface of Mansfield's conscious-ness, she also returned Mansfield to her unconscious depths, the source of the story's emotional truth.

Mansfield's letters to Brett, whom she called a "kindred spirit," were very much a part of her ongoing work.[58] They became sites of elabora-tion, strategy, and practice for her fiction. They became fictions them-selves, enacting the important idealization of their friendship. It is not the case that Mansfield did not care about or love Brett—she insisted she did, numerous times—but as Mansfield came to value work above every-thing else, as human imperfection and time pressed in on her, the essence of their exchange of letters, at least on Mansfield's side of it, was chiefly in her relationship to her own art projected through her absent but cor-respondent friend.

Absent, across the distance, Brett could be for Mansfield the kind of friend that Roland Barthes has described as "one who constructs around you the greatest possible resonance."[59] Without disruption, with no mood marred, Mansfield could write Brett her observations and thoughts that might feed into a story and be a stay against time and life's disap-pointments: "It is a very quiet day here, green and silver—the movement of the leaves is so secret so silent that I could watch them all day—I try to find words for how they lift and fall."[60]

57. To Dorothy Brett, February 26, 1922, in *Letters,* ed. Murry, II, 190. Some variant readings are given here from the MS in Newberry.
58. To Dorothy Brett [August 8, 1921], in Newberry. The version in *Letters,* ed. Murry, II, 393, omits this section.
59. Roland Barthes, *A Lover's Discourse,* trans. Richard Howard (New York, 1978), 167.
60. To Brett, July 29, 1919, in Newberry.

The Middle of the Note
Katherine Mansfield's "Glimpses"

SARAH SANDLEY

It is such strange delight to observe people and to try to understand them
[. . .] to push through the heavy door into little cafés and to watch the
pattern people make among tables & bottles and glasses, to watch women
when they are off their guard, and to get them to talk then, to smell flowers
and leaves and fruits and grass—all this—and all this is nothing—for there
is so much more.[1]

By the time Mansfield wrote this to Bertrand Russell late in 1916,
she had completed *The Aloe,* the first story in which she combined
free indirect discourse ("understanding") with the epiphany (an acute
sense of "so much more"). It was an innovative combination that was to
serve her in at least seventeen stories and fragments over the ensuing six
years.[2]

---

1. *Collected Letters,* I, 287–88. Because of Mansfield's characteristic use of three- and
four-dot suspensions, my excisions will be marked with square brackets: [. . .].
2. In order of composition, these are "Prelude," "A Dill Pickle," "Je ne parle pas fran-

Since the discovery of the manuscript of *Stephen Hero,* in 1944, the term *epiphany* has been retrospectively applied to a variety of moments in Modernist fiction. But in Mansfield's private writing, as in her criticism, she tended to refer to these moments as "glimpses": "But though one feels that her deliberate aim was to set down faithfully what she saw—the result is infinitely more than that. It is a revelation of her inner self [. . .] though her desire for expression was imperative and throughout the book there are signs of the writer's 'literary' longing to register the moment, the glimpse, the scene, it is evident that she had no wish to let her reserved, fastidious personality show through."[3]

Glimpse is Mansfield's own term, then. In her journal, she wrote, "And yet one has these 'glimpses' [. . .] The waves, as I drove home this afternoon, and the high foam, how it was suspended in the air before it fell, . . . What is it that happens in that moment of suspension? It is timeless. In that moment (what *do* I mean?) the whole life of the soul is contained."[4] She used such moments to structure her narratives, to bring central themes to a climax, and to express the widest variety of experiences, from intense, nondiscursive ecstasy, in "The Escape," to acute nihilistic suffering, in "A Married Man's Story." In that, she used intense moments in a manner different from other Modernist writers such as Virginia Woolf, whose "moments of being" uniformly flux and reflux in the narratives of *To the Lighthouse* and *Mrs. Dalloway.*

Mansfield's critical comments on writing and other forms of art are scattered in her letters, in the notebook jottings that have been brought together and published as *The Journal of Katherine Mansfield* and *The Scrapbook of Katherine Mansfield,* and in the reviews she wrote for the *Athenaeum,* collected and published as *Novels and Novelists.* But despite this dispersion and the fact that her sources are as diverse as film and music, there is a consistency between her comments, her practice of structuring stories through shifts in different characters' discourse, and the forms she let the glimpse take. Mansfield's exploitation

---

çais," "Bliss," "Psychology," "Carnation," "This Flower," "The Escape," "Revelations," "Miss Brill," "The Daughters of the Late Colonel," "Her First Ball," "The Voyage," "A Married Man's Story," "The Garden Party," "The Doll's House," and "Honeymoon."

3. *Novels and Novelists,* 12.

4. *Journal,* 202–203.

of the glimpse or epiphany is arguably the most complex and complete anywhere in Modernist writing.

Painting, Film, and the Short Story

When one has been working for a long stretch one begins to narrow ones vision a bit, to fine things down too much. And it is only when something else breaks through, a picture, or something seen out of doors that one realises it.[5]

With the exception of the occasional piece by D. H. Lawrence or Thomas Hardy, Mansfield found contemporary writing to be "little predigested books written by authors who have nothing to say," and thus of little stimulation in the search for her own prose and form.[6] But did she seek and gain inspiration from other art forms?

In her journal and letters there are certainly suggestions that Mansfield was aware of qualities that made other forms of art memorable for her and worthwhile. She offered perhaps the best-known of her comments several years after visiting the exhibition entitled "Manet and the Post-Impressionists" at the Grafton Galleries in London, in 1910. The exhibition, organized by Roger Fry, included 150 works, of which the brilliantly patterned van Goghs remained most forcibly in Mansfield's mind:[7] "[Sunflowers] seemed to reveal something that I hadn't realised before I saw it. It lived with me afterwards. It still does—that & another of a sea-captain in a flat cap. They taught me something about writing, which was queer—a kind of freedom—or rather, a shaking free."[8]

5. To Dorothy Brett, December 5, 1921, in *Letters*, ed. Murry, II, 160.

6. To S. S. Koteliansky, July 17, 1922, *ibid.*, 229.

7. Among the works were eight by Edouard Manet, twenty-one by Paul Cézanne, thirty-seven by Paul Gauguin, and twenty by Vincent van Gogh. See Harold Osborne, ed., *The Oxford Companion to Twentieth-Century Art* (Oxford, 1987), 208.

8. *Letters*, ed. Murry, II, 160. Compare "Hang it all Brett—a picture must have *charm*—or why look at it? It's the quality I call *tenderness* in writing—it's the tone one gets in a really first-chop musician" (*Ibid.*, 188–89).

Negative qualities that she perceived in an artist's work could also act as a catalyst for her, as in her dismissal of Renoir's treatment of flesh (see above, p. 66). The inner life always interested Mansfield, the "spirit," the revelation within the scene. Small wonder that it was van Gogh's vibrant energy, color, and inner spirit that taught her a "shaking free."

She came to writing, as Vincent O'Sullivan has said, on "the whole tide of Impressionism, with the thought not very far behind that a painting captures an object under the play of light as it is once, but can never be again; that what one looks at is both very private, and yet the world as indeed it is." Mansfield strikes many as a Literary Impressionist, for whom the focus is, as Julia van Gunsteren describes it, "on perception. . . . This fragmentary, momentary, evocative reality *is* or *becomes* reality for the Literary Impressionist."[9]

Certainly Mansfield saw the connection between the Impressionist painters' depiction of the particular outward moment and her evocation of a character's inner life at a particular moment. She said of Cézanne, "One of his men gave me quite a shock. He is the *spit* of a man Ive just written about—one Jonathan Trout. To the life. I wish I could cut him out & put him in my book."[10] She had a tendency to recall scenes in what, taking her phrase from William Wordsworth, she called "flashes" on her "inward eye."[11] In 1920, she transcribed a passage from Samuel Taylor Coleridge's *Essays on Shakespeare* into her notebook: "Or again imagination acts by so carrying on the eye of the reader as to make him almost lose the consciousness of words,—to make him see everything flashed, as '*Flashed* upon that inward eye./Which is the bliss of solitude.'"[12] Although Coleridge's comment predates Impressionism, it speaks to the effect that Impressionist painters sought, where the onlooker's apprehension is complete, sudden, and nondiscursive. Besides

9. Vincent O'Sullivan, ed., *The Aloe, with Prelude* (Wellington, 1982), 9; Julia van Gunsteren, *Katherine Mansfield and Literary Impressionism* (Amsterdam, 1990), 9.

10. Vincent O'Sullivan, ed., *Katherine Mansfield: Selected Letters* (Oxford, 1987), 225. *Letters*, ed. Murry, includes extracts only.

11. "How beautiful Garsington is. When I think of it my inward eye is a succession of flashes!" (*Letters*, ed. Murry, II, 319–20); "Ashelham [. . .] will flash upon one corner of my inward eye forever" (*Ibid.*, 327).

12. *Journal*, 223.

flash, the term Mansfield employed to describe that intense and intuitive apprehension was *glimpse*.[13]

Mansfield found guidance for her own creativity also in film. Between 1915 and 1918, black-and-white silent movies seem to have provided her with much of her entertainment.[14] Cinematic similes appeared in her private writing: "I am so sorry we only saw each other for such an interrupted moment; it was like a cinema!"[15] When overseas, without a motion-picture theater nearby, she was sent critical appraisals of new films like Charlie Chaplin's *The Kid*.[16]

Mansfield's work as an extra early in 1917 has to have given her an inside perspective on the way the finished film is assembled from segmented scenes and images—a structural technique not unlike the one she employed in longer stories such as "Prelude" and "At the Bay." As O'Sullivan remarks of *The Aloe,* "Its 'whole content,' if you like, is there in precise images—in the aloe itself, most obviously; in a small girl looking at the world through squares of coloured glass; a child diverted from thinking of death by a man's gold ear-ring. . . . These are almost all 'minor' images, in a sense even incidental. But they are what *The Aloe* is about, and how it is told. They are not symbols nor mere illustrations, but images *as* narrative progression."[17] Mansfield would also doubtless have noticed that the moving camera grants the director a certain license with perspective, allowing the presentation of different scenes or actions through the eyes of different characters, as well as having an overall perspective that takes in the whole scene. That is akin to the license that Mansfield employs as author to direct and

13. Examples are too numerous to list. She habitually used *glimpse* to emphasize the visual apprehension of a scene or object containing emotional significance. Consider: "Your precious sympathy, most dear Elizabeth I shall never forget. It made that glimpse of the open air twice as marvellous [. . .] I want to tell you what a perfect glimpse we had of the Chalet Soleil as we bumped here in the cold mountain rain" (O'Sullivan, ed., *Selected Letters,* 262–63).

14. For references to going to the cinema, see January 7, 1915, in *Journal,* 66; May 9–10, 1915, June 19, 1918, in *Collected Letters,* I, 182, II, 248; September, 1921, August 11, 1922, in *Letters,* ed. Murry, II, 136, 236. See also Vincent O'Sullivan, "Finding the Pattern, Solving the Problem: Katherine Mansfield the New Zealand European," in the present volume.

15. *Collected Letters,* I, 302.

16. *Letters,* ed. Murry, II, 136. *The Kid* was Charlie Chaplin's first major feature film.

17. Vincent O'Sullivan, ed., *The Aloe* (London, 1985), xviii.

structure the narrative through the minds of different characters, as well as through the narrator.

As the newest of narrative mediums, film presented a chronological, "transparent" window onto reality similar to that of realist fiction.[18] Even storyboards with the characters' dialogue written on them were readily accepted by the first audiences as continuous with familiar narrative devices. But that aspect of cinematography could not have offered much to Mansfield the writer. It is from innovations like the close-up that she could draw lessons. As a sharp focus on one object, the close-up is the cinematic equivalent of narrative symbolism, and sometimes, of synecdoche. The use of the close-up to impart clues about a character's state of mind has its counterpart in Mansfield's focusing of a character on a significant symbol in the stories that climax with a glimpse. Filmic close-ups on character's faces, combined with appropriate music—usually at a time of great peril, or extreme emotion—invite an emotional response from the viewer, much as Mansfield's narratives at glimpse climaxes contrive to be poetically resonant and emotionally charged.[19] In "The Garden Party," there is such a glimpse: "There lay a young man, fast asleep—sleeping so soundly, so deeply, that he was far, far away from them both. Oh, so remote, so peaceful. He was dreaming. Never wake him up again" (498).

Mansfield also availed herself of the equivalent of the filmic pan shot at times, as in the opening lines of "At the Bay": "Very early morning. The sun was not yet risen, and the whole of Crescent Bay was hidden under a white sea-mist. The big bush-covered hills at the back were smothered" (441). She deployed narrative "long shots" effectively, too, as in "The Wind Blows": "Look, Bogey, there's the town. Doesn't it look small?" (194). There is also a long shot in "The Stranger": "You could just see little couples parading—little flies walking up and down the dish on the grey crinkled tablecloth. Other flies clustered and swarmed at the edge" (364).

Lighting effects to create atmosphere doubtless commanded Mansfield's attention. In one of her reviews, she showed how she perceived

18. For a more detailed discussion of film and fictional realism, see David Lodge, "Thomas Hardy as a Cinematic Novelist," in *Working with Structuralism* (London, 1981).

19. The same point might be made of flashlight photography, another nascent art form in Mansfield's time and one that also captures "significant moments." She wrote of it in 1922. See *Journal*, 315.

light as an external signal of the moment: "For when the sun is over the sea and the waves high a trembling brilliance flashes over the town, now illuminating this part, now that [. . .] It is, and something is caught in it, dazzling fine, and then it is gone to be back again for another glittering moment [. . .] Brilliant light, but not deep light, not a steady shining—a light by which one can register the moment but not discover and explore it." [20] Consistently with that, in "Bliss" descriptions of light assist in the achievement of a glimpse: [21]

> And the two women stood side by side looking at the slender, flowering tree. Although it was so still it seemed, like the flame of a candle, to stretch up, to point, to quiver in the bright air, to grow taller and taller as they gazed—almost to touch the rim of the round, silver moon.
>   How long did they stand there? Both, as it were, caught in that circle of unearthly light. (312)

Or light may shift with a character's inner life, as in "The Daughters of the Late Colonel":

> On the Indian carpet there fell a square of sunlight, pale red; it came and went and came—and stayed, deepened—until it shone almost golden.
>   "The sun's out," said Josephine, as though it really mattered [. . .]
>   Josephine was silent a moment. She stared at a big cloud where the sun had been. Then she replied shortly, "I've forgotten too." (400, 402)

Mansfield's writing can be considered filmic in other, less obvious ways as well. Two consistent style markers in Mansfield's prose are the use of several adjectives before a headword, and the addition to the main clause of further right-branching clauses, usually with the conjunctions *or* and *and*. Of themselves, such artifices are not unusual. What is out of

---

20. Review of Joseph Hergesheimer's *Java Head*, June 13, 1919, in *Novels and Novelists*, 38.

21. Mansfield's connection of light effects with atmosphere is recurrent in the journal: "So I have drawn the curtains across my windows, and the light is intensely fascinating. A perpetual twilight broods here. The atmosphere is heavy with morbid charm" (*Journal*, 9); "I want to remember how the light fades from a room—and one fades with it, is *expunged*, sitting still, knees together, hands in pockets" (*Ibid.*, 279). Such light effects are similar to techniques of the French *symboliste* poets.

the ordinary is the way Mansfield manipulates her "layering" of pictorial adjectival detail, and her provision of information in further clauses, to contradict information already offered, or to be so profuse that accurate visualization becomes difficult. "The Escape" illustrates this: "It was an immense tree with a round, thick silver stem and a great arc of copper leaves that gave back the light and yet were sombre. There was something beyond the tree—a whiteness, a softness, an opaque mass, half-hidden—with delicate pillars" (349). In "A Married Man's Story," there is something similar: "We gaze at the slim lady in a red dress hitting a dark gentleman over the head with her parasol, or at the tiger peering through the jungle while the clown, close by, balances a bottle on his nose, or at a little golden-haired girl sitting on the knee of an old black man in a broad cotton hat" (482). It is as if an entirely different order of perception is required, reminiscent of the Romantics' aim to have the meaning flash upon the "inward eye" of the reader. Mansfield's layering technique might be said to engage the same quality of nonverbal comprehension that is the norm for audiences of rapidly moving, multistaged visual events on the screen. In Mansfield's case, the technique is for creating atmosphere; in film, it is usually for the sake of plot.

Poetry and the Prose of the Short Story

In 1907, back in Wellington after time at Queen's College, Mansfield planned a volume of "child-verse," to be illustrated by an artist friend, Edith Bendall. The verses she wrote were imitative of those in *A Child's Garden of Verses,* by one of her then preferred poets, Robert Louis Stevenson. The project never came to fruition, but Mansfield continued to write the occasional piece of poetry and to draw inspiration from her favorite poets, among whom she numbered Shakespeare, Coleridge, Wordsworth, and Hardy. (She also expressed admiration for Arthur Whaley's translations of Chinese poetry.) [22] But if Mansfield looked to the past for inspiration, she also kept a firm eye on active poets' work. In "Night Scented Stock," she parodied T. S. Eliot's "The Love Song of J. Alfred Prufrock," imitating perhaps most effectively the form and subject matter, and the startling use of metaphors and similes:

22. For a fuller discussion of Mansfield and poetry, see Vincent O'Sullivan's introduction to *Poems.*

"I can't dance to that Hungarian stuff
The rhythm in it is not passionate enough"
Said somebody. "I absolutely refuse . ."
But he shook off his socks and shoes
And round he spun. "It's like Hungarian fruit dishes
Hard and bright—a mechanical blue"
His white feet flicked in the grass like fishes . .
Some one cried: "I want to dance, too!"

[. . .] It shone in the gloom,
His round grey hat like a wet mushroom.[23]

She was conscious of a link between poetry and the short story, saying to Virginia Woolf of Eliot's poem, which she read aloud at Garsington shortly after it was published in June, 1917, "Prufrock is, after all, a short story."[24]

In searching for a "new word,"[25] Mansfield was aware of the potential that lay in the fusion of poetry and prose. In 1916, she recorded, "I feel always trembling on the brink of poetry [. . .] I want to write a kind of long elegy to you. . . . perhaps not in poetry. Nor perhaps in prose. Almost certainly in a kind of *special prose*."[26] Mansfield's attempt to write in a "kind of special prose" affects the entire form and structure of her stories. The "special prose" in "Prelude" and "At the Bay" conveys a sense of the characters' inner life, melting different levels of the characters' consciousness, different time scales and tenses, and different levels of reality. A "special prose" is also evident in the stories that climax in a glimpse, where a full range of conventional poetic effects is put to use to convey the felt quality of the experience, to imply that the characters are transcending their everyday condition of consciousness, and to mark the passages out as climactic. Consider "Carnation": "And as he whistled,

---

23. "Night Scented Stock," in *Poems*, 61.
24. *Collected Letters*, II, 318.
25. *Ibid.*, 343. See also Mansfield's review of F. Brett Young's *The Young Physicians*, October 24, 1919: "We live in an age of experiment [. . .] Writers are seeking after new forms in which to express something more subtle, more complex, 'nearer' the truth; when a few of them feel that perhaps after all prose is an almost undiscovered medium and that there are extraordinary, thrilling possibilities" (*Novels and Novelists*, 92).
26. *Journal*, 94.

loud and free, and as he moved, swooping and bending, Hugo-Wugo's voice began to warm, to deepen, to gather together, to swing, to rise—somehow or other to keep time with the man outside (Oh, the scent of Eve's carnation!) until they became one great rushing, rising, triumphant thing, bursting into light" (317).

That Mansfield's prose resulted from meticulous selection is attested by this comment regarding "The Man Without a Temperament": "I must see the proofs *myself* before it is printed. If it is typed 10 to 1 there will be mistakes and at any rate I cant expect anyone to go through it as I must go through. Every word matters. This is *not* conceit—but it must be so [. . .] where I intend a space there is a space [. . .] I *cant* afford mistakes. Another word wont do. I chose every single word."[27] And if she selected the words meticulously, it was in order to structure the story through the *character's* perception of reality, and thus to try to "efface" herself as narrator: "I bow down to you. I efface myself so that you may live again through me in your richness and beauty. And one feels *possessed*. And then the peace where it all happens."[28]

Mansfield's use of punctuation, particularly of three- and four-dot suspensions, is frequently acknowledged as a skillful style marker; it conveys characters' strategies of mental evasion and deferral. But Mansfield was sensible to the certain superficial vogue for suggestive suspension that had developed in the novel of her day: "About the punctuation in *The Stranger*. No, my dash isn't quite the feminine dash. (Certainly when I was young it was). But it was intentional in that story. I was trying to do away with the three dots. They have been so abused by female and male writers that I fight shy of them—*much* tho' I need them. The truth is—punctuation is infernally difficult."[29] In both the selection of words and the punctuation, Mansfield strove to present a mental profile of the characters, to fit them "on that day at that very moment."[30]

---

27. *Collected Letters*, III, 204. See also Mansfield's letter to Murry, October, 1920: "You know how I *choose* my words; they can't be changed. And if you don't like it or think it wrong *just as it is* I'd rather you didn't print it" (*Letters*, ed. Murry, II, 52).

28. To Dorothy Brett, September 12, 1921, in *Letters*, ed. Murry, II, 134.

29. To J. M. Murry, November, 1920, *ibid.*, 81. See also Mansfield's review of C. A. Dawson-Scott's *The Headland*, October 22, 1920: "There are no hard words in this novel, and there are an immense number of dots; they are so many and so frequent that we believe they must mean more than we have understood" (*Novels and Novelists*, 278).

30. To Richard Murry, January 17, 1921, in *Letters*, ed. Murry, II, 88. Mansfield was writing about "Miss Brill."

Musicality, Voice, and Tone

Closely related was Mansfield's application of musical concepts to her writing: "Bogey, I think the Oxford Book of English Verse is *very* poor [. . .] except for Shakespeare & Marvell & just a handful of others it seems to me to be a mass of falsity. Musically speaking, hardly anyone seems to *even understand* what the middle of the note is—what the sound is like."[31] In the early 1900s, Mansfield had considered becoming a professional cellist, taking lessons in Wellington from the Trowells' father, before deciding in favor of writing.[32]

The comparison of writing to different art forms was current in the early 1900s. When Murry cofounded a consciously Modernist journal in 1911, he chose to call it *Rhythm*. As David Lodge writes, "One way of defining . . . modernist literature, is to say that it intuitively accepted or anticipated Saussure's view of the relationship between signs and reality. Modernism turned its back on the traditional idea of art as imitation and substituted the idea of art as an autonomous activity. One of its most characteristic slogans was Walter Pater's assertion, 'All art constantly aspires to the condition of music'—music being, of all the arts, the most purely formal, the least referential, a system of signifiers without signifieds, one might say."[33] For a brief period in 1908, Mansfield had earned money by entertaining at society functions with recitations, mimicry, and music. In 1908, she wrote to Garnet Trowell that she had an ambition to recite what she wrote on stage, with a particular emphasis on tone: "Revolutionise and revive the art of elocution [. . .] A darkened stage—a great—high backed oak chair—flowers—shaded lights—a low table filled with curious books—and to wear a simple, beautifully coloured dress [. . .] Then to study *tone* effects in the voice [. . .] and express in the voice and face and atmosphere all that you say. *Tone* should be my secret—each word a variety of tone."[34] Twelve years after that comment, her interest in such recitation was unabated; in a letter to Murry in 1920, she wrote, "I think I'll learn plays by heart and give representations like Mrs Hannibal Williams used to."[35]

31. *Collected Letters,* I, 205.
32. *Ibid.,* I, 18; Alpers, *Life,* 21.
33. Lodge, *Working with Structuralism,* 5.
34. Alpers, *Life,* 71; *Collected Letters,* I, 84.
35. *Collected Letters,* III, 291. Mr. and Mrs. Hannibal Williams were elocutionists from

Mansfield's interest in performance was further expressed in the dramatic sketches she wrote between about 1906 and 1917, and in the dramatic pieces she wrote off the cuff for performance at Garsington.[36] She and Murry read poems and stories aloud to their friends and to each other. She retained a love of well-performed music, and an appreciation of the "tone one gets in a really first-chop musician."[37]

The idea of writing a story in sections, as a piece of music might be composed in movements, clearly appealed to her, for in the original manuscripts of "Je ne parle pas français" and "A Married Man's Story" she marked the end of sections with the use of an upper clef.[38] It is the question of tone, though, of being in the "middle of the note" that has the clearest connection with Mansfield's writing. Tone in music is closely allied to the idea of voice, which to Mansfield represented the degree to which she had succeeded in presenting the characters' discourse—their perceptions and thoughts in their words—rather than a controlling narrator's discourse: "In *Miss Brill* I choose not only the length of every sentence, but even the sound of every sentence. I choose the rise and fall of every paragraph to fit her, and to fit her on that day at that very moment. After I'd written it I read it aloud—numbers of times—just as one would *play over* a musical composition—trying to get it nearer and nearer to the expression of Miss Brill—until it fitted her."[39] Her belief that the author should be immersed in the characters' inner reality in order to write their discourse is stated time and again in her journal and letters: "I find my great difficulty in writing is to learn to submit. Not that one ought to be without resistance—of course I don't mean that. But when I am writing of "another" I want to so lose myself in the soul of the other that I am not."[40]

Evidently, she did not think attaining that was easy: "Whenever I have

---

New York whose tour had carried them to Wellington in the winter of 1900. The Williamses took all the parts when they recited plays by Shakespeare.

36. See David Dowling, ed., *Katherine Mansfield: Dramatic Sketches* (Palmerston North, N.Z., 1988). Several sketches were successfully revived in performance at the Katherine Mansfield Centennial Conference, at Victoria University of Wellington, in October, 1988.

37. To Dorothy Brett, February 26, 1922, in *Letters*, ed. Murry, II, 189.

38. In Newberry.

39. To Richard Murry, January 17, 1922, in *Letters*, ed. Murry, II, 88.

40. To Sylvia Lynd, January, 1921, *ibid.*, 93.

a conversation about Art which is more or less interesting I begin to wish to God I could destroy all that I have written and start again: it seems like so many 'false starts.' Musically speaking, it is not—has not been—in the middle of the note—you know what I mean?"[41] By 1914, when she wrote "The Little Governess" and "The Wind Blows," she had evolved the key technique of the glimpse stories. That technique structures the story around the inner lives of characters. Its dynamic is contained in various forms of interplay between those lives. There is interplay between direct (conscious) thought and free indirect (unconscious) thought; between those forms of thought and direct speech; and between the thought processes of the various characters. The interaction is complex, the contrapuntal effects pleasing and challenging. Mansfield had indeed become a "first-chop musician" in the manipulation of tones of voice and levels of thought.

External Atmosphere and a State of Soul

It is strange how content most writers are to ignore the influence of the weather upon the feelings and the emotions of their characters [. . .] But by "the weather" we do not mean a kind of ocean at our feet [. . .] into which we can plunge or not plunge, at will; we mean an external atmosphere which is in harmony or discordant with a state of soul; poet's weather, perhaps we might call it. But why not prose-writer's weather, too?[42]

In Mansfield's journal notes from her trip to the Ureweras late in 1907, there is a marked concentration on scenic, pictorial detail, and there is experimentation in the way the detail is described. Initial entries are highly personal: "I lean out of the window—the breeze blows, buffeting and friendly against my face—and the child spirit, hidden away under a thousand and one grey City wrappings bursts its bonds—and exults within me." These are followed by relatively impersonal snatches: "[. . .] the plain—rain, long threading—purple mountains, river ducks—the

---

41. *Journal*, 143–44.
42. Review of William Hay's *The Escape of Sir William Heans*, July 18, 1919, in *Novels and Novelists*, 50.

clumps of broom—wild horses—the great pumice fire—larks in the sun—orchids, fluff on the manuka, strawberries." Still later, a fictionalized third-person account blends personal feeling with external description: "They climb on to a great black rock and sit huddled up there alone—fiercely almost brutally thinking—like Wagner—Behind them the sky was faintly heliotrope—and then suddenly from behind a cloud a little silver moon shone through—One sudden exquisite note in the night terza. The sky changed—glowed again and the river sounded more thundering—more deafening."[43]

In this teenage notebook, Mansfield can be seen experimenting with what she came to call atmosphere. In the mature stories, this atmosphere, the fusing of external detail and a character's inner life, was central to her artistic objectives. Perception of significant external detail can provide insights into thought or feelings the character may not consciously acknowledge. It helped enable Mansfield to dispense with a narrator who colors and controls the narrative. It also assisted in building structure and form so that the stories lead to an all-important climax without the need for conventional crisis and resolution.

The narrative glimpse is a moment of enhanced inner significance, often channeled through a character's perception of an object or scene. It is the most intense rendering of atmosphere in Mansfield's fiction. Mansfield seemed to consider writing about or "telling" stories prior to finishing their composition counterproductive, a kind of betrayal that could prevent her from writing them out. But once well into the composition of "The Doll's House," just three days from its completion, she made a note from which it would appear that the atmospheric climax, or the glimpse, had been her starting point: "N.Z. *At Karori:* 'The little lamp. I seen it.' And then they were silent."[44]

In a review Mansfield wrote in November, 1920, there is further evidence that the atmospheric moment could be the catalyst for stories:

The old theatrical star is tempted to go to see the show one night. . . . Again she lifts the glass to her lips, but there is no wine. Just a breath, a sweet-

43. Katherine Mansfield, *The Urewera Notebook*, ed. Ian A. Gordon (London, 1978), 33–34, 46–47, 74.
44. *Journal*, 268.

ness—a memory that she sips—and then all is over. Well—mightn't that be a marvellous story? Isn't it one of the stories that we all keep, unwritten, to write some day, when we have realized more fully that moment, perhaps, when she steps out of the theatre into the cold, indifferent dark, or perhaps, that moment when the light breaks along the edge of the curtain and the music sinks down, lower, lower, until the fiddles are sounding from under the sea?[45]

Mansfield repeatedly pointed up in her fiction the superficial aesthetic trickery of taking external detail or effects for their own sake while affecting that they have a deeper significance. In "Je ne parle pas français," the cynical Raoul Duquette is satirized as the author of "False Coins, Wrong Doors, Left Umbrellas, and two in preparation." Beatrice, in "Poison," plumps a liqueur bottle and sweets down on a table with her "long gloves and a basket of figs" and stagily attempts to describe them as "The Luncheon Table. Short Story by—by—." Bertha, in "Bliss," thinks of her guests as a "decorative group [who] seemed to set one another off [. . .] and [. . .] reminded her of a play by Tchekof!" Later in the same story, Eddie, Mug, Face, and Harry mention a play called "Love in False Teeth" and invent the title "Stomach Trouble" for another, and just prior to the denouement, the effete poet Eddie waxes lyrical about a "new poem called *Table d'Hôte* [that] begins with an *incredibly* beautiful line 'Why must it always be Tomato Soup?'" In "Marriage à la Mode," Dennis Hill, one of the indolent young bohemians with whom Isabel is infatuated, shows himself practiced in describing momentary visual scenes such as "A Lady in Love with a Pineapple," "A Lady With a Box of Sardines," and "A Lady Reading a Letter."

Although Mansfield was sure enough of herself to expose such literary poseurs in her fiction, she was also aware that she was capable of using suggestive external detail to gratuitous effect from time to time: "I finished *Mr. and Mrs. Dove* yesterday. I am not altogether pleased with it. It's a little bit made up. It's not inevitable [. . .] it's not *strong* enough [. . .] I have a sneaking notion that I have, at the end, used the Doves *unwarrantably* [. . .] I used them to round off something—didn't I?"[46]

45. Review of W. Pett Ridge's *Just Open*, November 26, 1920, in *Novels and Novelists*, 299–300.

46. *Journal*, 256.

Mind Time

What I want to stress chiefly is: Which is the real life—that or this?—late afternoon, these thoughts—the garden—the beauty—how all things pass—and how the end seems to come too soon [. . .] And there seems to be a moment when all is to be discovered. Yes, that is the feeling.[47]

The fictional manipulation of time, through tense, and the presentation of characters who attempt to evade their existing situation by recourse to alternate times or realities is a consistent feature of Mansfield's fiction from 1915, and is particularly prominent in stories written after 1918. Of a very late fragment, "The Weak Heart," Mansfield wrote, "What I feel it needs so peculiarly is a very subtle variation of 'tense' from the present to the past and back again."[48]

"Variation of tense" is realized in sentences like "The week after was one of the busiest weeks of their lives" (386) and "Exactly when the ball began Leila would have found it hard to say" (426) and "And then, after six years, she saw him again" (271). The *in medias res* openings to Mansfield's stories are justly celebrated, for she deftly avoided the expository detail about characters that realist writers considered de rigueur, instead plunging the reader straight into the characters' minds, with the use of their idiom in free indirect thought, thus drawing the reader into an immediate attempt to locate the meaning of the statement in the *characters'* reality: the week after what? when did the ball begin? which ball? six years after what?

Mansfield held to a post-Paterian belief that each of us is "ringed around by that thick wall of personality," a wall that protects our own version of reality, making communication with others almost an impossibility.[49] The conflict of memories in "A Dill Pickle" is an illustration:

"How well I remember one night [. . .] telling you all about my childhood [. . .]"

But of that evening she had remembered a little pot of caviare. It had

47. *Ibid.*, 314.
48. *Ibid.*, 271.
49. Walter Pater, *The Renaissance: Studies in Art and Poetry* (1868), Conclusion. At times, Mansfield seemed to support an older, Aristotelian image. See *Collected Letters*, I, 14.

cost seven and sixpence. He could not get over it. Think of it—a tiny jar like that costing seven and sixpence. (274–75)

A "subtle variation of tense" was a necessary part of the structure of the stories that flow from the mind and reality of one character into the different mind and reality of another, like "Prelude":

> She hugged her folded arms and began to laugh silently. How absurd life was—it was laughable, simply laughable. And why this mania of hers to keep alive at all? For it really was a mania, she thought, mocking and laughing [. . .]
> "What have you been thinking about?" said Linda. "Tell me."
> "I haven't really been thinking of anything. I wondered as we passed the orchard what the fruit trees were like and whether we should be able to make much jam this autumn." (255)

The flow of tenses was also essential for presenting the shifting of realities within the consciousness of a single character, say, Beryl, in "At the Bay":

> Oh why, oh why doesn't "he" come soon?
> If I go on living here, thought Beryl, anything may happen to me.
> "But how do you know he is coming at all?" mocked a small voice within her.
> But Beryl dismissed it. She couldn't be left. Other people, perhaps, but not she. It wasn't possible to think that Beryl Fairfield never married, that lovely fascinating girl.
> "Do you remember Beryl Fairfield?"
> "Remember her! As if I could forget her! It was one summer at the Bay that I saw her. She was standing on the beach in a blue"—no, pink—"muslin frock, holding on a big cream"—no, black—"straw hat. But it's years ago now."
> "She's as lovely as ever, more so if anything." Beryl smiled, bit her lip, and gazed over the garden. As she gazed, she saw somebody, a man, leave the road, step along the paddock beside their palings as if he was coming straight towards her. Her heart beat. Who was it? Who could it be? (468)

The complex shifts of tense, from the present progressive ("go on living"), to the future modal ("may happen"), simple perfect ("dismissed"), future perfect ("couldn't be . . . wasn't possible"), and the conditional ("as if he were"), are used to convey Beryl's dizzying shift of times and realities. She evokes not one but two fictional males who—sometime in the future—conduct a nostalgic conversation about Beryl as she perceives herself to be now. What Beryl does in both "Prelude" and "At the Bay" is create a whole other self whose fictitious past, present, and future exist alongside her everyday self's present. It is only in "Prelude" that Beryl recalls glimpses in which there has been a sudden fusion of her various selves, allowing a painful recognition of her own duality: "If she had been happy and leading her own life, her false life would cease to be. She saw the real Beryl—a shadow . . . a shadow. Faint and unsubstantial she shone. What was there of her except the radiance? And for what tiny moments she was really she. Beryl could almost remember every one of them. At those times she had felt: 'Life is rich and mysterious and good, and I am rich and mysterious and good, too.' Shall I ever be that Beryl for ever? Shall I?" (258).

Mansfield's own preference for the past is a consistent theme in her personal and critical writings: "I have given up on the idea of Time. There is no such person. There is the Past. Thats true. But the Present and the Future are all one."[50] In her fiction, the mind time of dreams and daydreams—the past and future the fiction accommodates—is more "real" than the present. Mansfield practiced writing out that idea in her notebooks:

> He woke, but did not move [. . .] In that long moment he sprang out of bed, bathed, dressed, reached the wharf, boarded the ferry boat, crossed the harbour and was waving—waving to Isabel and Maisie who stood there, waiting for him on the pier [. . .] And all this moment (vision) was so clear and bright and tiny, he might with his flesh and pout and solemn eyes have been a baby watching a bubble.
>
> "I'm there—I'm there. Why do I have to start and do it all so slowly over again?" But as he thought he moved and the bubble vanished and was forgotten. He sat up in bed smiling, pulling down his pyjama sleeves.[51]

In the stories, characters' awareness of the present is rarely what forms their existence in the present. The notable exceptions involve

50. To Dorothy Brett, February 26, 1922, in *Selected Letters*, ed. O'Sullivan, 247. The version in *Letters*, ed. Murry, II, 188–90, omits this section.

51. *Journal*, 131. See also p. 141.

businessman characters like Stanley Burnell, in "Prelude" and "At the Bay," and Harry Young, in "Bliss," who live in a chronological series of nows, ruled by the clock: "'I've just got twenty-five minutes,' he said. 'You might go and see if the porridge is ready, Beryl?' [. . .] 'You might *cut* me a slice of that bread, mother,' said Stanley. 'I've only twelve and a half minutes before the coach passes. Has anyone given my shoes to the servant girl?'" (444–45). Usually, however, characters are shown to live in a discontinuous time of half-thoughts, daydreams, fantasies, and remembrances. In stories such as "Je ne parle pas français," "Bliss," "Miss Brill," and "Revelations," the narrative is directed either wholly or principally through the consciousness of a main character who is experienced at evading the present reality of a besetting situation to the degree that the narrative becomes *about* the very process of creating narrative fiction. The intense glimpse climaxes of the characters are thus structures of their imaginations, used to fill an emotional vacuum and to import false significance into their stories about themselves. Raoul Duquette, in "Je ne parle pas français," says, "If you think what I've written is merely superficial and impudent and cheap you're wrong. I'll admit it does sound so, but then it is not all. If it were, how could I have experienced what I did when I read that stale little phrase written in green ink, in the writing pad? That proves there's more in me and that I really am important, doesn't it?" (283). On the other hand, the glimpses experienced by Connie and Jug, in "The Daughters of the Late Colonel," by Linda, in "Prelude," and by Fanny, in "Honeymoon," represent a sudden fusing of different levels of mental reality, offering them a sudden almost omniscient ability to interpret their earlier narrative:

> Until the barrel-organ stopped playing Constantia stayed before the Buddha, wondering, but not as usual, not vaguely. This time her wonder was like longing [. . .] There had been this other life, running out, bringing things home in bags, getting things on approval, discussing them with Jug, and taking them back to get more things on approval, and arranging father's trays and trying not to annoy father. But it all seemed to have happened in a kind of tunnel. It wasn't real. It was only when she came out of the tunnel into the moonlight or by the sea or into a thunderstorm that she really felt herself. What did it mean? What was it she was always wanting? What did it all lead to? Now? Now? (402)

The climaxes of "The Garden Party" and "The Escape" are unique in the characters' inner life, and they are unique in Mansfield's stories, for they mark the only time that there is a deep apprehension of a now that is not related to clock time. Paradoxically, the glimpses have a timeless quality: "He was dreaming. Never wake him up again [. . .] What did garden parties and baskets and lace frocks matter to him? He was far from all those things [. . .] All is well, said that sleeping face. This is just as it should be. I am content" (498–99).

When *Bliss and Other Stories* appeared, in December, 1920, James Joyce's *Ulysses* was over a year away from its publication, in February, 1922, and Virginia Woolf's *Mrs Dalloway* almost five years away from its, in 1925. Yet it is Joyce and Woolf who are credited with the experimental development of free indirect discourse, and who have become synonymous with the use of the moment.[52] Mansfield operated on the margins of contemporary literary culture. An eclectic and individual thinker, she created a unique brand of the interior monologue and the glimpse that predated the use of those narrative devices by other Modernists and in some respects remain more innovative and varied.

52. Free indirect discourse, or interior monologue, sometimes called *erlebte Rede,* is discernible in literature as early as that of the Middle Ages. See R. Pascal, *The Dual Voice: Free Indirect Speech and Its Functioning in the Nineteenth-Century Novel* (London, 1977). It was not until the Modernist era, however, that free indirect discourse became a dominant narrative mode.

Reading "The Escape"

W. H. NEW

*I choose to examine "The Escape" partly because it has long been ig-*nored, and partly because a close reading of the story reveals a great deal about how Mansfield used narrative form.[1] "The Escape" is a deceptively simple story, with what looks at first like a conventional beginning, middle, and end, but the reader has constantly to adjust, to interpret anew what has just been read. The ending, moreover, is ambivalent,

1. Most comments on "The Escape" have been made in passing. Marvin Magalener, for example, asserts that because Mansfield equated love with childhood, her fiction "eliminates the likelihood of philosophical consideration, effectively reduces history to the immediate present, and denies the validity of relevant intellectual speculation." That, he suggests, explains why "stories like . . . 'The Escape' . . . suffer from treatment too one-dimensional and simplistic" (*The Fiction of Katherine Mansfield* [Carbondale, Ill., 1971], 124). Sylvia Berkman refers to "The Escape" as one of some "uncharitable studies of neurotic women . . . of highly irritable nervous sensibility" (*Katherine Mansfield: A Critical Study* [New Haven, 1951], 121). Further, Berkman says, "Miss Mansfield had no affection for the modern metropolitan young wom[e]n. . . . They demand the servile, undeviating attention of their men; their hypersensitive nerves cannot endure the slightest strain. It is in the delineation of these self-conscious, egocentric beings that she utilizes the syncopated accent of their own speech" (p. 180).

throwing into question everything that has seemed obvious on first reading, including the personality of the characters and the course of the narrative. But such an ending should not be a total surprise, for "adjustment" has been built into the *form* of "The Escape" from the beginning.
The story asks us to recognize the deceptiveness of absolutes and at the
same time the power of illusion. Reading the story requires us to interpret
how the forms of deception and adjustment connect with the events in
the narrative.

Thematically, the story focuses on the uneasy relationships between
men and women. Technically, it dramatizes how those relationships repeatedly surface in language and in the control over conventional systems
of social authority. In concentrating first upon technique, I will examine
ways in which form in this story constructs, and then reconstructs, the
character of events and the dimensions of personal relations. I will then
go on to consider some of the ramifications of the formal patterns, particularly as they bear upon an interpretation of the ending, and hence
upon a fuller appreciation of the text.

"The Escape" is a story with a limited known history. It first appeared
in the *Athenaeum* on July 9, 1920, and it was used, Antony Alpers observes, "as a late addition to *Bliss and Other Stories*."[2] It is the concluding story in that volume, which appeared in December, 1920. Alpers
adds, "No MS is known." The exact date of composition seems also
uncertain—Alpers leaves it out of his chronology—but there is evidence
in the text and in Mansfield's journal that suggests it was written close to
the time of publication.[3] The setting, for one thing, suggests Mediterra-

---

2. *Stories*, 563.

3. The tree scene may derive from observations in the south of France. Mansfield's journal for February 5, 1920, reads, "Saw an orange-tree, an exquisite shape against the sky:
when the fruit is ripe the leaves are pale yellow" (*Journal*, 198). Another entry, entitled
"The Glimpse," partly quoted by Sarah Sandley in "The Middle of the Note: Mansfield's
'Glimpses,'" p. 71 above, adds to the context for reading the epiphany scene: "In that
moment . . . the whole life of the soul is contained. One is flung up—out of life—one is
'held,' and then, —down, bright, broken, glittering on to the rocks, tossed back, part of the
ebb and flow. . . . But while one hangs, suspended in the air, held—while I watched the
spray, I was conscious *for* life of the . . . flowers on the tree I was passing; and more—of a
huge cavern where my selves (who were like ancient sea-weed gatherers) mumbled, indifferent and intimate . . . and this other self apart in the carriage, grasping the cold knob of
her umbrella, thinking of a ship, of ropes stiffened with white paint and the wet, flapping
oilskins of sailors. . . . Shall one ever be at peace with oneself? Ever quiet and uninter-

nean France, where Mansfield lived in early 1918, the year of her marriage to John Middleton Murry. The story was presumably written after
that time, possibly in 1919, a year of almost no story writing by Mansfield, or more likely, as Clare Hanson and Andrew Gurr argue, in Hampstead in 1920.[4] Possibly it was written in Ospedaletti or Menton, to
which Mansfield went in September, 1919, seeking a sunshine cure for
her tuberculosis, and where she remained through the spring of 1920.[5]

Motif and technique in the story also link it with others of this period.
A story involving marriage, with the focus on the man as well as the
woman, it can be compared with "Je ne parle pas français," of 1918,
with "The Man Without a Temperament," designed in January, 1920,
and completed in Ospedaletti, with "Marriage à la Mode," of 1921, and
in a kind of inverse way, with "Mr and Mrs Dove," also of 1921. A
central image of a tree in a closed garden—an image of transcendent or
epiphanic illumination—also suggests connections with "Bliss," which
had been completed in southern France in early 1918.[6] Noting the am-

---

rupted—without pain—with the one whom one loves under the same roof?" (*Journal*,
203). Gillian Boddy, commenting on Mansfield's pictorial abilities, cites a passage about
Bandol that may also be relevant: "The wind died down at sunset. Half a ring of moon
hangs in the hollow air. It is very quiet. Somewhere I can hear a woman crooning a song"
(*Katherine Mansfield: The Woman and the Writer* [Ringwood, Austl., 1988], 108).

4. "The Escape," Clare Hanson and Andrew Gurr assert, was "written at Hampstead
in the summer of 1920" (*Katherine Mansfield* [London, 1981], 57). Vincent O'Sullivan
told me in a letter in 1988 that there are no *direct* references to the story in Mansfield's
letters of 1920, though Peter Halter quotes a possibly relevant statement from a letter to
Richard Murry a month before the story appeared: "People today are simply cursed by
what I call the *personal* . . . What is happening to ME. Look at ME. This is what has been
done to ME. It's just as though you tried to run and all the while an enormous black serpent
fastened on to you (*Katherine Mansfield und die Kurzgeschichte* [Bern, 1972], 135).

5. The woman in the story uses masks—the makeup, the veil, the parasol—as rejections
of or resistance to the sun. Her habit is perhaps to be read as an unconscious denial of the
need for treatment. The combination of musical motifs, the south of France, and the threat
of tuberculosis may also suggest parallels with *La Traviata*.

6. Berkman points out the symbolic value of the copper-leafed tree, in *Katherine
Mansfield*, 192. Martin Armstrong makes the same point; according to him, "The Escape"
and "Bliss" are "prose poems [that use] symbolism. . . . [T]he idea of the story is embodied,
or partly embodied, in a tree. Just as in poetry, those trees stand for an emotion, a state
of mind, which, as beautiful visual images, they translate directly and emotionally to the
reader. It is, as it were, a short-circuiting of emotion from writer to reader without any coil
of analysis and generalization" ("The Art of Katherine Mansfield," *Fortnightly Review*,

bivalent ending, Alpers suggests a direct formal link between "The Escape" and the story called "Revelations," which immediately precedes it in *Bliss and Other Stories* and which had also been published in the *Athenaeum* in 1920, on June 11.[7] "The Escape," like "Revelations," makes use of a contrast between a desire for freedom and a commitment to enclosure or safety, a tension that takes figurative form in tropes and images of fashion, appearance, and travel. Such comparisons suggest the frame of mind in which these stories were composed. They only hint, however, at the particularities of text.

The story tells of a man and a woman, both unnamed, who have missed the train that will take them away from where they are. It begins—and for most of the narrative continues—within the woman's perspective. She blames her husband for all the mistakes, difficulties, and failures with which she feels she has to contend. As the story continues, it exposes their quarrels, or their suppressed quarrels, or at least her inner quarrels with him, while a driver with an open carriage takes them over a hill from one bay to another, to catch another train. After an abrupt stop along the way, which is separately perceived by the husband and the wife and which affects them differently, the story even more abruptly shifts time and place, and ends aboard the second train. The wife, who speaks both English and French, is in a compartment with another couple—a man, who speaks some English, and his wife, who appears to speak French only. The husband stands in the corridor, silent, just outside the open door.

The escape of the title can refer to their simple—or complicated, depending on one's point of view—process of departure. It can also refer to the main characters' separation from the past, to their different techniques for removing the self from, or denying, the present, and to their separate flights from themselves and from each other. Such escapes are

---

n.s., CXIII [1923], 488). This subject is fully discussed by Halter in *Mansfield und die Kurzgeschichte*, 133–35. Like Berkman, Halter stresses the metaphysics of the epiphany, focusing on the man's escape. He reads the epiphany first as a regressive, effectively suicidal flight, and second as a release from the weight of a restricted personal identity which is achieved by folding into the radiant harmony of all natural being. See also Sarah Sandley's discussion of prose poetry, and of glimpses and epiphanies, pp. 70–72, 77–79 above.

7. *Stories*, 563.

worked out in part thematically, insofar as the reader is explicitly alerted to the theme of responsibility and is sometimes told directly of changes and of failures to change. But for both the reader and the characters, the escapes seem problematic. The characters are travelers, in transit. But though movement would seem to imply change, mere travel sometimes changes little except place. Contrarily, sometimes a declaration of changelessness in the story has to be scrutinized, as when the wife says that her husband never alters and never learns. That judgment has first of all to be heard as *her* assertion: it embodies a perspective, not an absolute judgment, and may be incomplete. Sometimes, further, an image implies change, as when the wind blows, although at other times change occurs—or seems to occur—in the still moment in the middle of movement rather than in movement itself. (From that arises one of the apparent functions of the copper-colored tree in the story, which the husband sees, not the wife.) But *seems* is as important a word here as *change*. In many ways the story is more fundamentally concerned with the forms of escap*ism* than with escape. It is concerned with illusion—that is, with people's resistance to the things that go by the names of fact and logic, with their reluctance to escape self and embrace change, despite their declared longing to do so, and with their occasional refusal even to recognize when a real opportunity to escape presents itself. This thematic dimension of "The Escape," moreover, shows in the story's narrative syntax.

The story's approach is conspicuous in its opening paragraph:

> It was his fault, wholly and solely his fault, that they had missed the train. What if the idiotic hotel people had refused to produce the bill? Wasn't that simply because he hadn't impressed upon the waiter at lunch that they must have it by two o'clock? Any other man would have sat there and refused to move until they handed it over. But no! His exquisite belief in human nature had allowed him to get up and expect one of those idiots to bring it to their room. . . . And then, when the *voiture* did arrive, while they were still (Oh, Heavens!) waiting for change, why hadn't he seen to the arrangement of the boxes so that they could, at least, have started the moment the money had come? Had he expected her to go outside, to stand under the awning in the heat and point with her parasol? Very amusing picture of English domestic life. Even when the driver had been told how fast he had to drive he had paid no attention whatsoever—just smiled. "Oh," she

groaned, "if she'd been a driver she couldn't have stopped smiling herself at the absurd, ridiculous way he was urged to hurry." And she sat back and imitated his voice: "*Allez, vite, vite*"—and begged the driver's pardon for troubling him. (346)

The paragraph is remarkably tightly constructed. The point of view is established as the wife's; the illusion of speech is to be read as an internal monologue; speech itself is in a foreign tongue and in that form is to be heard as an imitation; the train and the parasol are introduced as images; the waiter is contrasted with the driver, both as figures and as roles; the words *still* and *change,* and all their intricate echoes, are punningly connected; and the intertwined themes of possibility and security, of the mix of certainties and uncertainties that attends the attribution of responsibility, are revealed by the entire scene.

That mix also shows up in the sequence of syntactic structures. Repeatedly, exception succeeds absolute. *If* and *what if* intersplice with *wholly and solely, paid no attention whatsoever, any other man,* and *couldn't have stopped,* so that the paragraph reveals, formally, the contrary desires that have generated the woman's plaintive irascibility: her desire for freedom from other people's tempo and opinion and order, and her desire for other people to construct the world around her. She seeks to be free to live by her own terms, but at the same time she refuses the responsibility for her own actions. Repeatedly she redesigns reality subjectively, one result being that she can impute blame elsewhere. The first sentence announces this attitude: "It was his fault, wholly and solely his fault, that they had missed the train." To read this sentence carefully is to see how its syntax also articulates the process of reconstruction by which she rewords events, and so reworks experience, until they establish her in the thwarted role that she chooses to play. "It was his fault" is her reading of events, but it is a first draft of the reality she wants; "wholly and solely his fault," she adds, reconstructing in order to allow no possibility of an alternative. She thereby reinvents what has happened; she also invents a fiction into which she can escape. Inside it, she can—from a superior vantage point—see herself as a victim of others, a victim of their stupidity (she calls them idiots), or their indifference, or their calculated malevolence. At the same time, she can feel safe from them, for she lays simultaneous claim to being a respectable English matron, secure if not serene in the mantle of her public identity and station.

95

That her restructuring of events, the fictionalizing of her life, is deliberate is apparent from the way the story proceeds. Each time the woman apprehends a new event or occasion, her observation takes a preliminary and then a second form. The whole story reveals the effects of *revision*, in more than one sense of the word. Sometimes the woman directly alters her initial perception; sometimes through free indirect discourse the narrative follows the woman's shift in posture or behavior. Always the story emphasizes what seems to be a greater clarity of observation, only by the sheer repetition to reveal the degree to which the clarity is an illusion wrought by rationalization and desire. The process, that is, is less additive than it is adjustive; it is designed more to reshape than to represent the dimensions of the real.

Several techniques contribute to the effect of revision, including five structural patterns:

1. The noun with a calorific modifier following: "And then the station—unforgettable" (347).

2. The intensifying alteration of a verb: "Oh, to care as I care—to feel as I feel" (347). "Her voice had changed. It was shaking now—crying now" (347).

3. The repetition of a phrase with the addition of adjectival detail: "the last of the houses, those small straggling houses with bits of broken pots flung among the flower-beds" (347). "he wore a new, a shining new straw hat" (347). "'Oh, the dust,' she breathed, 'the disgusting, revolting dust'" (347).

4. The alteration of number to intensifying effect: "Every five minutes, every two minutes the driver trailed the whip across them" (347).

5. The use of nominal and verbal lists, to account—almost cinematically—for swift sequential perceptions: "They swung down the road that fell into a small valley, skirted the sea coast . . . , and then coiled over a gentle ridge on the other side. . . . The carriage swung down the hill, bumped, shook. . . . She clutched the sides of the seat, she closed her eyes, and he knew she felt this was happening on purpose; this swinging and bumping, this was all done—and he was responsible for it, somehow—to spite her because she had asked if they couldn't go a little faster" (348–49; note how "this was all done," a passive, with no agent

named, unfolds into the naming of an agent, into an absolute ascription of responsibility, and into a connection between the naming of a possibility by the woman and the occurrence of dislocating consequences).

The text makes plain the effects of intensification and reconstruction. By rewording events, the woman validates her version of them and her reaction to them. What she does not notice is the degree to which she has involved her husband in her methods of seeing, and what she does not accept is the degree to which her claims to independence are thwarted by her own behavior. Throughout, she is irritated by dust and smoke, and by her husband—till, within her mind and the text, he becomes equated with them. In addition, he is so restructured by her speech patterns that after a while they become his own, forcing him to reassess himself and then almost to believe in his own diminishment. In her absence, just before his moment of revelation, for instance, "he felt himself, lying there, a hollow man, a parched, withered man, as it were, of ashes" (349). But Mansfield uses that result to paradoxical ends. The man's reduction to nothing gives him on the surface a sustaining spiritual power, whereas the woman's verbal absolutes and her confidence in accurate identifications consign her ultimately to dependence. It is not what she seems to want, but it is what she establishes claim to, leaving her confined by her willed misapprehensions. The reconstructing fiction leads him into an experience he thinks of as clarity; her claim to clarity leads her resolutely into fiction.

The story does not, however, work out a simple chiasmic exchange. And it is hard, finally, to accept either of the characters as hero, heroine, underdog, or sole victim. Indeed, why Mansfield analyzed the couple as she did seems to have less to do with contrast and balance than with the ambivalence of consequence and desire. How that is so becomes clear from the story's imagery, especially the images of train, tree, parasol, and veil.

The parasol is present in the first paragraph, a pointer in more ways than one. It is the instrument the woman refuses to use to call up a carriage. It is also the item that permits what she later calls "escape" (349) from her husband—and that hence gives rise to the separation permitting his metaphysical escape from her. The parasol appears three times in the story: first as the thematic pointer; next in a narrative ploy, made out to be the apparent cause of a quarrel between the man and the woman; and third as the agent of cinematic separation. Working in all three cases as a sign of the couple's marital tensions, it also functions—in concert with the images with which it is textually associated—to suggest why the woman finds herself behaving as she does.

The stylistic features of the story's opening suggest that the woman is particularly articulate: the man is the one whose command of language and tone of voice are affirmed to be ineffectual. But repeatedly when the woman speaks—that is, when the text puts her speech into quotation marks, signaling statement, though it is not always clear that she speaks aloud—her statements tail off into fragments.[8] On one such occasion— an occasion of one of her ongoing restructurings of reality—the quarrel is set in motion, though not directly and not immediately:

> "Oh, to care as I care—to feel as I feel, and never to be saved anything—never to know for one moment what it was to . . . to . . ."
>
> Her voice had changed. It was shaking now—crying now. She fumbled with her bag, and produced from its little maw a scented handkerchief. She put up her veil and, as though she were saying for somebody else: "I know, my darling," she pressed the handkerchief to her eyes. (347)

The veil is lifted. And the little bag, with its animal-like open "jaws" (347), displays its contents to the man, who identifies them not simply as toiletries but as the artifacts of her life and the accoutrements of a god-ruler's afterlife: "The little bag, with its shiny, silvery jaws open, lay on her lap. He could see her powder-puff, her rouge stick, a bundle of letters, a phial of tiny black pills like seeds, a broken cigarette, a mirror, white ivory tablets with lists on them that had been heavily scored through. He thought: 'In Egypt she would be buried with those things.'" (347). At this point, a tiny wind blows, just enough to cause a "whirling, twirling

---

8. Given the concern with mirrors, mimicry, and fragmentation, it is well to consider Toril Moi's comments on Luce Irigaray, in *Sexual/Textual Politics* (New York, 1985), as another context for reading "The Escape." As Moi understands Irigaray, she argues that women's writing uses mimicry and incomplete statements to parody the normative assumptions of patriarchal rhetoric, in its concern for "wholeness" and "centre," and to claim for women freedom from the "logical" strictures of consistency, identity, and limited meaning. In "The Escape," however, incomplete utterance seems rather to reinforce the woman's dependence.

snatch of dust" to settle "on their clothes like the finest ash" (347). She takes out a powder puff, the powder flies over them both, and she recoils at what she inconsistently calls "the disgusting, revolting dust" (347). It is her own action that causes the powder to fly, but by calling the powder dust, she resists acknowledging that. When he suggests she use her parasol to protect herself, she "blazed again. 'Please leave my parasol alone! I don't want my parasol! And anyone who was not utterly insensitive would know that I'm far, far too exhausted to hold up a parasol. And with a wind like this tugging at it. . . . Put it down at once,' she flashed, and then snatched the parasol from him, tossed it into the crumpled hood behind, and subsided, panting" (347). She reads subsequent events in a way that extends the quarrel. He buys her flowers from some children running alongside the carriage; she interprets his action as an insult, and as a reward for the children, whom she calls "horrid little monkeys" and "beggars" (348). So she hurls the flowers away. Each character misperceives the other as weak, and acts accordingly; they misconstrue each other's behavior, finding deliberate malice or cruelty where sometimes there is only petulance and self-absorption.

Obliquely duplicating her action with her bag, he takes out his cigarette case; she reminds him theatrically that she suffers anguish when smoke floats across her face. Smoke, dust, powder, and ash, in their association, alter the way the natural landscape is seen. The wind begins to blow "stronger" (348), and the roadside gardens take on "bright, burning" colors (348). The landscape burns; language blazes. Then the carriage goes over another bump, the parasol falls out, and the woman bursts into another incomplete statement, which she concludes quietly but with a false-seeming, mimic gentleness, again blaming her husband:

> "My parasol. It's gone. The parasol that belonged to my mother. The parasol that I prize more than—more than. . . ." She was simply beside herself. . . .
>
> "Look here," he said, "it can't be gone. If it fell out it will be there still. Stay where you are. I'll fetch it."
>
> But she saw through that. Oh, how she saw through it! "No, thank you." And she bent her spiteful, smiling eyes upon him, regardless of the driver. "I'll go myself. I'll walk back and find it, and trust you not to follow. For"—knowing the driver did not understand, she spoke softly, gently—"if I don't escape from you for a minute I shall go mad." (349)

The story continues its gradual shift to the man's point of view. He has his epiphany by the copper-colored tree, and the narrative closes.

The quarrel involving the parasol constitutes the main body of the story. It might be enough to dismiss the whole exchange as the sentimental excess Virginia Woolf and some other readers found in *Bliss and Other Stories* were it not for the way that the images, the objects, the events, and the structures of language in the sequence are coordinated to emphasize gender, role, and theatricality.[9] Accompanying the accounts of events aboard the carriage, a series of passages that describe the changing landscape creates the illusion of backdrop, of a changing set design against which the actions occur. The *staging* of the actions has to be read as part of the narrative form, and as integral to the story's achievement.

To start with, the contents of the woman's bag are no random collection. Some of the items—the powder, the rouge stick, the mirror—are part of a theater of masking and disguise. Along with the other items—the broken cigarette, the black pills, the bundled letters, and the ivory tablets—they bring together various modalities of alteration. But in the process, power is denied both to pills and to language. The pills are only seed*like,* the letters *bundled,* the lists on the tablets *scored-through,* their fertility or potency or potentiality removed from them. All that is left is paint and "dust"—the image of change and the image of identity but not the reality. The effect is reinforced by the mirror.

The actions aboard the shaking carriage begin, moreover, when the woman lifts her veil—that other mask of fashion's theater. She would be opening her face to view except that beneath the veil is the powdered face, or the face accustomed to powder—mask covering mask in an indefinitely extended implied layering of disguise. She refuses the parasol, another revelatory covering of the conscious coquette, but the man has offered it outside the accepted social context, suggesting it as protection against wind and dust rather than sun. She later claims it as her own, from her mother, after it is gone. There appears to be a power in possession, but there is a question whether the power rests in the object itself, in the illusion created by the object, or in the language that is used to articulate either object or illusion. Here there is theater in the *action* as well as in the *image.* For the woman is torn between acting in accordance with precept, which confines, and acting in accordance with convention,

9. On Virginia Woolf's opinion, see Claire Tomalin, *Katherine Mansfield: A Secret Life* (London, 1987), 218.

which also confines. It seems she cannot win. To use the parasol is to hide; to throw it away is to put on a false face; to possess it is to hold it through the identity of another; to escape in order to retrieve it is to withdraw. All actions involve role playing. And all roles, here, cause language to stutter into fragments or silence.

The veil and the parasol have to yield more if the ending of the story is to amount to anything beyond superficial portraiture. Consider first of all the image the woman projects, in a story from 1920. She is married: that gives her conventional status. She also smokes, or did once, though she does not like her husband to do so near her. She wears rouge: that makes her smart, to conventional eyes. The ambivalence of the imagery stems directly from the dichotomy between a woman who clearly claims all the privilege that marriage accords her and one who seems to blame her husband for her attraction toward, or at least dependence on, him. The makeup is a mask, but it is put on at once to declare her fashionable independence from convention and to impress or appeal to others around her, including men. The parasol—a "woman's object"—is spurned when her husband offers it to her, that is, when he establishes her role for her. But she is also at some level conscious that to give up the parasol—to declare her independence, perhaps—is to give up the kind of role her mother has set for her. To lift the veil, moreover, is potentially to give up the constraints of a traditional role, but it may also signify the giving up of mystery or power or both. In any event, she has lowered the veil again before she refuses the parasol, and she lies back, as the text has it, "as if overcome" (347), the theater of imitation ruling her action as well as her appearance. Her dark eyes look immense and imploring "behind the veil" (348) when she asks him not to smoke, but her voice, though "calm," is "weak" (348). Neither the characters nor their circumstances are as they seem. Hence the possibility for other kinds of reversal, or reconstruction, is strong.

Sandra Gilbert and Susan Gubar comment explicitly on the significance of veil imagery, in *The Madwoman in the Attic*. The veil, they write, is an "image of confinement . . . related to the imagery of enclosure that constantly threatens to stifle the heroines of women's fiction. . . . Unlike a door, which is either open or shut . . . , [a veil] is always potentially both—always holding out the mystery of imminent revelation."[10]

10. The imminence of revelation, Sandra Gilbert and Susan Gubar go on, is conceived as either a promise or a threat that the viewer will be able to see through the veil from one

In nineteenth-century literature, the veil is associated with Romantic fantasies about the "myth of penetrating vision," and "it makes perfect sense," they add, "that the ambiguity of the veil . . . should associate it in male minds with that repository of mysterious otherness, the female. As an inspiration and source of imaginative power, the presence behind the veil for many a poet is the female muse."[11] The "veiled lady of male literature," moreover, "frequently identified with spiritual powers," is usually angelic, though this muse, in male writing, often turns into the hag Medusa. But for women writers, say Gilbert and Gubar,

> the exceptional insight, with resultant duplicity, of a veiled lady, becomes a strategy for survival in a hostile, male-dominated world. Denied the freedom to act openly out in the world, their heroines exploit their intuitive understanding of the needs of the male ego in order to provide comfortable places for themselves in society. . . . Those cut off from political power may exploit their passivity by becoming instruments compelled by higher forces, even as they are drawn to what constitutes a shortcut to authority through a personal relationship with spiritual powers presumably beyond the control of men. . . .
>
> Finally, . . . the recording of what exists behind the veil is distinctively female because it is the woman who exists behind the veil in patriarchal society, inhabiting a private sphere invisible to public view.[12]

These comments appear in an essay on George Eliot's "The Lifted Veil," a short story that first appeared in *Blackwood's Magazine* in 1859. Eliot's story tells of the miserable life and impending death of a man named Latimer, from the point of view of the man himself. Cursed rather than blessed by the gift of foresight, Latimer early in the story imagines himself in mortal conflict with the wife he has not yet married. But he marries her anyway, and then lives to know—in a gothic deathbed

---

sphere to a second, between, for example, the "phenomenal and noumenal; culture and nature; two consciousnesses; life and death; public appearance and private reality; conscious and unconscious impulses; past and present, present and future" (*The Madwoman in the Attic* [New Haven, 1984], 468–69).

11. *Ibid.*, 470–71.

12. *Ibid.*, 473–74. The authors refer here to Louisa May Alcott, Mary Elizabeth Braddon, Harriet Beecher Stowe, and Charlotte Brontë.

scene involving medical experiment and a revived corpse—of his wife's actual plans to poison him. Now the connection between this story and Mansfield's "The Escape" might seem tenuous, and I have not been able to determine whether Mansfield even knew Eliot's story.

Mansfield's biographers have drawn some connections between Mansfield and Eliot, which, if to all appearances not immediately consequential, do establish a frame of reference. Claire Tomalin asserts that Mansfield "rather enjoy[ed] her role of free woman of letters, living outside the confines of convention like George Eliot." In a letter written to Dorothy Brett on June 10, 1919, Mansfield herself observed that she had to break a Friday appointment because "I quite forgot Virginia is coming to talk over the Centenary of George Eliot with me."[13] Virginia, of course, was Virginia Woolf, whose subsequent essay "George Eliot" appeared first in the *Times Literary Supplement,* on November 20, 1919, and then, revised, in *The Common Reader,* in 1925. Woolf commented specifically on the ramifications of trying to live outside social codes. She mentioned the effects of Eliot's social choices, of her health, her gender, and the unconventionality of her connection with George Henry Lewes: "Her union with Lewes had surrounded her with affection, but in view of the circumstances and of the conventions it had also isolated her."[14] Given that Woolf later, in 1931, told Vita Sackville-West that she had thought Mansfield "cheap," it is hard not to hear a comment on Mansfield also in Woolf's judgment of Eliot's personal circumstances. And it is impossible not to read into "The Escape" some revelation of Mansfield's personal association with John Middleton Murry.[15] The images of the ineffectual man married to the shrew, and of the would-be rebel who desires safety, and of the ill woman, with ineffective pills, who has ambivalent attitudes to childhood and children: all are testimonies to the complex desires of her own experience, though not all readers, of course, have found complexity in the story. Sylvia Berkman's adjectives for the woman in "The Escape"—*callous, temperamental, selfish, unreasonable, nervous, irritable, neurotic,* and *rapacious*—do not allow for many alter-

13. Tomalin, *Katherine Mansfield,* 104; *Collected Letters,* II, 328. See also Mary K. Benet, *Writers in Love* (New York, 1977).

14. Virginia Woolf, *The Common Reader* (1925; rpr. New York, 1953), 170.

15. The musical sensitivity of the husband in his moment of epiphany also suggests parallels with Garnet Trowell and George Bowden. For Woolf's comment to Sackville-West, see above, 47*n*36.

natives. But though to Berkman these adjectives suggest that Mansfield, out of her "specialized knowledge of exacerbation," was "turning the knife on herself," it seems impossible to accept "The Escape" simply as unmediated autobiography.[16] Instead, the functions and effects of the story's form must be acknowledged.

It is apparent that Mansfield deliberately chose to cast her story as she did. In some ways, too, her choice follows a line of writing that the nineteenth century made familiar. Gilbert and Gubar outline a pattern, adapting a Romantic mythology of the "fallen woman" to their reading of "The Lifted Veil." In a fallen woman's relationship with a man, they say, quoting Mario Praz, "he is obscure, and inferior either in condition or in physical exuberance to the woman, who stands in the same relation to him as do the female spider, the praying mantis, etc., to their respective males."[17] Mansfield's woman, with her open-jawed bag, occupies at least an analogous position. Gilbert and Gubar go so far as to describe Eliot as "an outsider, a fallen female viewing respectable society, an insect watching provincial life," whose "unique perspective gains by its obliqueness."[18] They argue that Latimer, the narrator of "The Lifted Veil"—a sensitive man on the outskirts of "ordinary" society, who is the second and "odd" child of an "intensely orderly" banker[19]—bears a kind of parodic relationship with Eliot, the author. The reader of Mansfield might well hear anticipatory echoes of another kind. Gilbert and Gubar argue that

> the ability of Latimer and George Eliot to see into a dreadful future which they are then helpless to avoid corresponds to the feeling among women that they are trapped in stories, unable to evade plots created for them by alien, if not hostile, authors and authorities. Mute despite their extraordinary gifts, Latimer and George Eliot remind us of the powerlessness of, say, Cassandra, whose expressive exertions never alter the events of the past or the future and whose speech is therefore as ineffectual as silence.

16. Berkman, *Katherine Mansfield*, 180, 121.

17. Gilbert and Gubar, *The Madwoman in the Attic*, 460–61. Gilbert and Gubar refer to Eliot against a backdrop that at this point includes Eve, Cleopatra, Lucrezia Borgia, Goethe's *Faust*, Shelley's Medusa, Keats's Belle Dame sans Merci, and figures in Coleridge and Wordsworth.

18. Gilbert and Gubar, *The Madwoman in the Attic*, 475.

19. George Eliot, "The Lifted Veil," in *A George Eliot Miscellany*, ed. F. B. Pinion (London, 1982), 31.

Latimer's essentially feminine qualities—his sensitivity, his physical weakness, his secondary status in the family, his dispossession, his passivity, and his intense need to be loved—are a source of anguish because they make it impossible for him actually to become a poet. Granted poetic abilities but denied the power to create, Latimer lives out the classic role of women who are denied the status of artist because they are supposed somehow to become works of art themselves.[20]

In part, one might add, they do so by wearing conventional theatrical masks. When Mansfield's woman is "beside herself" over the loss of the parasol, it is possible to read the statement, therefore, as more than a sentimental cliché. The phrase reiterates the tensions that rise from the division or doubling of the creative personality when it is pressured simultaneously to rebel and to conform. And as Gilbert and Gubar observe, "Imagery of enclosure and the use of doubles in women's literature . . . both are complementary signs of female victimization."[21] In the incident of the smoking case in "The Escape," the woman uses submissive forms of language, like "I beg and implore you" (348), that she has just associated with the flower children she calls beggars. But in the succeeding incident, involving the lurch that loses the parasol, the verbs tell a different story: "her eyes blaze at him, and she positively hissed" (399). Still, the categorical division between muse and Medusa, angel and monster, submissive and assertive, is part of traditional male literary design. Gilbert and Gubar go on to maintain that the female self, so divided— and they are referring to both characters and authors—will hence "explode" or dissolve into a "paralysis" of "self-loathing,"[22] perhaps of the kind that Berkman had in mind. "The Lifted Veil" implies, in Gilbert and Gubar's words, that the insights of realism, the appreciation of another's point of view, while sometimes identified "with the honesty of the dispossessed," may also "diminish the self, inundating it in the trivial pettiness of humankind . . . and paralyzing it with the experience of contradictory needs and perspectives."[23] The dislocation of personality, the construction of a fiction of woman, constitutes both a problem and an

20. Gilbert and Gubar, *The Madwoman in the Attic,* 449–50.
21. *Ibid.,* 443.
22. *Ibid.,* 465–66.
23. *Ibid.,* 474–75.

escape from confronting the problem. If authors, like characters, are trapped in alien stories, who takes responsibility for the fiction of experience? Who has authority over it, in other words? The questions Gilbert and Gubar raise refer to Eliot but also relate to Mansfield.

Clearly, "The Escape" is at most a kind of closet gothic, if any parallels with Eliot hold at all. But the doubling of character and the role reversals that accompany this division reconfirm that Mansfield's story is to be read as more than a simple realistic portrayal of a marital spat; they also bear directly on the story's ending. "The Escape," unlike "The Lifted Veil," does not narrate events primarily from a man's point of view, but it is the men in both stories who are given the visionary capability. Over the course of "The Escape," too, the roles of the man and the woman— and the conventional associations with those roles—begin to blur, becoming part of an authorial comment on the ambivalence of authority and fictional invention.

Eliot's Latimer, at his moment of insight, finds nothing. Able to see through everything except Bertha, his wife, he finally discovers that the veil that encloses her encloses nothing but pettiness and negation: "The terrible moment of complete illumination had come to me, and I saw that the darkness had hidden no landscape from me, but only a blank prosaic wall."[24] Bertha's shallowness, he realizes to himself, has interpreted his sensibility as weakness, as a quality that would put him in her power, whereas it turns out to be a strength that has kept him separate from her grasp. But Eliot also explains why his recognition does not free him, and why "complete illumination" cannot free anyone: "So absolute is our soul's need of something hidden and uncertain for the maintenance of that doubt and hope and effort which are the breath of its life, that if the whole future were laid bare to us beyond to-day, the interest of all mankind would be bent on the hours that lie between."[25] When the woman in "The Escape" walks back to reclaim her parasol, however, and the man has his moment of revelation, what he finds seems on the surface to

24. Eliot, "The Lifted Veil," in *A George Eliot Miscellany*, ed. Pinion, 55.
25. *Ibid.*, 52. The passage continues, "Conceive the condition of the human mind if all propositions whatsoever were self-evident except one, which was to become self-evident at the close of a summer's day, but in the meantime might be the subject of question, of hypothesis, of debate. Art and philosophy, literature and science, would fasten like bees on that one proposition which had the honey of probability in it, and be the more eager because their enjoyment would end at sunset."

be some sensibility to life that is missing in the daily routine. But this passage of Mansfield's story is full of paradoxes. He sees the tree, lit by its "great arc of copper leaves" with "a whiteness, a softness, an opaque mass ["with delicate pillars"], half-hidden" beyond it. And "as he looked at the tree he felt his breathing die away and he became part of the silence. It seemed to grow, it seemed to expand in the quivering heat until the great carved leaves hid the sky, and yet it was motionless. Then from within its depths or from beyond there came the sound of a woman's voice. A woman was singing. The warm untroubled voice floated upon the air, and it was all part of the silence as he was part of it" (349–50). For his "revelation" to take place, he apparently has to surrender to the visionary experience completely, to be "enfolded" by an element that he identifies not only as female but also as "dark . . . unbearable and dreadful," something floating "like a great weed . . . warm, stifling," which nonetheless in due course gives him "heavenly happiness" (350). The question is, is this the man's discovery of his nascent sensibility, or is it a retaliatory escape from his wife, or is it something else? Is it a revelation or a reveiling?[26] Is Mansfield on his side in a marital war or really on the wife's, if on either character's side? Is the man responding to an empirical woman or to a convention of woman, a mix of sibyl and siren and mother?[27] And where does power finally rest: with sensibility, silence, or speech? Pointedly, the "epiphany" is not a conclusion, and not the end of the story.

The text shifts abruptly from the still moment to the activity aboard the train. The woman is in the compartment, talking; the man is in the corridor, both hands gripping the brass rail as the train rushes and roars through the dark.[28] The voices of the woman and her fellow passengers come out to him but do not reach him. His epiphany seems to have separated him even farther from others. Nevertheless, if the husband seems solitary, occupying the margins of the compartment, he remains self-contained. He continues to be a presence. In public, it is the woman who

26. The root word for revelation means, paradoxically, "reveiling," as though mystery defers not to clarity but to another mystery; it must be emphasized, however, that the Latin prefix *re-,* in this context, means "back from" rather than "again."

27. The pillars in the vision suggest an oracle.

28. He is reenacting in some degree the position his wife took in the carriage, gripping her seat against the shaking motion. Both appear to be *cradled,* rocking; hence both appear to be working out their connection with a mother figure as well as with the other.

has effectively disappeared as an individual—into her role as middle-class wife. For all her comments are now focused on her husband, and as the story moves to a close, they dissolve into lies and half-truths and fragmentary reconstructions of truth that come to no conclusions at all: "Do not disturb yourself, Monsieur. He will come in and sit down when he wants to. He likes—he likes—it is his habit. . . . *Oui, Madame, je suis un peu souffrante. . . . Mes nerfs.* Oh, but my husband is never so happy as when he is travelling. He likes roughing it. . . . My husband. . . . My husband. . . ." (350). In silence, the husband has surrendered to some mysterious female force and found happiness; in words, the wife escapes from herself only into incomplete utterances that declare her dependence upon a man. It seems he finds happiness not in traveling at all but in stillness. He now wears his "habit" like a cloak, a veil. It is she who seeks to move on, but travel gives her no satisfaction, for despite moving, she remains in an enclosure, defined by herself but from without.

This scene does not resolve matters. The man is still ineffectual, despite his presumed insight—for perhaps the insight, because he is a man, is made to seem somehow a conventional attribute of his presumed inef-fectuality.[29] The woman, swinging from vulnerability to shrewishness, gradually draws some of the reader's sympathy, because she shows herself over the course of the story to be as much a victim of physical discomfort and a pawn of the social pressures around her as a deliberate designer of discord. The problem, if there is one, lies in the reader's expectation of a resolution. But Mansfield's language has throughout insisted on ex-posing the limits of reconstruction, dramatizing artifice and effect, and undercutting the validity of absolutes, absolute conclusions, and absolute reversals.

The story "Bliss," completed in 1918, provides a paradigm by which to read the epiphany scene of "The Escape." In "Bliss," the ecstatic, ro-mantic, epiphanic glimpse of the pear tree is given to Bertha—who has the same first name as Latimer's wife.[30] In Bertha Young's case, too, in "Bliss," the power to see past surface into luminescence is deceptive. It is an escape from reality, not to it. (In "At the Bay," which Mansfield com-

29. See Moi, writing about Hélène Cixous: "It is . . . patriarchy, not feminism, that insists on labelling women as emotional, intuitive and imaginative, while jealously convert-ing reason and rationality into an exclusively male preserve" (*Sexual/Textual Politics*, 123).

30. She is Bertha Grant before her marriage to Latimer. Bertha is also the name of Rochester's "mad wife" in *Jane Eyre*.

pleted in 1921, the year after "The Escape," it is the men who need conventional language, and the women who discover in silence an alternative
form of expression that renders conventional language to some degree
irrelevant.) "The Escape" thus incorporates a formal variation on a literary theme that Mansfield has employed elsewhere. In "The Escape,"
she appears to have asked what kind of story would result if an author
gave silence to a man and speech to a woman. One result might well have
been to reverse roles altogether and so produce something that might,
given the attitudes of the time, have read as a fantastic or ironic critique
of the status quo. Overtly reversing the options presented to men and
women might well have exposed the limits the status quo regularly imposed upon their behavior. "The Escape" hints at that, but for all its
reversals, it is not so straightforward a story. It suggests that men, put
into an apparently secondary, "female," role, even given the creative
power of silence, will transform it into an absolute, either on their own
or by absorbing the structures of the language of power, and that women,
given what seems to be the dominant role, and control over speech, are
not so free from convention that power will not also limit them. Given
the story's concern from the beginning with reworking and revising experiences, the man's putative epiphany can be read as yet another reconstruction of events—an escape, not a recognition—one that, even though
it does not happen directly to the woman, is framed by her language
patterns, which are derived from those of conventional male literature.
Authority can remain powerful by remaining articulate.

But for neither character does authority bring freedom. For the man,
at the end of the story, reconstruction dissolves into absolute repetition:
"The voices murmured, murmured," says the text. After that comes the
last—and I think sardonic—statement in the story, and therefore in the
collection in which "The Escape" appears: "So great was his heavenly
happiness as he stood there he wished he might live for ever" (350). For
both the characters, to accept the absolute is to refuse to face the reality
of the alteration that is represented in the motions of their lives; it is to
accept fiction as though complete and true. In the woman's words at the
end of the story, her husband becomes a fiction. But in her compartment
she does not escape from enclosure either, for all that her voice and her
fellow passengers' are "never still" (350). The story obliquely suggests
that if women espouse the language of convention, they too will become
fictions, enclosed by the very language in which, even as they have at-

tempted to reconstruct it, they have invested authority. Given that paradox, how, then, does the reader finally respond to the "revelations" of "The Escape"—and to the veils of illusion that revelations contrive? Tomalin observes about Mansfield that she

> was a liar all her life . . . and her lies went quite beyond conventional social lying. Whereas Murry "forgot" things or distorted subtly, she was a bold and elaborate inventor of false versions. A charitable view of the origin of this habit could be that it was a bid for attention, a response to feeling obscured and overlooked in a large family with an inattentive mother; this may then have developed into a pleasure in dramatizing for its own sake, making herself into the heroine of a story. If the truth was dull, it could be artistically embroidered; and if she was the heroine of her own life story, lies became not lies but fiction, a perfectly respectable thing.[31]

This paragraph reads in some ways like a commentary on "The Escape." But "The Escape" argues that not all fictions are, finally, acceptable. Although fictions can instruct, they can also mislead. They can articulate alternatives, or they can be contained by the power of the conventions they employ. Sometimes fictions simply reconstruct the limits of the status quo, and are all the more seductive when they seem most to promise escape. Hence story making—the temptation that invites both the woman and the man to reinvent their own and each other's lives—can be a temptation for an author as well as for the characters. "The Escape" dramatizes the interconnection between the desire to escape from reality and the desire to change it, between wish fulfillment and reform. It demonstrates that articulateness and illumination are both sometimes notional rather than substantive, imitations of power rather than indices of possessing it, requiring always to be read carefully. But the fact that reading, too, is a reconstructive process seems to me, in this context, finally to spell out an interpretive dilemma. One of the many fascinations of "The Escape" is that it not only delineates, by means of its narrative, some familiar paradigms of power but also provides within its textual method some ways of commenting on the narrative and questioning the authority of the paradigms it uses. Cogently addressing the nature of in-

31. Tomalin, *Katherine Mansfield,* 57.

terpretation, this story refuses to resolve all the questions it raises. The refusal is part of the narrative design, suggesting that in this, as in other ways, Mansfield was at the forefront of fashion, using words to contrive an illusion of life, and using writing to speak about the contrary appeals of fiction itself.

What the Reader Knows; or, The French One

Perry Meisel

Though we customarily honor Mansfield for her craft, we too often let its mechanisms elude or escape us. Let us pay homage to Mansfield, then, by trying to be clear—a little bit clear anyway—not only about how her texts provoke, assuage, upset, and pacify but also about the way they are made as narrative structures. Two stories will do better than one, especially if they are very different.

First published in 1919, Mansfield's ironic and unforgiving tale "Je ne parle pas français" may strike us as galling and even cruel, certainly in comparison with the almost superhuman pathos of a tale like "Bliss," first published in 1918. If we read the stories in relation to each other, however—they were begun, by the way, less than two weeks apart, in late January and early February, 1918, respectively—we may be surprised by the kind of implicit dialogue they conduct, and in the process discover something precise about the way Mansfield's stories function, both as moral exercises and as narratological ones. Indeed, it may well be the case that narrative economy of the highest order—the kind of economy for which we customarily celebrate Mansfield's peculiar kind of genius—is the identity, or at least the parallelism, of the moral and the narratological. I will try to elaborate that identity or parallelism in Mansfield's work.

While "Bliss" is, of course, well known, "Je ne parle pas français" presents special and unexpected complexities. The story itself is simple enough: Raoul Duquette, a twenty-six-year-old French writer of astonishing pretension and surprising success, befriends a foreigner visiting Paris, an English writer named Dick Harmon. Raoul secures rooms in Paris for Dick on his next visit, which he makes in the company of a beautiful and delicate woman—his fiancée, as it turns out—who, at least by her own testimony, does not speak French; as she puts it, in the only line delivered in French in the story, "Je ne parle pas français." The kick of the tale comes when Dick deserts her, leaving behind a letter that she shares with Raoul, and with us, giving as the reason for Dick's desertion his mother's unwillingness to accept the match. The beautiful and delicate woman—she is given no proper name, only the generic nickname Mouse—is left desolate and alone in Paris, with only the dubious friendship of Raoul. But though Raoul promises to return on the morning after Dick's flight, he fails to do so. He announces his decision to us with a perverse pride in collapsing all decency of feeling—the kind of pride that marks his attitude toward everything in his derisive monologue, which is at one and the same time out of all whack with our customary sense of Mansfield and yet somehow peculiarly representative of certain impulses in her fiction.

The story's real tradition is not so much that of the reflexive or self-conscious *récit*—a story about writing a story—though it has sure elements of that, as it is of the bad or unpublished tale. The story is a sort of burlesque on both bad fiction and the pop mythology of the rakish aesthete which is among the very real raw materials of the Parisian demimonde—the "submerged life," as Mansfield describes it—that the story represents. It particularly mocks the unsavory Raoul, against whose ugly nature we rather automatically react.

In what direction does the story's viciousness cut? Where is its irony to be located? Or to put it another way, where does its irony locate its reader?

One way of answering such a question is to say that what the reader knows in "Je ne parle pas français" are all the things that the story itself derides: an innate sense of compassion, a sense of human worth, a sense of human sharing. All the things that the pretentious narrator maintains *are* the case are *not* the case, cannot possibly be the case; all our decency says no. Central here is Raoul's notion that people are, as he puts it, like portmanteaus. "I don't believe in the human soul," says Raoul. "I never have. I believe that people are like portmanteaux—packed with certain things, started going, thrown about, tossed away, dumped down, lost and found, half emptied suddenly, or squeezed fatter than ever, until finally the Ultimate Porter swings them on to the Ultimate Train and away they rattle" (277). Echoing E. M. Forster's indictment of modern life as the "civilization of luggage" in *Howards End,* of 1910, Raoul's metaphor reduces people to inhuman parcels, and their mortal care, or lack of it, to a kind of indifferent and haphazard registry.

Only such a cynical belief would allow for the callousness of Raoul's behavior, and yet it is a belief that is sustained throughout by a consistent if distasteful vision of how experience is structured. Raoul elaborates, through the logic of his figures of speech, an entire theory of character that is extraordinarily cogent from an abstract point of view.

"People are like portmanteaux," like pieces of luggage, devoid of innate or indwelling essence, because life, or at least our perception of it, is structured in or by a temporal chain whose functioning requires the contrast and comparison of what Raoul calls "moments" or "instants" one with another. "You never do recover the same thing that you lose," says Raoul. "It's always a new thing. The moment it leaves you it's changed" (280). While this may sound, on the one hand, like a lovely theory of the constant freshness of experience—and in some degree it is—it is, on the other hand, really a grindingly desperate theory of the evanescent flux of all things beneath our feet. Only by the play of relations, between one moment and another, or between one "habit" and another, can what we ordinarily call an essence or an absolute quality be established as such. The theory of signification implicit here is one familiar to structural linguists under the name of difference, and to psychoanalysts under the name of deferred action, even though Mansfield's own vocabulary derives from the Romantic tradition of Walter Pater and his privileged moments, and before him, of William Wordsworth and his "spots of time" in Book 12 of *The Prelude.* Raoul even explains, disparagingly though logically enough, that his bitterness against life is, as he puts it, the "direct result of the American cinema acting upon a weak mind" (278)—that life is a function of the ideologies into which we are inscribed rather than of any indwelling sanctity it may be said to muster from beyond the bounds of culture. "Everything," says Raoul, "is arranged for you—waiting for you" (278). Hence one's character is, from the ground up, a "pose," as Raoul puts it, which becomes a "habit"; even poor Dick doesn't just "look . . . the part," whatever part that may be, "he was the part" (288).

Such a perspective deracinates all notions of authenticity, not just in the temperamental way we might expect in any case of Raoul but in a seriously persuasive way no matter our moral evaluation of Raoul himself. Authenticity of self—or of world—is no more than a fiction, no less real for being so but surely less secure metaphysically. Indeed, self and world are, from Raoul's point of view, almost entirely without any metaphysical dimension whatsoever.

How far we are from the delectable universe of Bertha in "Bliss," where the human soul, as Mansfield puts it, has a "shower of little sparks coming from it" (305). In Bertha's "bosom," says Mansfield, "there was still that bright glowing place" (305). The difference could not be more exact; Bertha's tropes—"shower of sparks," "bright glowing place"—insist on a human essence, recalling Wordsworth's wishful image of the human spirit in the Intimations ode as well as a whole tradition of Platonic signs for the soul that stands behind it.

At the same time, though, "Bliss," too, is structured by irony. If "Je ne parle pas français" makes us feel, by dint of the reactive thinking irony classically induces as a rhetorical device, that just the reverse of its assertions is true—that there is a human soul, not just people as portmanteaus—then "Bliss" also requires an equal and opposite reaction: the feeling that despite its manifest claims, there is no Wordsworthian or Platonic "shower of sparks." In fact, poor Bertha is disabused of precisely the comforting notion that there is when her recognition of Harry's secret arrangement with Miss Fulton—an almost high-Victorian moment of knowledge, perhaps the reason Virginia Woolf felt obliged to criticize it—punctures her bliss at tale's end.

If in "Je ne parle pas français" the reader is all love and goodness, in "Bliss" the reader is all worldly guile and suspicion. The very first line of "Bliss" makes us prophets of contingency and caution; Bertha's pace is so breathless—like her running in the scenes she imagines—that we want to slow it down for fear she will fall and hurt herself, as she indeed does at the story's close. The story finds the suspicion in us by the force of its negation: "Although Bertha Young was thirty she still had moments like this when she wanted to run instead of walk, to take dancing steps on and off the pavement, and to bowl a hoop, to throw something up in the air and catch it again, or to stand still and laugh at—nothing—at nothing, simply" (305). By contrast, the opening lines of "Je ne parle pas français" fill us with the kind of gray rain we later associate with Jean Luc Godard's early *hommages* to film noir; the story finds the sunshine in us by the force of its negation: "I do not know why I have such a fancy for this little café. It's dirty and sad, sad. It's not as if it had anything to distinguish it from a hundred others—it hasn't" (277).

In "Bliss," what the reader knows is that people are indeed like portmanteaus. Despite Bertha's radiant optimism, they do not wear their essences on their sleeves; their sleeves are packed away in boxes of signification—in portmanteaus like those Raoul describes—that are the rhetorical tokens by means of which narrative allows us to know them and by which it allows Bertha to know them through a painful education. Bertha's fatal blindness or innocence of vision is in reading her surroundings, her husband included, too straightforwardly, reading them as though there were no necessity for reading—until the secret is made so palpable as to shock her into her realization. In this sense the story is an allegory of reading, disabusing the reader as well as Bertha of the notion that the notion of a human essence—whether in life or in a story—is secure.

But in "Je ne parle pas français" what the reader knows is that people are not at all like portmanteaus: that is the tug of the heart against which the story works. We can go up and back like this all day. It is as though Bertha's wishes are fulfilled by the negation of Raoul's view of the world, and Raoul's wishes fulfilled by the negation of Bertha's view of the world. This kind of dialogical play between the two stories is probably endless. But how can both these claims be true? How can the reaction prompted by one tale be the opposite of that produced by the other? How can one writer exhibit so discordant, so internally divergent a sense of what we ordinarily call character? How can Bertha's naïve Platonism give way to a darker sense of the instability of essences, while Raoul's nasty sense of the instability of essences gives way to a brighter, perhaps even genuinely Platonic, sense of the real stability of essences?

Well, if each reaction produces its opposite in the play of the reader's mind, it is likely the case that each category in fact needs the other to be what it is. Both can be true at the same time because each claim—so

Mansfield's epistemology goes—needs the other for what coherence each may be said to have. One is reminded of Harold Bloom's paradox that if God created the world out of nothing, then he must have created the void at the same time that he created the world. In a curious but implacable logic, Raoul's irony requires the truth of the heart he rejects, much as Bertha's belief in essence requires its violation by a duplicitous world. Each notion of character depends for its sense upon the other.

In both cases, too, what is dramatized is not so much discordance as the calculated disposition of the structuring trope of irony in a very precise sense: the enactment of the reverse of what is narrated in what the reader knows rather than in what the character shows or tells. Each story represents a falling away from the state that it names. "Bliss" is so named because that is *not* what the story transacts—not bliss but its sudden opposite. "Je ne parle pas français" is so named because what the story does is speak French, even while announcing that it does not.

Speak French, even while announcing that it does not. Mansfield thereby gives us a wonderfully appropriate figure for the operation that is responsible for what the reader knows. Recall that in the Parisian story the words spoken by the fiancée—"Je ne parle pas français"—are the only words spoken in French in a story that, by all logical implication and necessity, must of course be written in French. It is, after all, a story by the French writer Raoul Duquette, even though it is of course written in English, since it is really a story by the anglophone writer Katherine Mansfield.

The real but absent text of "Je ne parle pas français"—the French one—is, I would argue, a sign or cipher for the structure of Mansfield's reader, in whom resides the necessary illusion of a French text that finds its prior cause in Mansfield's English text. A French text is what the reader ultimately presumes—a text that exists nowhere but that has to exist everywhere if Mansfield's story is to sustain its illusion. The French one must be supposed: the real text that is missing, that has somehow been translated but that "retains"—the very word choice conveys the sense that there really is a French text—an aura of presence, like the one that attends the Greek whose authoritative absence Virginia Woolf will similarly lament, in a different context, some six years later.

For Mansfield, moreover, the importance of the reader's activity cannot be overestimated. It is the reader that is the active instrument or channel supplementing what is lacking in both texts. The reader is a kind of supplemental intersection between the text and the characters that it pretends, as part of its strategy, to be separate from, merely transcribing their self-sufficient essence, even though, as with all literary figures—as distinct from what we call historical ones—there are, strictly speaking, no such originals in fact. Bertha, Raoul, Harry, Mouse, even the Norman Knights, who humorously enough invade Bertha's home in "Bliss"— these are all figures in the reader's mind. They are the result of the work the reader does to exact from the text a stable illusion of character, which exists nowhere but in the reader's apprehension. By this unconscious work on the reader's part, the story takes on what mimetic attributes it may have, the result, not of an unmediated mimesis, but of Mansfield's technique of writing, and of writing her real text—her French one— through the orchestrated play of her reader's moral assumptions.

After all, narrative at large—and Mansfield in particular—constructs readers and, through them, worlds; it does not express, through a discourse of simple correspondence, characters that it projects as real and with whom the reader, as the saying goes, identifies. Rather, narrative opposes, through a discourse of transaction, the image of characters against whom the reader measures himself or herself. It is this revisionary ratio—the one between the reader and the subjective others he or she confronts in narrative—that structures what the reader knows, and it is here that narrative finds its true destination.

What makes Mansfield so special, then, is the precision with which she both exploits this ratio and clarifies its nature as the active pivot or mechanism of the art of fiction. She shares with some of her contemporaries—D. H. Lawrence and Wyndham Lewis especially—an identifiable Modernist strategy of alienating her reader in calculated and specific ways. The difference, however, is that Mansfield's technique is finally a conservative one that exploits the reader's unconscious and its assumptions rather than upbraids them.

My *Katherine Mansfield*

ALEX CALDER

KM to JMM, October 4, 1920:

> I am *no* critic of the homely kind. "If you would only explain quietly and in simple language," as L.M. said to me yesterday. Good heavens, that *is* out of my power.[1]

My Katherine Mansfield is no writer of the homely kind. Unhomely then? Perhaps the word has more of a ring in Freud's German: *unheimlich,* which his translators call the uncanny. As for the homely, let that term characterize some of the more familiar constructions of Katherine. She is homely because she writes about her and my home, about a New Zealand that shapes her as a writer; because she is a symbolist, a writer who presents the fleeting, the intangible, the transcendent, in terms of the close-to-home, the concrete detail; finally, and no doubt too obviously, because she is a "women's writer," someone essentially attuned to wom-

1. To J. M. Murry, October 4, 1920, in *Letters,* ed. Murry, II, 49.

en's experience, women's concerns. But my Katherine Mansfield is none of these: to describe her as homely is out of my power.

A claim like this puts me in bad company. There is nothing homely, for instance, in the following tribute to Katherine Mansfield.

> She will come back—she will come back again
> And linger here among our leafy ways,
> When tuis sing their gay-glad song of praise
> To lovely Spring and all her merry train.
> When sweet expectant notes of love and pain
> Trill out their message she will come to gaze
> On what we, purblind, see but through a haze
> And only dimly hear in minor strain.
>
> 'Neath moonless skies, her little torch held high,
> She'll walk afar through dusky forest trees,
> Where baby owls give out their wistful cry
> And night is full of husky melodies.
> Only nocturnal things, like Kiwis shy,
> Will see her pass on nights like these.[2]

The poet had to be in the grip of something to write like that. Perhaps, putting aside a volume of stories, he wanted to express a mood that seemed to come over his reading, but the poem he wrote exceeds its conventions and occasion. The evoked return—with its baby owls, its wistful cries and husky melodies—is like a return to the sounds and scenes of the nursery. More symptomatic, perhaps, is that image of a Thumbelina-sized Katherine Mansfield, "her little torch held high," flitting through the New Zealand bush. What makes the poem ludicrous is not so much its naïveté as the poet's blindness to the literal. There is another name for this symptom: the blindness of love.

Any reading of Katherine Mansfield means imagining something like this ethereal wood sprite, "seen but through a haze." The author is patently absent and yet "she will return, she will return again," whenever

---

2. The poem "Katherine Mansfield" is by R. E. Rawlinson. It was first published in the *Sydney Bulletin* and is reprinted in *The Mystery of Maata*, by P. A. Lawlor (Wellington, 1946), 4.

we care to read her. An author is a function of a discourse, but that does not quite mean that this figure is constructed habitually, neutrally, by a reader. The process is affective as well. Reading, we might say, is a variety of transference just as transference is a variety of reading.

Let me unpack that tautology a little. Freud used to ask his patients to tell him a story, "the whole story," as he put it, of the patient's life and illness. But that was not what they told him. "Patients," he observed in the Dora case history, "are incapable of giving such reports about themselves." Pieces of the story were missing, fragments were implausibly connected, even events apparently open to view were uncertain. The story as narrated concealed another story that was subject to repression. Over time, Freud wrote, "the patient supplies the facts which, though he had known them all along, had been kept back by him or had not occurred to his mind. The paramnesias prove untenable and the gaps in his memory are filled in. It is only towards the end of the treatment that we have before us an intelligible, consistent, and unbroken case history."[3] Of course, as Freud found to his cost with Dora, it was never enough for him simply to listen, interpret and construe, and then say to his patient, Here at last is the real story behind your narrative. What happened instead in the telling of and listening to stories was more dynamic, more interactive than that: the channel was noisy and, in a postscript to the case history, Freud explained the informative noises: "What are transferences? They are new editions or facsimiles of the impulses and phantasies which are aroused and made conscious during the progress of the analysis; but they have this peculiarity, which is characteristic for their species, that they replace some earlier person by the person of the physician."[4]

New editions, facsimiles: the textual metaphor seems unavoidable. To use those two little words which preface all stories, transference belongs to the realm of "as if": the physician is not the earlier person, there are only signs that he is being taken for or is acting as such. Peter Brooks comments, "The transference is textual because it presents the past in symbolic form, in signs, thus as something that is really absent but textually present, and which furthermore, must be shaped by the work of interpretation carried on by both teller and listener."[5]

3. Sigmund Freud, "Fragment of an Analysis of a Case of Hysteria," trans. Alix Strachey and James Strachey, in *Pelican Freud Library,* VIII (Harmondsworth, Eng., 1977), 45–47.

4. *Ibid.,* 157.

5. Peter Brooks, "Psychoanalytic Constructions and Narrative Meanings," *Paragraph,*

My Katherine Mansfield, then, is very much a partial construction—partial, no doubt, in that I do not aim to do more than sketch a few scenes of writing and transference in her stories; partial, of course, because it will be a construction the stories and I make, just as analyst and analysand between them conjure the special "as if" space of the transference. If the psychoanalytic parallel has any force, however, there can be no telling who has the upper hand in this process: both reader and text dispute and exchange their available positions in the transference, the one analyzing, the one analyzed, the one reading, the one read. If that means one can but follow the example of the author of that poetic tribute to Mansfield, one might still hope not to repeat his husky melodies and wistful cries. Instead, we might look to another of those unhomely returns Katherine Mansfield makes in the writing of others, this in Ian Wedde's *Symmes Hole,* a novel about a character with several authors inside his head:

> And here comes Kathleen, with her white clavicles and her dark eyes and her smile that enters your heart like a sentence so perfect it has no sound, no more than the deadly soft click of a pearl-handled pistol being primed in a dark ambuscade: your blood freezes, and then you hear the breath of her laugh, you see maybe a dim gleam of slick on teeth or lipstick or eyeball, hear a rustle of clothing, somehow the lights are up again and you can smell the charnel byre and piss-straw of her rotting lungs' breath.[6]

That's my Katherine Mansfield.

"Poison"

KM to JMM, November, 1920:

> And about *Poison.* I could write about that for pages. But I'll try and condense what I've got to say. The story is told by (evidently) a worldly, rather

---

VII (March, 1986), 57. My remarks on writing and transference are thoroughly indebted to Brooks—both to the article cited and to his major work, *Reading for the Plot* (Oxford, 1984).

6. Ian Wedde, *Symmes Hole* (Auckland, 1986), 278.

cynical (not wholly cynical) man *against* himself (but not altogether) when he was so absurdly young. You know how young by his idea of what woman is. She has been up to now, only the *vision*, only she who passes. You realize that? And here he has put *all* his passion into this Beatrice. It's *promiscuous* love, not understood as such by him; perfectly understood as such by her. But you realize the vie de luxe they are living. . . . And you realize? she expects a letter from someone calling her away? *Fully* expects it?[7]

There are four question marks in this passage, but always the same question asked: Do you realize? Can you see? Or as New Zealanders say on the telephone, "Are you there?" Narratives, Brooks argues, "speak repeatedly of the transferential condition—of their anxiety concerning transmissibility, of their need to be heard, of their desire to become the story of the listener as much as the teller."[8] Mansfield's letter, from her to a particular reader, supplements the short story's own concern with the transmission of messages that are not what they seem to be—with poisoned communications. The narrator (you remember?) is drinking with Beatrice on the terrace of a luxurious hotel. She waits anxiously for the post, but all that arrives is a newspaper with a report of a poison trial. Beatrice asks him, "Haven't you ever thought . . . of the amount of poisoning that goes on? It's the exception to find married people who don't poison each other—married people and lovers. Oh, . . . the number of cups of tea, glasses of wine, cups of coffee that are just tainted. . . . The only reason why so many couples . . . *survive,* is because the one is frightened of giving the other the fatal dose. That dose takes nerve! But it's bound to come sooner or later" (381). The story ends with a twist:

I lifted my glass and drank, sipped rather—sipped slowly, deliberately, looking at that dark head and thinking of—postmen and blue beetles and farewells that were not farewells and . . .

Good God! Was it fancy? No, it wasn't fancy. The drink tasted chill, bitter, *queer.* (382)

The narrator has been poisoned by a letter that does not arrive yet acts as if it had arrived. Its absence is semiotically present, a trace that con-

7. *Letters,* ed. Murry, II, 81.
8. Brooks, "Psychoanalytic Constructions," 55.

taminates the exchange of all other messages that are sent and received in the present. But this is only to allegorize a transferential situation: the transference becomes active when the pattern is repeated in the exchange of messages between the teller of the story and its listener or reader.

Every narrative, we know, has a narrator, yet we tend to overlook the inevitable presence of the narrator's counterpart, the narratee. "Poison," a retrospective first-person narration, retains something of the structure of a framed tale. In a framed tale, the narrator, sitting perhaps in front of a log fire on a cold winter evening, addresses his story to a companion and, as we read the story the narrator has to tell, we readers never quite forget our surrogate, the narratee companionably sitting in front of the fire. In "Poison," the narrator is similarly telling his story to another character. She—let us say she—is not named, not addressed directly, but her presence is registered in the narrator's many allusions to the time of narration and his trick of anticipating the responses of the person he is talking to. We gather, for example, that the narratee has no prior knowledge of Beatrice, that her friendship with the narrator, though not of long standing, is one that allows confessions of an intimate sort. She is single, possibly in her thirties, the narrator just a little older. Often, we notice, he pays a flattering kind of attention to her knowledge of the ways of the world. When his talk turns to marriage, however, he is careful that his narratee should not suppose that his wish to have been married to Beatrice indicates a current interest in permanent relationships. This, then, is the context in which the narrator tells his story about Beatrice's covert farewell and, as he talks, it is the turn of his listener to be poisoned.

Does the narratee know? Does her drink, in turn, taste chill, bitter, queer? We never find out. The narratee's presence fades before the end of the story, yet perhaps her situation is no different from the reader's. Whether one sees through the narrator or falls for the narrator, one is poisoned just the same. The reader who recognizes a taint in the message has no other remedy than to repeat the story, to acknowledge the force of the poison by passing it on. The reader who simply swallows the story pays an even more satisfying tribute to the poisoner's art.

Deadly Poison

When Freud said that his patients were unable to give a full account of their life and illness, that the fuller version was jointly constructed in the relation of teller to listener, he anticipated a distinction that is fundamental to any theory of narrative: the distinction between story and discourse. Story is the universe of events, characters, places, and items of setting referred to in a discourse telling of them. Discourse, the means by which a story is communicated, is routinely thought to involve the selection and ordering of possibilities offered by the larger universe of the story. But we should be careful not to assume that story is that which comes first, the foundation over which a discourse is laid. Rather, there is no story without discourse, no intelligible consistent and unbroken case history except in the wake of a discourse as it passes from one to another. With "Poison," we saw that there is an opportunity in that passing for something to be slipped in, for someone to poison another with the uncertainty of a message sent or not sent. But sometimes story itself travels away from the discourse, and the inevitable illusion of counterfactuality is raised to a higher power in a deadlier game where not knowing one's story commits one to risk poison as cure.

Take the case of "A Married Man's Story." A man writes an account of his life and unease, but his story slips away from him. He is not sure, and we are not sure, where accurate memory stops and something beyond accuracy takes over. Perhaps his mother did come to his bed one night, all those years ago, to whisper that his father had poisoned her; perhaps it is only a dream he remembers; perhaps everything the narrator says is, as he warns us, the "plain truth, as only a liar can tell it" (481). He is not sure, and we are not sure, why he writes, whom he writes for, or even what it is he is writing. Nor do we have the whole story: whatever it is he is saying, it seems to stop rather than come to an end. This, however, is how the narrator begins his story: "It is evening. Supper is over. We have left the small, cold dining room; we have come back to the sitting room where there is a fire. All is as usual. I am sitting at my writing table which is placed across a corner so that I am behind it, as it were, and facing the room. The lamp with the green shade is alight; I have before me two large books of reference, both open, a pile of papers. . . . All the paraphernalia, in fact, of an extremely occupied man" (476). Four dots quietly separate the last two sentences of this passage. The intrusion of this small suspension is a reminder that it is always impossible to begin at the beginning. A beginning always carries with it the seeds of an ending, an ending that must be staved off by the dilatory space of the narrative but that also acquires the force of a vanishing point bringing detail into lines of order and significance. Although the two large books of reference will not be mentioned again, mentioning them so pointedly at the outset opens an enigma—What books of reference?—while invoking the ghost of an ending that might answer.

The opening paragraph continues, "My wife, with her little boy on her lap, is in a low chair before the fire. . . . The warmth, the quiet, and the sleepy baby, have made her dreamy. One of his red woollen boots is off; one is on. She sits, bent forward, clasping the little bare foot, staring into the glow, and as the fire quickens, falls, flares again, her shadow—an immense *Mother and Child*—is here and gone again upon the wall" (476–77). The shadow of this immense *Mother and Child* is not thrown haphazardly. The detail forecasts significance. Later, we learn that something happened the previous autumn to sour the marriage. What this was we are never told, but the shadow portrait confirms C. K. Stead's hunch that the elided catastrophe is the birth of the narrator's son. The story he means to tell, Stead suggests, is that having become a father, he becomes like his father, and has begun, metaphorically at least, to poison his wife.[9] Perhaps we may suppose further than that. If the story the narrator means to tell concerns the birth of his son, the story Mansfield began to write might have ended by closing an enigma: the narrator turning, perhaps, to those two books of reference, a pharmacology text, a handbook of forensic pathology.

But I think we are spared both of those twists. Instead, both the story the narrator begins telling and the story Mansfield begins writing find another set of rails to run on. The crossover occurs in the last paragraph of the third section:

> You know those stories of little children who are suckled by wolves and accepted by the tribe, and how for ever after they move freely among their fleet grey brothers? Something like that has happened to me. But wait—that about the wolves won't do. Curious! Before I wrote it down, while it was still in my head, I was delighted with it. It seemed to express, and more, to suggest, just what I wanted to say. But written, I can smell the falseness immediately and the . . . . source of the smell is in that word fleet. Don't you agree? Fleet, grey brothers! "Fleet." A word I never use. When I wrote "wolves" it skimmed across my mind like a shadow and

9. C. K. Stead, *In the Glass Case: Essays on New Zealand Fiction* (Auckland, 1981), 45.

I couldn't resist it. Tell me! Tell me! Why is it so difficult to write simply—and not only simply but *sotto voce,* if you know what I mean? That is how I long to write. No fine effects—no bravuras. But just the plain truth, as only a liar can tell it. (480–81)

Hitherto the narrator has been addressing a no one in particular who may, someday, happen across the confession confided to the pages. Descriptions of the household, comments like "You know how soft and crumbling the wood of a summer house is in the rain," as well as the more direct pleas and expostulations—"Oh, don't misunderstand me!"—are all addressed to this other person, the future reader. Though this narratee is repeatedly addressed in the passage just quoted—"Don't you agree?" the narrator asks him—the deliberation about the word *fleet* suggests that the future reader is in fact a screen narratee. The person the narrator writes for, the one listening acutely to what is said, is himself.

There follows, too, a reversal in the object of the narrator's aggression. Often he is smugly congratulatory about the effect his language has on his wife. He fancies he poisons his wife with his little barbs, yet there never is any certainty that his words and silences find their mark. Instead, with that word *fleet,* his own discourse starts to smell, to turn on him like a poisoner who drinks the cup he thought to offer to another. It is at this point, too, that the story the narrator means to tell—about marital unhappiness caused by the birth of a son—begins to move toward the story of another birth, of the narrator's own coming into the world. "You know those stories of little children who are suckled by wolves and accepted by the tribe, and how for ever after they move freely among their fleet grey brothers? Something like that has happened to me." This is the story that takes over from the story he meant to tell, but there is also a sense in which it is a story that steers away from the narrator's discourse, a story the narrator does not know he is telling. Like the recollections of Freud's patients, this account of his childhood is marked by fantasy, by chronological instability, by repression. There is the fantasy, partly disavowed, of not being the child of one's parents. When the narrator refers to little children suckled by wolves, he surely means very little children—like Romulus and Remus—yet the origin of his sense of brotherhood with the wolves is also placed much later: it dates from an evening, after his mother's death, when he was thirteen years old. We learn that from the last sentence of the final fragment of text: "but I from that night did beyond words consciously turn toward my silent brothers. . . ." When we recall those fleet, grey brothers from the earlier section, two points of blockage, of proximity to the repressed, fold into each other. Symptomatically, the chronology seems to waver, seems to loop back on itself, while an earlier failure to write is repeated, giving this manifestly discontinued text a latent circuit of closure.

Can we reconstruct what is closed off and return a full, coherent, and intelligible story to the narrator? There is certainly a story about mothers and fathers he does not know he is telling, but that does not mean it is hidden exactly. Consider the following passage:

> But really to explain what happened [last autumn] I should have to go back and back, I should have to dwindle until my two hands clutched the bannisters, the stair-rail was higher than my head, and I peered through to watch my father padding softly up and down. There were coloured windows on the landings. As he came up, first his bald head was scarlet; then it was yellow. How frightened I was! And when they put me to bed, it was to dream that we were living inside one of my father's big coloured bottles. For he was a chemist. I was born nine years after my parents were married; I was an only child, and the effort to produce even me—small, withered bud I must have been—sapped all my mother's strength. (482)

Freud dreamed a lot about climbing stairs; indeed, that dream symbol acquires a notoriously catechetical interpretation as a displacement for sexual activity. So that was what the young child was watching as he watched father padding softly up and down? Sometimes even vulgar Freudianism seems to get it right. The narrator's thoughts immediately turn to his own conception and the slip—"I was an only child, but the effort to produce *even* me"—again discloses an observed primal scene. Then, if one starts bracketing the chronology of the manifest story, other details follow. "I stared at my father so long it's as though his image, cut off at the waist by the counter, has remained solid in my memory" (482). The work of censorship here is accompanied by a displacement onto another paternal figure: "I hide in the dark passage, where the coats hang, and am discovered there by one of the masters. 'What are you doing there in the dark?' His terrible voice kills me; I die before his eyes" (483). As for the mother, it is her voice that the narrator recalls in a dream, saying,

"Little sneak! Little sneak!" Still, it was "not as if she were angry"; it was "as if she understood, and her smile somehow was like a rat . . . . hateful!" (486). The tale of poisoning, in this reading, conflates memories of her illness with her. Perhaps this is why the father becomes a donor of sinister fluids, the little "pick-me-ups" he sells to the women of the street—why he becomes the man who looks like a bottle, "Deadly Poison, or old D.P.," as the narrator calls him. Perhaps this is also the source of the narrator's inability to connect his child with his wife and himself: "My wife doesn't seem to me the sort of woman who bears children in her own body" (478), he confides.

But these suggestions have yet to take transference into account. There can be little point in inventing a past for the narrator unless it is possible to show how that story is unconsciously repeated in the narrator's discourse—how that primal scene acts as if it were present as the narrator tells of his own belated entry into the world and as he turns, beyond words, to his silent brothers the wolves. To begin with, we might consider a moment when the narrator tries to summarize his past. "The Past—what is the Past?" he asks himself. "I might say the star-shaped flake of soot on a leaf of the poor-looking plant, and the bird lying on the quilted lining of my cap, and my father's pestle and my mother's cushion, belong to it" (484). A number of image clusters need to be followed here, but I must be content to stress one: the "poor-looking plant." It begins as a "small withered bud"—the narrator's image of himself as a baby—and continues with a description of his childhood: "I seem to have spent most of my time like a plant in a cupboard. Now and again, when the sun shone, a careless hand thrust me out on to the window-sill, and a careless hand whipped me in again—and that was all. But what happened in the darkness—I wonder? Did one grow?" (483).

One moment of growth occurred when his school fellows placed a dead bird in his pocket:

> How tightly the beak was shut; I could not see the mark where it was divided. I stretched out one wing and touched the soft, secret down underneath; I tried to make the claws curl round my little finger. But I didn't feel sorry for it—no! I wondered. The smoke from our kitchen chimney poured downwards, and flakes of soot floated—soft, light in the air. Through a big crack in the cement yard a poor-looking plant with dull, reddish flowers

had pushed its way. I looked at the dead bird again. . . . And that is the first time I remember singing, rather . . . . listening to a silent voice inside a little cage that was me. (484)

The singing is worth noting. In an earlier passage commenting on the time of narration, he asks himself, "Aren't those just the signs, the traces of my feeling? The bright green streaks made by someone who walks over the dewy grass? Not the feeling itself. And as I think that, a mournful, glorious voice begins to sing in my bosom. Yes, perhaps that is nearer what I mean. What a voice! What power! What velvety softness!" (477). This is a singing beyond words; it is with this voice that he will turn toward his silent brothers, the wolves. The narrator's identification with that dead bird gives us an origin for his song. The "silent voice inside a little cage that was me" is the voice of the dead one inside him.

In the passage about the dead bird, the narrator mentions that a "poor-looking plant" has pushed through the cement. That plant continues to grow along with the story. After the mother's death, it is "a creeper with small, bunched up pink and purple flowers," growing "close up against the window." He says, "These, when I touched them at night, welcomed my fingers; the little tendrils, so weak, so delicate, knew I would not hurt them. . . . When I came to the window, it seemed to me the flowers said among themselves, 'The boy is here'" (485). The night after the dream in which his mother calls him a little sneak, there is a moment of birth:

Then the shrivelled case of the bud split and fell, the plant in the cupboard came into flower. "Who am I?" I thought. "What is all this?" And I looked at my room, at the broken bust of the man called Hahnemann on top of the cupboard, at my little bed with the pillow like an envelope. I saw it all, but not as I had seen before. . . . Everything lived, but everything. But that was not all. I was equally alive and—it's the only way I can express it—the barriers were down between us—I had come into my own world!

This moment of birth might be understood as a moment of division. "The barriers were down between us," the narrator says, but between whom and whom? The imagery divides the narrator between two correlatives—one the poor-looking plant in the cupboard that has, at last, come into flower, and the other the creeper that has pushed its way through the cement at the time of the passage about the dead bird, the plant that, after the death of the mother, climbed the wall of the house, its flowers saying among themselves, "The boy is here." Something damaging to the father happens when these two come together, and something is born. The sign of the father in this passage is the bust of the man called Hahnemann. It's as if this Hahnemann—Cocksman is a literal translation of the name—is somehow broken by the rocking of the cupboard as the plant delivers its strange flower. As for what is born, it is the collapse of another division inside the one and the same: the voice that speaks language, and the voice beyond words. With it, the barriers are down, too, between the narrator and the narratee: that internal distinction within the same disappears, for quite simply the possibility of discourse ends with that birth, there can be no more to say.

"A Married Man's Story" is a text that breaks down barriers or, as I prefer to call them, boundaries—boundaries of the self, of language, of ends and beginnings. But let me continue to pattern the detail of the text just a little longer. The birth passage is preceded by a curious game in which boundaries are breached and restored, a game played with fascination but also leading to the moment of awful dreariness out of which the narrator's new self is born.

> I lighted the candle and sat down at the table instead. By and by, as the flame steadied, there was a small lake of liquid wax, surrounded by a white, smooth wall. I took a pin and made little holes in this wall and then sealed them up faster than the wax could escape. After a time I fancied the candle flame joined in the game; it leapt up, quivered, wagged; it even seemed to laugh. But while I played with the candle . . . a feeling of awful dreariness fastened on me—yes, that is the word. (486)

Fleet, fast, fastened. Between fleet and fastened, between that which goes and that which stays, is abjection. The narrator calls it a feeling of awful dreariness. Julia Kristeva elaborates:

> There looms, within abjection, one of those violent, dark revolts of being, directed against a threat that seems to emanate from an exorbitant outside or inside, ejected beyond the scope of the possible, the tolerable, the thinkable. It lies there, quite close, but it cannot be assimilated. It beseeches, worries, and fascinates desire, which, nevertheless, does not let itself be

seduced. Apprehensive, desire turns aside; sickened, it rejects. A certainty protects it from the shameful—a certainty of which it is proud holds on to it. But simultaneously, just the same, that impetus, that spasm, that leap is drawn toward an elsewhere as tempting as it is condemned. Unflaggingly, like an inescapable boomerang, a vortex of summons and repulsions places the one haunted by it literally beside himself.[10]

Abjection rings, or permeates, the border between the pure and the impure, the me and the not-me; you will recognize it most readily in that reaction of nausea, of a retching that turns you aside, that keeps your clean and proper body on the outside of "defilement, sewage and muck," and in the various ways cultures construct complex rites and practices that police the inevitable strayings across those borders, preserving identity, system, and order. Kristeva is also the theorist of an obscure pathology of subjectivity she terms the abjection of self:

If it be true that the abject simultaneously beseeches and pulverizes the subject, one can understand that it is experienced at the peak of its strength when that subject, weary of fruitless attempts to identify with something on the outside, finds the impossible within; when it finds that the impossible constitutes its very *being*, that it *is* none other than abject. The abjection of self would be the culminating form of that experience of the subject to which it is revealed that all its objects are based merely on the inaugural *loss* that laid the foundation of its own being.[11]

Let me elaborate this by returning to the image of the plant in the cupboard. The important component is the cupboard, the wall or border surrounding a kind of vacancy whose only positive is the drive to expel, to exclude. On the far side of that border is the dead mother, the mother killed or expelled too soon. Hers is the realm of the prelinguistic, of a wolf language beyond words. Her emblems in the story are as various as the cruel indifferent star the narrator gazes at, as the creeper growing on the outside wall of the house, as the dead bird, as the floral cushion embroidered with the tombstone words *sweet repose*. But there can be no border without the father—without Herr Cocksman, phallic representa-

10. Julia Kristeva, *Powers of Horror,* trans. Leon S. Roudiez (New York, 1982), 1.
11. *Ibid.,* 5.

tive of the language and gendered sexuality toward whom a subject is propelled in the order of symbolic relations. It is from this fortress that the narrator speaks, from the walls separating an emptiness inside from an abjected outside. And yet, as he speaks, the plant in the cupboard grows. What "feeds" it is the fascination and repugnance of the abject, compelling and impeding a search for origins, for the primal scene that will undermine the logic of the boundaries its repression has long since thrown up. It is a scene in which life is already infected with death, with its deadly poison. Though not consciously recognized, the consequences of that scene are the symptoms of the narrator's discourse. It is as if what started as an itch, a tickle in the throat, had the undifferentiating and deconstituting force of cyanide swallowed. The impossible that ought to have been outside is within, and when the barriers are down, the possibility of language and identity is held between the points of suspension that truly complete "A Married Man's Story."

Sweet Repose

I have told a story about "A Married Man's Story"—an "as if" account of the narrator's past that underscores the act and trajectory of his discourse. But it was not as simple as that: in talking about narrators and narrating, I have always had—such is transference—some earlier person than a narrator in mind. I call her my Katherine Mansfield. My reader will know that one way to pass from a text to the figure that wrote it is to suppose that the text is confessional, but that is not my business at all. Instead, let me explain how it is that "A Married Man's Story" is a text in which my Mansfield comes at—or against—the conditions of her writing at all.

"The sooner the books are written," Mansfield confided to her journal, "the sooner I shall be well." [12] It never did work, but still there is a connection between the beginnings and ends of writing and those of life. Freud called transference an "intermediate region between illness and real life through which the transition from one to another is made." [13] One might say that writing, for Mansfield, became an intermediate re-

12. *Journal,* 271.
13. Brooks, "Psychoanalytic Constructions," 56.

gion between illness and *represented* life through which the transition from one to another was made. Sometimes, as in bad writing, the transition effected by sublimation does not work: a false note is struck. Let me give one example. On completing "At the Bay," in September, 1921, Mansfield wrote to Dorothy Brett, "It is so strange to bring the dead to life again. There's my Grandmother, back in her chair with her pink knitting, there stalks my uncle over the grass; I feel as I write, 'You are not dead, my darlings. All is remembered. I bow down to you. I efface myself so that you may live again through me in your richness and beauty.'"[14] There is something too naked about a statement like that: it lays bare the abjection that edges all reachings to the sublime.

"At the Bay" is almost a case in point. What saves the story for me is the ugliness of its final section. Morning has passed to evening, the tide is full once more, a "cloud, small, serene, float[s] across the moon," and the vile Harry Kember invites Beryl over to the fuchsia bush. There is a sense in which "A Married Man's Story" may have made that ending possible. Mansfield began writing "At the Bay" in July or August, 1921. By August 14, however, she put it aside to write one of her nicer stories, "The Voyage." That concerns a little girl, Fenella, who has recently lost her mother, and the voyage she and her grandmother make from Wellington to Picton, between the two islands of New Zealand. It is a voyage from darkness into light, and the use of a young child's point of view further assists the mood of reconciliation with death. Mansfield then wrote another story about a dead mother—"A Married Man's Story"—became ill, and completed "At the Bay," in September, 1921.[15] One text nudges another. It is possible to suppose that the seventh section of "At the Bay"—the one where Kezia and her grandmother have their conversation about death—acted as a springboard for "The Voyage"; more definitely, there are echoes of "The Voyage" in the narrator's reverie in the first section of "A Married Man's Story" and echoes of "A Married Man's Story" in the opening paragraph of the last section of "At the Bay."

All these stories are, as we say, haunted by death. It is as if the sense of an ending impelled a return to beginnings, to the childhood memories of "At the Bay." Autobiography is invariably a mode of mourning, but the grief of a life coming to an end does not find solace in its beginnings;

14. To Dorothy Brett, September, 1921, in *Letters*, ed. Murry, II, 134.
15. For discussion of these dates of composition, see Stead, *In the Glass Case*, 44, 280.

instead, loss is compounded as the writer meets an anxiety peculiar to beginnings. To ask, Where do I start? is to be reminded of a gap that is always there between representation and the plenitude of what might be represented. If we suppose some such crisis stopped the composition of "At the Bay," then "The Voyage" represents one type of recovery. It is the sublime consolation of putting death in its place amid the splendid and persistent cycles of nature, a gesture that also etches writing's own resistance to the onslaught of time. But you do not have to cough blood to feel how pathetic, how tawdry, these gestures can seem. One response might well be the countersublime of "A Married Man's Story." There a search for beginnings finds that life is poisoned by death, but the response is far from the traditional consolation offered by the immortality of writing. Instead, there is another way of coming against the ends of mortality and discourse. Freud called it the death drive, the fundamental impulse of all life to return to an earlier state of things. For the narrator of "A Married Man's Story," the return is a catastrophe won by his discourse, a shuddering birth in which the walls of the self are undone and language plummets into the presymbolic. And perhaps as the narrator turns to his silent brothers, the wolves, we may hear an author's silent, howling protest at writing, at the writing that ought to protect her from death but appears as its cold and frozen analogue.

Kristeva writes, "The corpse, seen without God and outside science, is the utmost of abjection. It is death infecting life. Abject. It is something rejected from which one does not part, from which one does not protect oneself as from an object. Imaginary uncanniness and real threat, it beckons to us and ends up engulfing us."[16] Art protects us from that.

I was walking along Tinakori Road, in Wellington, and turned in at number 25. Mansfield's birthplace was just as I had imagined it, lovingly preserved, a perfect small pocket in time. Manuscripts, first editions invited perusal. Among them was a favorite of mine, a page of trial signatures from the 1904 notebook:

Kathleen

K

Kathleen M. BeuChamp

16. Kristeva, *Powers of Horror,* 4.

athleen BeauChamp
K   M Beauchamp ?
KM Beauchamp ?

KM Beauchamp
                                        the best?
Kth. Beauchamp.

But what was that on the other side of the page? There, in black graffiti-like swirls of calligraphy, some poisoner had left these words of Artaud: "The dead little girl says, I am the one who guffaws in horror inside the lungs of the live one. Get me out of there at once!"[17]

17. *Ibid.*, 25.

The French Connection: Francis Carco

CHRISTIANE MORTELIER

> Only connect the prose and the passion. . . .
> Live in fragments no longer. . . . Only connect.
> —E. M. Forster, *Howards End*

Although Katherine Mansfield traveled frequently to France in the last ten years of her life, she had few really close contacts with French people. In all, her time in France amounted to approximately three years, yet her personal references in her writings are confined to concierges and maids, petit-bourgeois denizens of the pensions and hotels where she stayed, and the anonymous people she saw in trains, streets, and restaurants.

There were no close friends, no attempts to join French literary circles, no sense of French conversation entering her internal language in any significant way.[1] Nor did the French environment become fundamental to the stories. There are vivid descriptive glimpses—in "Spring Pictures," for example—and snippets of backdrops of hotel rooms or streets, but

---

1. Mansfield met some French writers and critics through Carco during her stay in Paris in 1913–1914, but they seem to have left no trace in her journal or notebooks. Henri Clouard, a well-known critic of the prewar era, mentioned her in *Histoire de la littérature français du symbolisme à nos jours, 1914–1940* (Paris, 1949), 224–25. He also recalled her in a letter to Carco, April 9, 1932, as "cette belle jeune Anglaise silencieuse auprès de son mari" ("that beautiful, silent young Englishwoman close to her husband"; Francis Carco, *Montmartre à vingt ans* [Paris, 1938], 177).

those are never intrusive and never essential. France was presented in diminutive pictures of insectlike human activity from up high looking down, as in the vignettes that color the letters.[2]

So in France more perhaps than in England, Mansfield seems to have lived the self-contained life of a writer drawing her material from within herself, and from other literature, including, as I shall show, French. The main benefit to Mansfield of her visits to France—apart from the slight relief she may have enjoyed in her health—was the stimulus of reading in French. Her French reading was important to her. For us, it is instructive.

Mansfield mentions more than a dozen French authors. They include Georges Duhamel, Marcel Proust, Guy de Maupassant, Paul Verlaine, and Octave Mirbeau, all in her journal and letters.[3] Her response to Maupassant and Proust has received special attention. Her significant interest in Colette, and the connections and parallels between them, are beginning to be recognized, as in the essay in this volume by Ruth Parkin-Gounelas.[4] Colette remained prominent in Mansfield's mind at least from November, 1914, when her name appeared in the journal, to October, 1916, when Mansfield made a last reference to her in a letter to Mary Hutchinson.[5]

The other French connection was, of course, Francis Carco. Mansfield went to France twice with the express purpose of meeting French people. The first time, in the winter of 1913–1914, she and John Middleton Murry stayed in Paris, in the rue de Tournon, near the Luxembourg Gardens, and spent time with Francis Carco. The second time, in February, 1915, she braved wartime France for her few days' liaison with Carco at Gray, on the Saône near Besançon. The episode has become notorious

2. Many were written from the fourth floor, in Carco's apartment on the quai aux Fleurs, or from railroad cars. That goes some way toward explaining Mansfield's detached vision.

3. Murry, who had an excellent command of French and was well read in French literature, played an important role in guiding Mansfield's reading in that area. As coeditor of *Rhythm,* he was responsible for selecting iconographic and literary material, which was very often published in French.

4. The connections with Colette were fully explored in the original version of this paper, delivered at the Katherine Mansfield Centennial Conference, at Victoria University of Wellington, in October, 1988.

5. "Colette Willy is in my thoughts tonight" (*Journal,* 61). See also Ruth Parkin-Gounelas' discussion, pp. 37–41 above. "What will you think of Colette, I wonder. . . . For me she is more real than any woman I've ever known" (*Collected Letters,* I, 282).

both biographically and for Mansfield's apparently autobiographical use of it in "An Indiscreet Journey." It brought together, one might say, Mansfield in love, Mansfield at war, and Mansfield at work in a quite extraordinary way. It also had ramifications within French, as well as English, literature.

François Marie Alexandre Carcopino-Tusoli, known in literature as Francis Carco, was born in the Pacific, in Nouméa. His parents were both Corsican. His father was a civil servant in the French colony of New Caledonia, and Carco lived there until the age of ten.[6] Moving back to France, the family settled in Villefranche-de-Rouergue, then because of civil-service postings, in various places in the south of France: Marseille, Agen, Toulouse, Rodez. The young Carco was called up for a spell of military service in Grenoble and became Corporal Carco, holding the same rank as "le petit caporal" in "An Indiscreet Journey." Much against the wishes of his father, who wanted him to enter the civil service, he turned to literature, reading extensively, writing poetry, contributing to short-lived provincial literary magazines, and finally moving to the French capital.

He arrived in Paris in 1910 and began a bohemian life of dissipation and near-starvation. His good friends Pierre MacOrlan and Roland Dorgelès, however, helped him learn about Parisian life and enjoy the last years of the relaxed *vie de bohème* before the First World War.

The Butte Montmartre was a real village then. He often called at the Lapin Agile cabaret, where Frédé, the colorful proprietor, wore clogs, played the guitar, and frequently fed poor artists and poets for free. Spring brought the heady scents of lilacs growing in the cabaret's garden, inspiring poems from writers drinking wine under the arbor. He associated with needy young painters and poets destined to become famous: Maurice Utrillo, Pablo Picasso, Amedeo Modigliani, Jules Pascin, Max Jacob, Marie Laurencin, André Salmon, Guillaume Apollinaire. There were also others—the untold casualties of the *vie de bohème*—whose works are remembered neither in galleries nor in histories of French literature. Carco was to recall those years with much pleasure and some nostalgia in several volumes of reminiscences.[7]

6. His father was "chef de service de l'enregistrement, des domaines de l'état et du timbre," in Nouméa.
7. Francis Carco, *De Montmartre au Quartier Latin* (Paris, 1927); Francis Carco, *Mé-*

Carco's bohemia was less romantic than Henri Murger's, which Giacomo Puccini popularized in *La Bohème*. He did not seek out little seamstresses with a virgin heart. His contacts were partly with the lower strata of Parisian society, learning the language and manners of the apaches and often dressing like them. The Paris bohemia of the prewar years in Montmartre d'en bas, along the *boulevards extérieurs,* was, if picturesque, also fraught with real dangers. Many would-be artists and poets lost their health and lives through sordid love affairs, drink, and drugs.[8] They came in daily contact with thieves and violent characters who were quick to settle scores with a jackknife or a gun. All this was immensely fascinating to Carco, who was to draw the substance of many novels from his experiences.[9]

He quickly wrote his first novel of low life, *Jésus-la-Caille,* and was on his way to being the prime successor to Charles Louis Philippe, who had died in 1909, as chronicler of the Paris underworld. *Jésus-la-Caille,* published in installments in the magazine *Le Mercure de France* in 1914, and soon afterward in book form, benefited from the literary protection of another major French connection of Katherine Mansfield's, Rachilde.[10] Marguerite Vallette, cofounder and coeditor with her hus-

moires d'une autre vie (Paris, 1934); Carco, *Montmartre à vingt ans;* Francis Carco, *A voix basse* (Paris, 1938); Francis Carco, *Bohème d'artiste* (Paris, 1940).

8. Carco's disillusioned recollection of this life is worth setting alongside the more destructive cynicism attributed to Raoul Duquette: "Je menais à l'époque une existence absurde se partageant entre le *Lapin,* les boîtes de la Place Blanche et les bistros des Halles. . . . Toute de hasards, d'excès . . . La mode était alors à des départs chimériques, à des amours manquées, à d'immobiles voyages au fond d'un bar, devant des fioles d'alcool multicolores, tandis que l'on regardait tomber la pluie. Huysmans avait créé une sorte d'hypnotisme personnel dont notre génération fut consciemment victime. . . . nous ne vivions pas, nous nous imaginions vivre" (*Bohème d'artiste,* 164; "In those days I was leading an absurd existence divided between the Lapin, the nightclubs of the Place Blanche, and the bistros of Les Halles. . . . Risk and excess of every kind . . . The fashion then was for imaginary leave-takings, lost loves, immobile journeys on the floor of a bar surrounded by bottles of alcohol of many colors, all the while watching the rain fall. Huysmans had created a sort of personal hypnotism of which our generation was consciously the victim. . . . We did not live, we imagined ourselves living.")

9. Carco toward the end of his life suggested that the proximity of the convict prison in Nouméa had given him his fascination with the underworld, "la goût de la crapule." See his *Rendez-vous avec moi-même* (Paris, 1957).

10. The first part appeared in *Le Mercure de France* on January 16, 1914, and the

band of *Le Mercure de France,* and herself a prolific writer and critic under the pen name of Rachilde, was an important figure in the Paris literary world of the time.[11] She published about thirty novels from 1878 to 1942, and their alluring titles—*Monsieur Vénus,* of 1884, *La Virginité de Diane,* of 1886, *La Marquise de Sade,* of 1887, *L'Animale,* of 1893—indicate why they created some scandal. But she was energetic, too, in recognizing talent. She wrote articles in support of Colette, especially of the *Claudine* novels and *L'Entrave,* and she helped Carco become a published novelist.

In 1898, in *L'Heure sexuelle,* she portrayed a passionate and alluring young writer, Louis Rogès, for whom Paris no doubt supplied plenty of models, but the novel made a big impression on Mansfield, who read it in 1915 and called it "fascinating . . . far more interesting than *Colette* the *master.*"[12] Mansfield's fascination may have been just with the story, which tells of a passionate young idealist who aspires to a chaste love with a prostitute, whom he believes to be a reincarnation of Cleopatra and through whom he lives out a variety of colorful mystical oriental fantasies and perversions.[13] Or perhaps Louis Rogès reminded Mansfield of Carco and their own very recent, very colorful entanglement. Fully

---

second, from Chapter XXII, on February 1, 1914. An extract from a poem by François Villon introduced the text, which is slightly longer than the book form. Mansfield and Murry were in Paris at the time of publication in the magazine, and Carco must have taken them to the bars on the boulevard de Clichy, which are featured in the novel.

11. Rachilde lived from 1860 to 1953. She used other pen names, usually anagrams of *Rachilde,* such as Jean de Childra and Jenny Chibra. She "discovered" Colette, Alfred Jarry, and Jules Renard. She has been variously attached by critics to "l'école naturaliste des Goncourts" and to the symboliste and the decadent movements. See Ruth Parkin-Gounelas' discussion, p. 42 above.

12. *Collected Letters,* I, 162. Rachilde, as coeditor of *Le Mercure de France,* claimed she had interviewed the novel's author, Jean de Childra.

13. Claude Dauphiné, *Rachilde, femme de lettres, 1900* (Périgueux, 1985), 53. For comments on positive aspects of *L'Heure sexuelle,* see also Jennifer Waelti-Walters, *Feminist Novelists of the Belle Epoque: Love as Lifestyle* (Bloomington, Ind., 1990), esp. 214–16: "Rachilde writes a cynical criticism of society into an apparently scandalous and slightly erotic text. What society calls love is usually a commerce in bodies. . . . Only those persons who deal openly can remain pure because they can distinguish between prostitution and real love" (pp. 214–15). A similar distinction is made in Carco's novel *Les Innocents,* though not explicitly. Milord and Melle Savonnette, both prostituting themselves to Winnie Campbell, do love each other.

consummated in the war zone at Gray, this had begun in Carco's home territory—Montmartre, La Closerie des Lilas, and the Bal Vachier, on the Montagne Ste. Geneviève.

As coeditor of *Rhythm,* Mansfield had read some of Carco's early poetry: the prose poems of *Instincts,* from 1911, the verse of *La Bohème et Mon Coeur,* from 1912, and *Chansons Aigres-Douces* and the Verlainian *Au vent crispé du matin,* both from 1913. She seems to have found much of his verse congenial. Since Carco's verse has never been translated into English, it is worth providing a sample of the work of the young writer Mansfield was to meet and enjoy. Carco was listed as a foreign correspondent for *Rhythm* in France, along with his friend the poet Tristan Derème, who introduced the latest French poetic school as L'Ecole Fantaisiste and defined *la fantaisie* as "une manière de douce indépendance et parfois comme un air mélancolique que voile un sourire ambigu. Non pas une indépendance qui veuille tout démolir pour tout reconstruire . . . mais un souci d'agréable liberté spirituelle qui permette de donner au monde des aspects imprévus" ("a kind of sweet independence sometimes tinged with a melancholy that veils an ambiguous smile. It is not the kind of independence that proposes to break down everything in order to build anew . . . but a concern for a sort of pleasant spiritual freedom capable of revealing unexpected aspects of the world").[14]

"Les Huit Danseuses," the shortest of three prose poems from *Instincts,* which were published in Volume I of *Rhythm,* shows Carco's sensual mood and a clever surprise finale:

> Les huit danseuses, guidés par les flûtes, s'enlevaient et tournaient, puis s'enlaçaient avec leur voiles. Elles parurent de fines tanagréennes fragiles qu'un souffle eût brisées. Mais bientôt elles accoururent en se tenant les mains.
>
> Chacune m'attirait par son geste.
>
> Alors, d'un large mouvement mesuré par l'orchestre, elles levèrent les bras vers le ciel et l'écharpe dont elles étaient gardiennes se délia soudain comme une chevelure, se tordit, voltigea, claqua, puis sous le vent ne fut plus qu'une longue flamme vivante au poing des danseuses. Les robes moulaient ces huit corps, habiles et parfaits, qui tour à tour, s'offrirent et se dérobèrent, furent absolument nus.

14. Tristan Derème, "Lettre de Paris," *Rhythm,* II (1912), 113.

The eight dancing girls in their light veils, graceful and fragile, like Tanagra statuettes, were rising, spinning around, and holding hands to the sound of the flutes.

Each one drew me in with her movements.

Then, as they lifted their arms to the sky on an ample swell of the music, the scarf they held was suddenly released like tresses. Twisting, flying, flapping in the wind, it turned into a long flame, alive in the dancers' hands. Their apparel was clinging to eight perfect bodies, now offering themselves, now drawing back, stark-naked.[15]

Carco's verse in *La Bohème et Mon Coeur* is quite different from the clever prose poems and genre pieces of *Instincts*. He reminds us of Alfred de Musset, Jules Laforgue, and Verlaine in his predilection for short meters, impressionist techniques, and occasional touches of wit and humor. He shared their acute sensibility and uncovered the many nuances of "love"—a whole range of sense perceptions associated with feeling or not, a mixture of pain and pleasure, warmth and detachment, sensual enjoyment and nostalgia.

In a later "Lettre de France" to *Rhythm* devoted to the new French poets, Derème wrote, "Une âme lyrique qui se manifeste à travers un visage pâle et rasé comme des complets impeccables: c'est Francis Carco. Il chante les petits cabarets et les visages de la nature. . . . Le poète maintenant se réfugie dans les paysages; il les regarde, les sent, les goûte et les peint avec passion par petites touches vives et minutieuse. . . . Sa poésie est, avant tout, concrète; elle hait l'abstraction et, par une sorte d'intuition, épouse si étroitement la forme et la manière des choses, qu'elle donne l'impression d'être *une poésie physique,* beaucoup plus faite pour agir sur la sensibilité que pour émouvoir l'intelligence" ("A lyrical soul showing through a pale, closely shaven face and impeccable suits: that is Francis Carco. He sings about little cabarets and the faces of Nature. . . . Now the poet finds refuge in landscapes; he looks at them, feels, savors, and paints them with passion in bright meticulous little touches. . . . His poetry is concrete above all; it hates abstraction and espouses the shape

---

15. Francis Carco, "Les Huit Danseuses," *Rhythm*, I (1911), 25–27, 20, 21. "Les Huit Danseuses" followed "Après minuit" and "Aix-en-Provence." Carco, apart from his descriptions of Mansfield, has not previously been quoted in an English-language publication either in the French or in translation, so far as I am aware. Most translations here are mine.

and manner of things so closely, by a kind of intuition, that it gives the impression of being a *physical poetry,* created more to act on sensibility than to touch the intellect").[16]

The poems in *La Bohème et Mon Coeur* are short and predominantly written in octosyllabic lines, sometimes alternating with alexandrine. Much use is made of questions, precise short notations in a style that avoids poetic diction and tends naturally to simple colloquial terms, a style consciously reminiscent of the Verlaine of *Romances sans paroles.* Carco, though not displaying the extreme metrical variety of his master, inherited his fine sense of rhythm, and his taste for assonance, as illustrated by the *pluie* and *insomnie* in the second stanza of "Amour":

> Tu riais. Tu te renversais
> Dans mes bras et l'aube amoureuse
> Illuminait ma tête creuse
> Et lourde, mais je te berçais,
>
> En chantant. Le jour, dans la pluie,
> Se levait et n'en pouvait plus.
> Contre ta hanche étroite et nue,
> Je tombais enfin d'insomnie . . .
>
> Matins amers, amour charmant,
> Epuisante et trouble folie,
> Au réveil, la mélancolie
> Sépara plus tard ces amants.
>
> Pourquoi? Nul ne le sait. Lui-même
> Pleurait en s'éloignant de toi.
> Et, depuis ce jour, que de fois
> L'aube a fripé ses roses blêmes![17]

Nature is prominent in the verse of Carco, a conscious follower of Verlaine, and it is treated in a similar Impressionist manner in "Verlainien":

16. Tristan Derème, "Lettre de France," *Rhythm,* II (1912), 229–31. Derème's remarks could equally apply to Mansfield's fictional prose, in my view; they underline the affinities between the two.

17. Francis Carco, "Amour," in *La Bohème et Mon Coeur* (1912; rpr. Paris, 1939), 93.

Un arbre tremble sous le vent.
　　　Les volets claquent.
Comme il a plu, l'eau fait des flaques.

Des feuilles volent sous le vent
　　　Qui les disperse
Et, brusquement, il pleut à verse.

□

　　　Le jour décroit.
Sur l'horizon qui diminue,
Je vois la silhouette nue
D'un clocher mince avec sa croix.

　　　Dans le silence,
J'entends la cloche d'un couvent.
Elle s'élève, elle s'élance
Et puis retombe avec le vent.

□

Un arbre que le vent traverse
　　　Geint doucement,
Comme une floue et molle averse
Qui s'enfle et tombe à tout moment.

Du vieil amour mélancolique
　　　Que j'ai pour toi,
Restera-t-il que la musique
Monotone de cette voix ?[18]

Mansfield and Carco met, through Murry, in the winter of 1913–1914, when Mansfield and Murry were staying at rue de Tournon. Murry

18. Francis Carco, "Verlainien," in *La Bohème et Mon Coeur,* 114–15. Verlaine's familiar terms find an echo here and in other poems in this collection: *vent, voix, mélancolique* (rhyming with *musique*), and the long adverbs ending in *ment.*

reported that while he was toiling at "serious" articles, Carco was showing Mansfield the city.[19] Clearly they enjoyed each other's company, and their explorations were not of the usual tourist haunts. The Carco who had just completed *Jésus-la-Caille* was to be resurrected by Mansfield in the first part of "Je ne parle pas français," in a declaration by Raoul Duquette that reflects the young writer's confidence and clearly underlines the distinction between the real Carco and his unsavory fictionalized counterpart:

> The book that I shall bring out will simply stagger the critics. I am going to write about things that have never been touched before. I am going to make a name for myself as a writer about the submerged world. But not as others have done before me. Oh, no! Very naively, with a sort of tender humour and from the inside, as though it were all quite simple, quite natural. I see my way quite perfectly. Nobody has ever done it as I shall do it because none of the others have lived my experiences. I'm rich—I'm rich. (282)

In articles written ten years after Mansfield's death, Carco, despite his general concurrence with Murry's sanctifying posthumous transformation of her, wrote of their long walks at night through the outlying districts of Paris. They stopped at dingy bars and other underworld resorts.[20] Carco, born far from France, was enthralled by what Parisians scorn as Paris exoticism. For an itinerant young woman in conscious pursuit of life in the raw, he was the perfect tourist guide.

Murry, too, benefited from his guidance. *Between Two Worlds* tells of Carco's taking over the sale of furniture when Murry and Mansfield were leaving their flat: "His idea I gathered, in wide-eyed astonishment, was that the brothel-keepers would know the likeliest dealers, or, better still, offer to buy the things themselves. So with my pepper-and-salt trousers and my monocle, I trotted after him in a dream across Paris and back again."[21] Murry speculated that Carco may have been testing English phlegm, or gathering exotic copy. He described Carco as "something of a connoisseur in bizarre sensations" who took him "to desolate brothel-

19. John Middleton Murry, *Between Two Worlds* (London, 1935), 272–73.
20. Carco, *Montmartre à vingt ans*, Chap. X.
21. Murry, *Between Two Worlds*, 276.

bars in forlorn suburbs, with that queer tired atmosphere of dingily commercial vice, which he was himself to render so impressively in his novels." Murry's portrait of Carco's mixed qualities is judicious: "a touch of
the *voyou*, a touch of the singer at the *caf' concert,* an evident streak of
talent. . . . I couldn't help admiring the amazing audacity with which he
played his part. His cynicism enveloped everybody." [22]

Carco had indeed a touch of the caf'concert chanteur. He knew innu-
merable songs, both traditional French and the latest popular successes
sung at street corners and in music halls. At one time he scraped a living
by singing in cabarets. Later on, between the two world wars, some of
his poems served as lyrics to charming popular songs such as "Le Gai
Caboulot" and "Il pleut." [23] There were gaiety, charm, and music in this
bohemian colonial, as well as cynicism and audacity. No wonder his
"warm sensational life," as Mansfield put it in her journal, appealed to
her, searching as she was for experience with a literary flavor.

The details of their affair have been well documented.[24] In Cornwall,
living adjacent to the Lawrences, Mansfield and Murry reached an understanding that they would part. On November 15, 1914, Mansfield
reread Colette's *L'Entrave* and remarked, "I don't care a fig at present
for anyone I know except her." [25] The next day, a letter from Carco arrived, and for the next three months they wrote each other passionate
letters and exchanged photographs and locks of hair. "The opening pages
of her diary for 1915 are full of references to the Frenchman whom Jack
knew better than she," Antony Alpers remarks wryly. She wrote that
when she and Murry made love, "I felt I betrayed F." [26]

22. *Ibid.,* 276–77, 149.

23. "Il pleut," from *Petite Suite sentimentale* (Paris, 1936), was set to music by the
popular composer Jacques Larmanjat. The poem, in a tender mood, links the images of rain
and separation. It ends,

> Je t'aime. Oh! ce bruit d'eau qui pleure,
> Qui sanglote comme un adieu.
> Tu vas me quitter tout à l'heure:
> On dirait qu'il pleut dans tes yeux.

24. The best accounts are in Alpers, *Life,* 173–77; and before him, in Didier Merlin's
Le Drame secret de Katherine Mansfield (Paris, 1950). See also Merlin's translation of "An
Indiscreet Journey" and other stories from *The Doll's House,* published in French under
the title *Le Voyage indiscret* (Paris, 1950).

25. *Journal,* 62.

26. Alpers, *Life,* 174.

And so on February 15, 1915, Mansfield left England again, to join Corporal Carco at Gray, "within the zone of the armies and not allowed to women. The last old pa-man who saw my passport, 'M. le Colonel' . . . nearly sent me back."[27] The couple contrived to spend four days—or as much of those as Carco's duties in the military postal service permitted—in secret love and exciting talk. Then she sent Murry a telegram saying she would arrive the next day, February 25, at Victoria Station. The affair was over.[28]

There is a poem by Carco, entitled "Rengaine" (Familiar tune), collected in a later edition of *La Bohème et Mon Coeur,* with his *Vers retrouvés,* that could have been written by the poet when Mansfield was leaving Gray. The tone and words fit the occasion: it is also interesting as an example of Carco's use of dialogue and simple language in his poems:

Tu t'en vas et tu nous quittes.
—Adieu! Pense à moi, quelquefois.
—Je ne t'oublierai pas, petite!
Tu nous quittes et tu t'en vas.

Tu m'écriras trois semaines.
Le coeur y est, bien gentiment
Et puis tu berceras ta peine
Dans les bras d'un autre amant . . .

Tu sanglotes. Je suis triste.
Le train siffle. Ah! Mon Dieu, mon Dieu!
Je ne veux pas quie tu me quittes,
Maintenant que c'est sérieux.

Mansfield borrowed Carco's apartment on the quai aux Fleurs when she returned to Paris to write for two short periods between March and May, 1915. She wrote most of *The Aloe* on the quai aux Fleurs, returning to New Zealand in imagination. According to Alpers, she also wrote "An Indiscreet Journey" there, just before she fled back to Murry yet again on

27. *Collected Letters,* I, 150.
28. Alpers, *Life,* 177; Carco, *La Bohème et Mon Coeur,* 209.

May 19, having heard that Carco was on his way to Paris.[29] The story is a skillful, semifictionalized narrative of her adventure, incorporating some more recent impressions of the consequences of war. Carco was behind the "little corporal," perhaps little more than the embodiment of the frisson of illicitness with which the whole narrative trembles. Nor had she exhausted Carco's literary possibilities. "Je ne parle pas français" was still to come.

Entanglements between writers, of course, are always hazardous to both parties. Carco was at work equally quickly, writing *Les Innocents,* his second novel, which was published in 1916.[30] Its portrait of Winnie Campbell gives us a fictionalized version of Mansfield that is valuable for its physical portrayal of her, for its insight into her dedication and procedures as a writer, and for its psychological perception into traits not much noted by other contemporaries: "Winnie Campbell n'était pas riche et elle écrivait pour les journaux anglais des romans qu'un éditeur publiait à Londres dans une collection populaire. Cela lui donnait quelque argent. Elle avait 27 ans. Sa jeunesse n'était point celle des femmes de son âge ni de sa condition. Elle détestait Londres dont elle avait épuisé les curiosités et les saveurs défendues" ("Winnie Campbell was not well off. For English magazines, she wrote novels that were published in London in a popular series. That provided her with a small income. She was twenty-seven. She did not share the youthful life of women of her age and class. She hated London, whose sights and forbidden charms she had exhausted").[31]

Carco's physical description of Winnie confirms the delicate image of "innocence" and frailty that he saw in Mansfield at their first meeting and adds something more: "C'était une petite femme menue, gracieuse avec froideur et dont les immenses yeux noirs se posaient partout à la fois" ("She was a tiny woman, graceful yet cold, whose large black eyes looked everywhere at once"). But her clothes did not radiate femininity; they were more in keeping with a sporting or even a military or masculine look: "Elle n'était ni poudrée convenablement ni chaussée comme les filles de Paris. . . . De plus, . . . son manteau de coupe originale . . . était

29. *Collected Letters,* I, 188; Alpers, *Life,* 178.
30. *Les Innocents* was published by La Renaissance du Livre in 1916. An edition illustrated by Charles Laborde came out in 1921; that was republished by Ferenczi in 1924, with original woodcuts by André Dignimont.
31. Francis Carco, *Les Innocents* (1916; rpr. Paris, 1952), 100.

orné de rangées symétriques de boutons, ronds, en nickel" ("She did not wear face powder, nor did she have the same sort of shoes worn by Paris girls. . . . Moreover, her coat, in its unusual style, was decorated with symmetrical rows of round nickel buttons"). She did, however, wear a hat: "Enfin, Winnie portait, sur des cheveux admirables et coupés tout droits sur la nuque, un chapeau de feutre rond à grands bords qu'elle ôtait quelquefois pour secouer la tête" ("Finally, on her lovely hair, which was cut very straight at the nape of the neck, Winnie wore a round hat with a wide brim which she occasionally took off to shake her head"). She did not wear cheap perfume, and she smoked English cigarettes: "Elle lui parut appartenir à cette catégorie des 'poules de luxe' qu'il ignorait, parce qu'elle ne répandait pas ce parfum violent de verveine ou de muguet qu'il reniflait chez d'autres, avec délices. Une odeur de tabac 'riche' et de myrrhe lui flattait la narine" ("She did not seem to him to belong to the category of high-class tarts familiar to him, because she was not surrounded with the strong perfume of verbena and lily of the valley that he sniffed delightedly in other girls. A smell of tobacco 'for the rich' and of myrrh tickled his nose"). He held her interest: "Elle s'amusait de tous ses gestes et du sens qu'elle donnait à ses paroles. Le regard trouble et jaune de Milord l'attirait. Un bref frisson lui fit baisser les paupières" ("His movements and the meaning she gave to his words amused her. She was attracted by the dim look in his yellow eyes. She gave a short shiver and lowered her gaze").[32]

In *Les Innocents,* the literary Mansfield appears in a way that justifies Alpers' image of a "predatory" writer looking for "copy." Carco's Winnie was constantly asking questions of the young man she had chosen as the central character for a book she was writing and whom she paid for services rendered: "Winnie se servait de lui, comme le peintre d'un modèle dont il étudie le caractère et les mouvements. . . . Elle l'interrogeait avec détachement; elle se montrait d'une extrême habilité pour laisser au Milord le soin d'expliquer sa conduite aventureuse, les moeurs qu'il pratiquait et le sens qu'il découvrait aux détails de la vie" ("She used him just the way a painter uses a model, studying character and movements. She questioned him with detachment; she was extremely skillful and allowed Milord to explain his audacious behavior, his accustomed habits, and the meaning he found in the details of life"). She watched him care-

32. *Ibid.,* 62–64, 67.

fully: "Elle prenait le Milord tout entier dans son regard" ("She held Milord completely in her gaze"). And she was just as attentive to his words: "Winnie l'écoutait avec une avidité sensuelle qui crispait les ailes minces de son nez" ("Winnie listened to his tales of low life with a sensual eagerness that tensed her thin nostrils").[33]

She was accomplished at absorbing herself in roles: "Elle était mieux qu'une femme curieuse, le miroir exact et profond de l'homme qu'elle voulait refléter tout entier. Cela seul comptait à présent" ("She was more than a woman full of curiosity, she was the exact and deep mirror of the man she wanted to reflect totally. That was the only thing that really mattered to her now."). The young man's girlfriend, Melle Savonnette, gave an unflattering assessment of Winnie Campbell at work: "Melle Savonnette comprit que la femme près de qui elle était, ne se trouverait jamais capable d'éprouver aucun sentiment directement humain. Elle cherchait trop à dépasser les limites extrêmes de la pudeur et de la franchise" ("Melle Savonnette understood that the woman who was close to her would never be capable of experiencing a really human feeling. She was too intent on overreaching the farthest limits of decency and sincerity").[34]

Winnie told Milord she wanted to meet his girlfriend, Savonnette; she needed to see her for the book she was writing, for which she could not find a suitable ending. Carco conveyed Winnie's view of life and art in a passage of Mansfield's anglicized French:

> Il est bête . . . Oh! vraiment si bête d'imaginer seulement les choses, pensait Winnie. Il faut voir. Il est alors sur les visages les mots nécessaires et, l'expression change, c'est encore une parole qui n'est pas menteuse. Et, quand il se tait, ou sourit, ou bien fait son méchant regard, il me donne aussitôt les termes pour écrire: "Il se tait. Il sourit. Il tient ses yeux durement fixés sur elle." Oh! mon Dieu! On peut souvent n'avoir pas besoin de toucher les choses avec la main mais il est la joie d'écrire les mots qui sont exacts et toujours plus exacts, toujours plus, sans plus."

It is really silly to imagine things only, thought Winnie. One must see. Then one finds on faces words that are necessary, and when the facial expression

33. *Ibid.*, 88, 90, 92.
34. *Ibid.*, 199, 237.

changes, it is new words that do not lie. And when he is silent or smiles or
has a nasty look on his face, straightaway he gives me the words to write,
"He is silent, he smiles, he gave her a hard stare." Oh, Lord, one does not
often need to touch things, but there is a joy in writing words that are right
and always more right, always and nothing else.[35]

Carco provided other psychological insights into Mansfield. Winnie
Campbell, who looked so sweet, was a perverse creature at heart. She
enjoyed the brutal attentions of Milord, the young male prostitute she
financed, and was not against his beating and bruising her. She kept
pushing him and provoking him in all sorts of ways. She displayed her
ambivalent sexual urges shamelessly in front of him, provocatively saying
that her relationship with Beatrice, her woman friend and a kind of cubist
painter, who became a war photographer, like the real Beatrice Hastings,
on whom she was based, was not love:

> "Et votre copine de la rue Visconti?"
> ". . . Elle est une femme véritablement supérieure et elle dit toujours, s'il
> faut, les choses dans le moment. Elle connaît tous les pays et les hôtels et
> tous les bateaux . . . et tous les bars des colonies. . . . Mais ce n'est pas
> l'amour, Béatrice."

> "And what about your girlfriend from the rue Visconti?"
> ". . . She is a really superior woman and she always says the right things
> at the right time when she has to. She knows every country and every hotel
> and every ship . . . and every bar in the colonies . . . But Beatrice is not
> love."[36]

In the end, Winnie became intimate with Melle Savonnette, whom she
also paid for services rendered—not least in order to study the young
man's reactions to the unusual situation.

The sensational material in *Les Innocents* should not suggest that the
novel is badly written. Carco had a great concern for style and the right
words. The novel flows easily; it is economical and well-constructed. It is
not pornographic, just disquieting enough in its presentation of sexual

35. *Ibid.*, 228–29.
36. *Ibid.*, 95.

and sentimental urges as something quite *de fait*. It seems to say, This is what it is, this is life, the real thing.

Carco, trying to seize on the experienced reality of his unusual characters, broke down the barriers of bourgeois conventions. There is a point to the story, though it is only hinted at. The title is the first clue. The novel tells us that prostituting one's body does not, as one might assume, imply the corruption of the "soul." True love can develop despite prostitution. In *Les Innocents*, delicate feelings of moral responsibility develop between the two young protagonists, who eventually free themselves from the bondage of the perverse, coldhearted writer by killing her. They must then, of course, kill themselves.

In later years, Carco stressed the fictional nature of the characters and situations in *Les Innocents*, asserting that Mansfield had nothing to do with the perverse side of Winnie: "C'est à Katherine Mansfield que je dois d'avoir écrit mon meilleur livre, car elle m'en a, dans une certaine mesure, procuré tous les éléments. Si c'est elle qu'à maints détails on reconnaît dans la Winnie des *Innocents*, elle n'a posé du personnage que ce qu'il présente de pur, d'intact" ("I am indebted to Katherine Mansfield for inspiring my best book, for to a certain extent she gave me all its elements. If she can indeed be recognized in the Winnie of *Les Innocents*, she was the model only of that part of the character which is pure and untouched").[37] Yet his portrayal of Winnie the dedicated writer, fresh though it is in so many details, is consistent with the Mansfield who emerges from the journal, the letters, and other testimonies of her own. There is the well-known letter to Dorothy Brett of October 11, 1917, in which Mansfield talks about becoming the apple or the duck that she sees, and ends up by saying, "I believe in technique . . . because I don't see how art is going to make that divine *spring* into the bounding outlines of things if it hasn't passed through the process of trying to *become* these things before recreating them."[38] Carco, bad though his press has often been, saw Mansfield clearly enough to make a strong fictional character from the writer seeking to pass through just that process.

Les Innocents is dedicated to Rachilde as "ma marraine d'avant la guerre" ("my prewar godmother"), in a play on the expression *marraine de guerre*. The theme and characters of Carco's first novel, *Jésus-la-*

---

37. Carco, *Montmartre à vingt ans*, Chap. X.
38. *Collected Letters*, I, 330.

Caille, had been just the right kind to titillate Rachilde's editorial fancy. The novel revolves around the figure of a fine-featured young male prostitute with ambivalent proclivities who is such a picture of youthful innocence and beauty that he is known as Jesus the Quail. A regular female prostitute of the lower reaches of the Butte Montmartre is irresistibly attracted to him. To season matters further, a subplot introduces some "tough gentlemen" from the Milieu who rely for their living on thieving and the earnings of their "girls" and who are ready for violence and murder if insulted or betrayed. The novel is significant as a prototype of many novels and films devoted to the criminal Milieu.

If Mansfield felt an impulse to retaliate for Winnie Campbell, that was not her immediate reaction. She had first encountered Carco as a poet and continued to think of his poems. In the summer of 1917, she quoted in her journal the third stanza of "Province," from *La Bohème et Mon Coeur.* The complete poem reads,

> L'ombre du clocher noir entre dans la boutique.
> Un lilas, débordant les grilles d'un jardin,
> Se balance et je vois luire et trembler soudain
> Des fouillis bleus, la route et l'auberge rustique.
>
> Des pigeons, mollement arriveés sur le vent,
> Tournent dans l'azur pâle en éployant leurs ailes.
> Province! Ah! ce bonheur, que j'ai connu sans elle,
> Comme il pèse à mon coeur scrupuleux et fervent!
>
> Et pourtant, il faut bien s'habituer à vivre,
> Même seul, même triste, indifférent et las,
> Car, ô ma vision troublante, n'es-tu pas
> Un mirage incessant trop difficile à suivre?

In this mood piece, the first two stanzas are descriptive; they evoke the quiet atmosphere of a small provincial town, with its church steeple, lilac, lush vegetation, and a flight of pigeons, finally leading to a melancholy questioning in the third stanza:

> And yet, perforce one must get used to living,
> On one's own in sadness, indifferent and weary,

> For, oh disquieting vision of mine, are you not
> An endless mirage, far too hard to pursue?[39]

Carco's work owed much to Apollinaire, as well as Verlaine. Like Apollinaire, Carco elected autumn as his "mental" season and cultivated melancholy moods attuned to the October and November cityscapes of Paris. The resulting touches punctuate his narratives in both *Jésus-la-Caille* and *Les Innocents*. His Parisian fall does not accentuate the traditional elements of nature. Rather, he finds his *correspondances* in urban sidewalks glistening with rain, bitter winds in dingy streets, and tugboats hooting on the Seine. The waters of the river are in tune with feelings of solitude and the difficulties of artistic creation.

By Mansfield's difficult summer of 1917, she had followed endless mirages of her own. She shared the melancholy of the third stanza of "Province," unaware that she had given more permanence to the disquieting vision it speaks of than she knew.

A few months later, Mansfield returned to the mirage that had been her short-lived Gallic romance. "Je ne parle pas français" is partly a reprisal for *Les Innocents,* delayed by two years. She had been in France again, at Bandol, and wrote the story in ten days, between January 30 and February 10, 1918, at Hôtel Beau Rivage.[40] It was included in *Bliss and Other Stories* in December, 1920. Alpers has shown that the text was expurgated and that the editorial suppressions of 1920, which survived until Alpers' definitive edition of the stories in 1984, were very much against Mansfield's will. Carco had become more shadowy than she wished. The editor cut all realistic details "portraying the cynical attitudes towards love and sex of her narrator, Raoul Duquette."[41] Sensual descriptions and words that were thought too crude for a Katherine Mansfield story were omitted out of fear of shocking her readers. She had argued unsuccessfully that they were essential elements: "The outline would be all blurred. It must have those sharp lines" (561).

39. Carco, *La Bohème et Mon Coeur,* 96; *Journal,* 124. Mansfield quotes the third stanza only, probably from memory, since she omits *bien* in the ninth line, thus losing the twelve-syllable alexandrine. Carco acknowledged her choice of the quatrain, though he remarked aptly that she was attracted to it more by the "idea of mirage" than by appreciation of its poetic worth.

40. On Bandol, see Jacqueline Bardolph, "The French Connection: Bandol," in the present volume.

41. Alpers, *Stories,* 559–60.

The story, even in its reduced form, has layers of meaning. To suggest that it was in one respect a counterblow to Carco's less than flattering version of her as Winnie Campbell is simply to add a fold that must, even five years after their indiscreet four days, have had personal import for her. Duquette's bisexuality, in particular, was suitable revenge for Winnie's unstable proclivities in *Les Innocents*. There is also a likely double entendre, Alpers suggests, or at least a private meaning, in the title phrase: "On the subject of love, it seems to declare, the author and the French . . . don't speak the same language at all. In a letter to Murry, she called [it] 'a tribute to Love . . . you understand'" (559).

She submitted Carco to some sharp literary mockery, too, in the titles she gave Duquette's publications: a collection of poems called *False Coins,* a serial story entitled *Wrong Doors,* another collection grouped as *Left Umbrellas.* There seems no room after that for acknowledgment of the merits of some of Carco's early poems and stories.

Perhaps Mansfield gained more from Carco than she knew or admitted, however—or from the French connection more generally, through the work of the three French writers with whom she had a contemporary association, Carco, Colette, and Rachilde. "An Indiscreet Journey" and "Je ne parle pas français" both deal with self-identity, especially in relation to sensuality and sexual experience, in a way quite different from any earlier, or even any other, of Mansfield's work for publication. Clearly, they place Mansfield nearer to Colette and Maupassant than to Chekhov. The French treatment of life in its physical and less savory aspects is quite distinctive, and is common to Colette, Rachilde, and Carco. Colette addressed with unique freedom and honesty the problem of dependence and independence in matters of love. Rachilde could make serious fiction of sexual fantasies. And Carco presented the Paris underworld naturally and without moralizing, using direct dialogue and often local slang to color and authenticate the material. The place of realistic sexual experience in focusing identity in a fiction of contemporary life is a natural and central element in the work of all three. Mansfield also aspired to make it so in hers.

There may have been other things in her writing that derive from Carco, such as her use in the *New Age* series, from 1917, of Cockney dialogue, strongly reminiscent of his Parisian slang. Perhaps, too, it was Carco's economical way of foreclosing the narrative, curtailing and moving swiftly out of a chapter, that suggested to her the possibilities of suspended endings. At least the parallel is worth observing. So, too, is the way that her disjunctions, the repeated plungings of the reader into some new medias res, are also characteristic of this Pacific-born Frenchman. The affinity that provided four brief indiscreet days was present much longer in the texts they each produced. But even quite apart from that, Carco has earned the right to be known to readers of Mansfield as he really was, not merely as the "little corporal" or the unwholesome Duquette. And who is to say whether Carco's memories of childhood in Nouméa were not rekindled in the intense conversations he and Mansfield had at Gray while she was imaginatively rediscovering her own native land?[42]

In her French connections, Mansfield found an open though civilized discussion of topics that were still taboo in serious English writing of her time. Sensuality and sex were not yet acceptable as literary topics in spite of the efforts of Thomas Hardy, Olive Schreiner, H. G. Wells, and others. As Alpers comments with reference to the cuts from "Je ne parle pas français," "*The Rainbow* had been suppressed, and *Women in Love* had not yet appeared; *Ulysses* and *The Waste Land* were still two years away."[43] Mansfield, like many of her contemporaries, found in French writers an inspiration to tackle forthrightly the topics she felt impelled to investigate. "Bliss," also written in February, 1918, shows traces of the French connection in the incident chosen and the sensual feelings tentatively expressed by Bertha Young toward her husband, Harry, and Miss Fulton.

In finding Colette, Rachilde, and even more, Carco, Mansfield gained a stimulus at a time when her inspiration was at a low ebb. The French connection was a significant catalyst and may have been what enabled her to focus to consummate effect on the concerns most troubling her. Those concerns had beset her from adolescence and were resolved only through the even more serious affliction of her final illness, and through her eventual marriage to Murry. In the French, and the not insignificant Francis Carco in particular, she found the courage and literary models to carry into her writings the adventures she had repeatedly sought in her intimate relationships with men and women.

42. Francis Carco, *Maman Petitdoigt* (Paris, 1920).
43. Alpers, *Stories,* 561.

The French Connection: Bandol

JACQUELINE BARDOLPH

Bandol, in Katherine Mansfield's "unhoused condition," was a privileged place and time, "that country of her grief and joy." L.M. (Ida Baker) felt excluded when she joined her there.[1] Mansfield's stays at Bandol, in the winter of 1915–1916 and in 1918—the second very much illuminated by the memory of the first—were not very long, but they were moments of serenity and fertility in her writing life. That was not only because the woman who had twenty-six postal addresses in a few years could find better living conditions in the town. In the "unhoused," "unaccommodated" condition of the exile, and also of the artist, she organized her vision and her writings around essential themes and images that had much to do with place, with the sense of belonging, with her home in New Zealand, and with the home still to be created.[2]

Two extracts from Shakespeare copied in her scrapbook in 1916 show the two poles of her imaginary space: "When I was at home, I was in a

---

1. [Ida Baker], *Katherine Mansfield: The Memories of LM* (London, 1971), 107–109.
2. For the prevalence of the image of place and home, see Andrew Gurr, *Writers in Exile: The Identity of Home in Modern Literature* (Brighton, Eng., 1981), 33–60.

better place;/But travellers must be content"; and, "I like this place/And willingly would waste my time in it."[3] These lines will be my starting point in a ramble, partly personal, that will take me from the hills around Bandol, from the wind, the almond trees, to the little house and the short story "Sun and Moon," written on her second stay in 1918, when she also produced the better-known "Bliss."

Because I have known from adolescence the landscape on which Mansfield was projecting her dreams, testing her memories, getting in touch again with the "self which is continuous and permanent,"[4] I would like to conduct a visit to the place. I will show also, with the help of Mansfield's personal papers, how she fitted the experience of it that chance had given her into the continuity of her work, how she shaped some elements of that small area of France to the need of her artistic vision.

The place has changed brutally. Yet it is still possible to know what Mansfield knew, walk the paths she explored on her first stay, recognize the brilliance of her descriptions as she emerged from the first shock of her grief over her brother's death and decided to see and to put into words what her senses told her, as a kind of restorative discipline. At first, she was numb: "To tell you the truth these things that I have heard about him blind me to all that is happening here—All this is like a long uneasy ripple—nothing else—and below—in the still pool there is my little brother."[5] But then in December she could say, "My work is shaping for the first time today—I feel nearer it. I can see the people walking on the shore & the flowery clusters hanging on the trees—if you know what I mean. It has only been a dim coast & a glint of foam before—The days go by quickly."[6]

What did she see? Bandol was a fishing village with a few hotels, far from more fashionable places east or west on the Coast, and rather cheap. Fishing settlements and their inhabitants were marginal at that time to the Provençal economy and culture; the centers were in the agricultural countryside, inland. After the arrival of the railroad, the economy had been helped by the culture of flowers—roses, narcissus, immortelles. What she encountered was not very rich, not very friendly

3. *Scrapbook,* 51.
4. *Ibid.,* 137.
5. *Collected Letters,* I, 200.
6. *Ibid.,* 206.

people, less of a traditional community than existed a few miles inland. Mansfield rendered the populace vividly and accurately, down to local turns of speech. She also responded acutely to the place itself.

During her first stay, when she was able to walk around, she rediscovered the sea, and thus came back in touch with an essential part of herself, her New Zealand self. She described how she climbed rocks, followed the *sentier des douaniers,* listened to the sea, smelled the "sharp smell of the wet blue gum trees," felt the wind blow through her sleeve: "When the wind blows I go to the windiest possible place and I feel the cold come flying under my arms—When the sea is high I go down among the rocks where the spray reaches and I have games with the sea like I used to years ago. And to see the sun rise and set seems enough miracle." It is impossible to mistake the relief she obtained from this physical contact, revivifying and cleansing her: "Murry does not like this place, but in many ways I do. For one thing, and its awfully important, the sea is here—very clear and very blue. The sound of it after such a long silence is almost unbearable—a sweet agony, you know—like moonlight is sometimes. . . . In my *heart* I am happy—because I feel that I have come into my own. You understand me?"[7]

Above all, the winter months at Bandol provided her with an essential system of contrast. Bandol is not properly speaking on the Côte d'Azur, and her descriptions of the extremes of the winter climate are not the impressions of an oversensitive temperament. Between November and March, when she was there, it will be wind for a while, either the "bitter east wind" she mentions, full of the promise of rain, the "thousand knife-like airs" from which there is no shelter as they mill around trees and houses that, just as she says, "are not made for such rude times," or the notorious Mistral, no joke in winter, that ice-cold north wind that blows relentlessly, unflinchingly, night and day for three, six, or nine days of clear sky and bright, harsh light: "There seems to be a ring of light round everything."[8] At Mistral time there are more suicides, there is unrest in mental homes. Then one morning there will be a strange silence and the dawn of a glorious spring day, whether in December or January, with spring bulbs emerging before Christmas perhaps, a warm sun, blossoms everywhere.

7. *Ibid.,* 217, 238, 200–201.
8. *Ibid.,* II, 105, I, 211.

After the dark and drizzle of a London winter, that was country Mansfield could take to. The power of the elements connected her directly with her New Zealand self. Her native town of Wellington is a place of windswept contrasts and bright light. At Bandol, the sea is tideless, but it is the sea. We can see how her work was given shape not by circumstance but by the coherence of the imaginary world she created, for when she responded to the Mistral, wind was already a strong element in her work. The wind of Wellington had already given rhythm and emotional force to "The Wind Blows," that "tale of unrest" written in 1915 after finding her brother, Leslie, again.

For Mansfield, the wind became a Shelleyan force, liberating, cleansing, but often associated with death. That is a strong motif in her letters and journals, at first connected with themes of brother and family, and gradually associated in her dreams with a "hollow dread," the memory of her dead, a vision at once comforting and frightening. As she grew weaker during her second stay, in 1918, the wind's powerful breath seemed a threat to her own lungs: "Un peu de vent & that vent is like an iced knife"; "Terrific wind & cold"; "Never, not even on shipboard or in my own little country or anywhere have I heard such wind." [9]

In her poetic system, that dark motif contrasted with life images, increasingly vulnerable ones. When she described the landscape in Bandol in 1918, after a spell of Mistral, there was no cliché in her choice of words: "Every mortal thing looks to be sheathed in a glittering beauty." [10] In many stories the fragile beauty of life, and its promise of fertility, cohere around a fruit tree in blossom: she had written "The Apple Tree" and was to choose the pear tree for "Bliss." In Bandol, the full splendor of the almond tree in blossom was the source of such sensuous felicity, so many symbolic echoes, that the question arises whether the pear tree of "Bliss" was not somehow also the almond tree she observed in the town where she wrote the story—changed into a pear for a word game with Pearl and the pearl-handled knife of husband or father. In Provence, the first sign of the new cycle of life is the lavish white blossoms of the almond tree. On a landscape still brown with winter, the trees, sometimes quite large, explode in white in January, just before the mimosa, beginning a sequence that brings pear and quince, apricot and cherry to trans-

9. *Ibid.*, I, 207, II, 101, 115, 29.
10. *Ibid.*, II, 32.

form the countryside. Mansfield had an almond tree in La Petite Pauline, and like all Provençals learned to rejoice in its promise, for "les fruits passeront la promesse des fleurs." To rejoice but fear, because it is a yearly gamble: the Mistral might kill the new blossoms. She quoted from a bleak Provençal poem by Jean Henri Fabre: "pas de nougat pour le noël." If the wind wins, there is no traditional nougat at Christmas, none of the "nougat . . . made at Ollioules of the very almond trees *here*." [11]

In Bandol's climate, with its exaggerated contrasts, Mansfield enriched her perception of natural cycles. She saw afresh and wrote afresh about the old conceits of the garden and the winter. She would write ecstatically to Ottoline Morrell in 1916 about "this hour of bright moonlight, when the flowering almond tree hangs over our white stone verandah a blue shadow with long tassels," and in 1918 about "sitting on a stone in the sun and listening to the bees in the almond trees and the wild pear bushes." She quoted Percy Bysshe Shelley to her: "I dreamed that as I wandered by the way/Bare winter suddenly was changed to spring." [12] In the same letter to Ottoline Morrell from 1918, written in February, there is evident the sensuous enjoyment and possibly the undercurrent of jealousy that were to be transformed into fiction. The tree motif in "Bliss" is effective because the sensorial re-creation is so exact, and also because the symbol is not one-way but at the center of a network of meanings that Mansfield had been working upon in the "camping ground" of her private writings. The story thus can leave many questions unanswered about the sense of the promise of the lavish fecundity in the blossoms. At one level, all the white is no Mallarméan image of the sterile sheet of the writer but a figure of the promise and precarious joy of writing, as a letter on February 3, 1918, about the "writing game" expresses clearly; on the one hand, there is the intimation of "joy . . . the flower without thought of a frost or a cold breath," both a promise and a memory of the Pauline days, and on the other hand, an adumbration of despair, the image of the withering blossom and an "*extremely* deep sense of hopelessness—of everything doomed to disaster—almost wilfully, stupidly—like the almond tree and 'pas de nougat pour le noël.'" [13] In this letter, the famous "cry against corruption" is, in company with the image of the almond

---

11. *Ibid.*, 54, 131.
12. *Ibid.*, I, 245, II, 86.
13. *Ibid.*, II, 54.

tree, expressive of the mood of the three apparently dissimilar stories written in Bandol in 1918: "Bliss," "Je ne parle pas français," and "Sun and Moon."

In Bandol, Mansfield enjoyed an elemental simplicity, but she also found or chose another way of seeing, that of deliberate daydreaming. After the harsh experience of sophisticated life, the masks and the striving, she made the village a place of innocence, attempting to connect a bucolic description of unspoiled simplicity with the inner vision of her childhood, of the security of home prior to worldly experience. In order to move away from her recurring dreams about her dead relative, she found her work, as she called it, in learning to see reality, to be aware of the surface of things again. Her fight was against the image of the dead brother down below: "The associations that massed around the words 'home' and 'work' were the strongest supports available to her." [14] Like John Keats, she in words explored simple, sensuous joys: "sunshine which melts in one's mouth," the "air . . . like fruit," the "air . . . like silk today & . . . a sheen upon the world like the sheen on a bird's wing." Her letters and journal seem to be sketches, exercises in perception and definition to prepare for the fiction. The words paint the color and texture of the sea, the fruit and flowers, the abundance to be found in Bandol market, "in front of that square curious little church." [15]

The Edenic motif is often present in her descriptions but for complex reasons, perhaps partly to keep sentimentality at an ironical distance while playing with it. She deliberately indulged in fantasies that make of the whole Bandol area a kind of fairyland, in the mood of which she retrospectively said, "Being 'children' together gave us a practically unlimited chance to play at life—not to live." [16] At the worst, particularly for an eavesdropper to her letters to Murry, things become too whimsical, a not-so-private lovers' code with dolls and miniature artifacts: "My grown up self sees us like two little children who have been turned out into the garden." [17] But most of the time, the fiction that uses this material is both magical and sane, like that of Hans Christian Andersen and the Grimm brothers, whom she admired. She gets lost on purpose in her

14. *Collected Letters*, II, ix (in Introduction, by Vincent O'Sullivan).

15. *Ibid.*, 221, 223, 204, 227.

16. *Scrapbook*, 125.

17. *Collected Letters*, II, 46. For similar moments of perspective, see Cherry Hankin, "Katherine Mansfield and the Cult of Childhood," in the present volume.

forest walks, between high stone walls, is frightened by dogs on a chain and jumping goats: "Shall I 'enter those enchanted woods' do you think Boge"; "There are faeries, faeries everywhere." The village of Le Castellet is a Dürer, the peasants in the landscape are bright-colored and earthy miniatures just like the santons of the church's Christmas crib she extolled in the splendid letter to J. D. Fergusson.[18] Like a child playing at getting lost in the wild part of the garden, she creates for herself "'secret' places."[19] It was still possible to do that in this small cultivated landscape even twenty years ago, and it especially mattered to her, since she knew she was partly deceiving herself: the rocks she climbs were not Swiss peaks, the rather small forests were not wild New Zealand, so that the untouched places became important personal finds, necessary to the communion with the source of herself.

On her walks around Bandol she expanded and elaborated on another motif in her writings and fiction: the motif of the little house. The house she lived in, locally called La Petite Pauline because it was set in the shadow of La Grande Pauline, though delightful at the time, was in memory to become a dream house. In the woods, she had already seen the "house on chicken legs" of Russian tales. Another house she had looked at on her walks in search of a "minute villa" became "our house": "The little house is there, waiting for us. Its eyes are shut until I open them." It was the French avatar of The Heron, the fantasy cottage she tried to impose on Murry page after page as an image of future married bliss: "Weve got furniture, books, a lovely doll. Don't you want to be my mate & live with me in a tiny cottage & eat out of egg cups?"[20] The irony is that the actual house turned out to be The Elephant, in Hampstead.

The house motif is a particularly feminine one, of course, but the dimensions her fantasy chose for her dwelling, as it recurred in her dreams, her letters, and her fiction, are arresting. Everything was miniature in her mentions, part sentimental and part ironical, of the house she sought: a shaded terrace, a place for two people to sit and read, flowers and blossoms, innocence and privacy. Such houses were dotted all over the landscape. Each path, each walk could take her to a new one. It is possible to see, as with the wind and the almond tree, how the theme is binary, the

18. *Collected Letters*, I, 202, 236, II, 34–35.
19. *Ibid.*, I, 238.
20. *Ibid.*, I, 243, II, 76.

little house taking its meaning in contrast to the big house that was home and family, the populated home in New Zealand during her first eighteen years. During her first stay in Bandol, she was working on "Prelude," recreating, building the big family place in Karori, the one they moved to, the one that was to be miniaturized in its turn in "The Doll's House." All her creative self was engaged in that construction, regaining the inhabitants, the colors, and the smells of the house. Its inner geography from kitchen to upstairs rooms had to be made organically alive. Sometimes it had to be seen from the garden, or the other side of the road, the only light the lamp in her father's study ("The Garden Party"). Paradoxically, the mobile family's new house became a symbol of stability—a fortress, a nest, or a prison for its various members. It served as a complete metonym for the bourgeois patriarchal order, with its arrogance, its comforts, and its constraints. Mansfield resumed her work on "Prelude" at her writing table in the villa Pauline in 1916, building a bridge in words, constructing the mental home of the exile, but with such an awareness of the dangers of idealization and such clarity of purpose that it has become the *topos* of memories of the pains and joys of growing up.

On her second visit to Bandol, she lived in the memory both of the long-ago big house and of the villa Pauline, where two years before she had been happiest in her work and life. As she worked on "Je ne parle pas français" and "Bliss," she had a dream, she said, and made a short story out of it with only a few days' work. She dismissed "Sun and Moon" as easy and minor, and so do most critics. The story was done for money, because children's stories sell well. It is an idyllic tale, according to Murry, but the sign of pathological longing for childhood refuge, according to Jeffrey Meyers, and a "purely sentimental story of children," according to Claire Tomalin.[21] Yet maybe we should question Mansfield's flippant dismissal of a story so close to basic emotions. Fables like Andersen's and like "Hansel and Gretel" are not to be taken lightly, for they are expressions of natural human anxieties, attempts at creating mythological order out of the chaotic fears and rivalries in any family group. Most important, "Sun and Moon" works as a short story: it is compact, poetic, and disturbing. In Mansfield's life, Bandol was a place and a time of both mourning and creation. "Sun and Moon" has the force of her

---

21. Jeffrey Meyers, *Katherine Mansfield: A Biography* (London, 1978); Claire Tomalin, *Katherine Mansfield: A Secret Life* (London, 1987).

other works of the period. In its treatment of specific themes—the little house, the brother and sister, the loss of innocence—it connects with her major works: with "The Wind Blows," "The Apple Tree," and "Prelude," written before; with "Bliss," written at the same time; with "The Daughters of the Late Colonel," written afterward.

"Sun and Moon," which is clearly organized, like a fable, has a big house of parents and parties enclosing a small house of make-believe and dreams. Like "Je ne parle pas français," from the same period, the story uses the device of the unreliable witness. The internal focus and the occasional use of free indirect style make plain that the perception and judgment are those of the very young boy Sun. That allows for irony, as in "Her First Ball," through the ecstatic description of order, beauty, and wealth. In the food and the magnificent layout of the table before the party are all the signs of vulgarity and decay. What is constrained and artificial appears beautifully ordered to the child: "And all the lights were red roses. Red ribbons and bunches of roses tied up the table at the corners. In the middle was a lake with rose petals floating on it" (301). The bright colors and red ribbons more probably came across as a crass display, like the "pink sateen bows" in Tui's room, in the sketch "Kezia and Tui."[22] Mansfield's phrasing animates objects ("winking glasses"), humanizes food ("almond finger," "collar on the ham," "fishes, with their heads and eyes"), and objectifies the children ("unbuttoned," "undressed," "dressed," "rapped on the head," "picked up"). The intersection of categories gradually establishes a Hansel-and-Gretel atmosphere: "a man helping in a cap like blancmange." Often, desire and eating seem to be of a cannibal order, and the intimacy of the parents aggressive and threatening, as when Father "pretended to bite [Mother's] white shoulder."[23]

The little house is the centerpiece on the dining table, the focus of the children's joy: "Oh! Oh! Oh! It was a little house. It was a little pink house with white snow on the roof and green windows and a brown door and stuck in the door there was a nut for a handle" (301). The text presents the little house three times, following the pattern of folktales. The first time is as a promise, a vision that makes Sun nearly faint. The

22. *Scrapbook,* 47.
23. The point is C. A. Hankin's, in *Katherine Mansfield and Her Confessional Stories* (London, 1983), 63–64.

second time is in his dream as he falls asleep on the stairs and the man with gray whiskers points the handle, the nut, at him. If the whole story is a dream, this is a dream within a dream. The third time is after the party, when the ruins are shown to Sun, and Moon, willing to compromise and ingratiate herself with her father, eats the nut. At that, Sun lets out his own version of a "cry against corruption": "Suddenly he put up his head and gave a loud wail" (304).

The little house is an image of a fragile construction that lives only in anticipation or regret, never in the here and now. The narrative is elliptical, the feast and eating not shown but present in just an emblematic bottle "lying down with stuff coming out of it on to the cloth and nobody stood it up again" (304). From Mansfield's other writings, we know how pregnant an image the miniature house is for her. There are the little house of the grandma in Picton, in "The Voyage," and the little hut Kezia shares with her in "At the Bay"—a manageably sized retreat from the tensions of the big house, as in "Kezia and Tui": "Grannie and I are going to live by ourselves when I grow up." [24] The little house may also be part of an impossible dream of escaping from the tyranny of patriarchal order and the necessity of fertility and the production of males so constraining Linda Burnell in "Prelude."

For it is clear that this fragile dollhouse is conceived against social pressures and adult order. "Sun and Moon" is psychologically interesting because it shows from a child's point of view what it is to be brutalized, to be objectified by well-meaning adults and roughly handled by an insensitive "jolly father." As in the beginning of "Prelude," the children take second place to possessions and are part of the adults' goods and chattels to be occasionally shown off: "I'll ring for them when I want them, Nurse." They are designated in reductive terms: "my lamb," "sweet little cherub of a picture of a powder puff," "the ducks! . . . Oh, the sweets," "the pets," "my precious babies." The recurrent use of the passive emphasizes their powerlessness. They are "dressed" in fancy costumes for display to the guests, as the ham is dressed "and the little red table napkins made into roses." The description is merciless and goes beyond anecdotal childhood reminiscence. The story, like others from the same time, is a cry against a brutal and indifferent power. The father of the New Zealand stories, seen through the child's eyes, is getting closer

24. *Scrapbook,* 46.

in his callousness to the boss, in "The Fly," who, "killing for his sport," absentmindedly tortures a fly. Because "Sun and Moon" is so anchored in the little boy's perception, it is more a nightmare than a dream; the little house is lost, its key eaten up. In a letter Mansfield wrote in 1915, she included an aside: "All Im feeling? Ah, I cant—Ive lost The Key just for the minute—you know how things do get lost in bed." And in a letter she wrote in 1918, she voiced the wish to escape: "I want you to come with a key youve made yourself & let me out and then we should tiptoe away together into a kinder place where everybody was more of our heart and size."[25]

"Sun and Moon" bears the stamp of Bandol in that it deals with a brother and sister. "The Wind Blows," written soon after Mansfield's reunion with Leslie, demonstrated the strong emotional force the subject had for her. "Sun and Moon," coming after his death, controlled the emotional flux by removing the characters to very early childhood and by using the format of the fable. The title can be taken as mock emphatic or as straight poetry or as both, inasmuch as the lyrical and ironical are often held in balance.

Perhaps there is biographical significance in the connection of the brother and sister and the little house. Many of the letters that Mansfield wrote at Bandol, especially to Murry, established a strange fiction in which roles seemed to fuse and interchange. Much psychological speculation has attended Mansfield's proposal to create a house for the "three of us," including husband and dead brother, and her giving her improbable husband her brother's pet name, Bogey, and an honorary brotherly status. At other times, Mansfield seemed to impersonate her brother as a pal to Murry: "We are two little boys walking with our arms (which won't quite reach) round each others shoulders."[26] In her make-believe world, the memory of her brother could comfortably inhabit a world of fairies. In her letters to others, which were of a less wishfully fictive cast, she stated plainly how important the reunion had been: "Oh, Vera, I loved him—more than I can say—and we understood each other wonderfully—When we talked together, we were like 'one being.'"[27] After becoming aware of the solitude of exile, of the solitude in her love life,

---

25. *Collected Letters*, I, 215, II, 81.
26. *Ibid.*, II, 220. Cherry Hankin quotes this more fully, p. 31 above.
27. *Collected Letters*, I, 246.

she acknowledged that she had found in Leslie the bridge that led her home and to her deeper self.

But the writer, the artist, uses such facts and emotions and reshapes them. Only one story depicts the childhood relationship in which the older sister mercifully teases the baby boy: the sketch "Love-Lies-Bleeding."[28] But the fictional brother and sister in "Sun and Moon" embody in their symmetry a pattern on which Mansfield worked with many variations from story to story. In "The Wind Blows," the New Zealand wind—before she had known the Mistral—connected her with her brother. The second half of the story opposes the brother and sister's exhilaration to the atmosphere around the piano teacher, who is thrilling and frightening in his adult sexuality. The brotherly bond, consciously idealized, stands in telling contrast with the *mauvaise foi* of flirtatious contacts with the piano teacher. The brotherly couple, dressed alike like Sieglunde and Sigmund, are symmetrical images. Their complicity changes the meaning of the wind, which halfway through the story becomes a portent of freedom, opening up to the sea, where, in a sort of mirror image, a couple escaping the small island on board a liner beckons to them, from the future, or the future in the past, in a complicated time warp. "*They* are on board leaning over the rail arm in arm" (194). The abandoned New Zealand town becomes a toy town, in the same way the big house of memory will shrink to a plaything in the "Doll's House."

In "The Apple Tree," another brother and sister, symmetrically coupled, play a cruel game on the father.[29] The apple tree, in the wild part of his garden, is a surprise he had not bargained for. "It had not been counted in, hadn't in a way been paid for." When he lets the children have the first taste of the apple of knowledge, which he has cut into portions for himself and them with his pearl-handled knife, they hide their disgust at its sourness in order to enjoy the revenge of letting him experience the disappointing astringency himself. "Sun and Moon" is less didactic but likewise shows brotherly complicity as comforting but powerless. The children are together, they can see corruption, they are watchers, nearly voyeurs, of adult sexual aggression. This structure is close to that of "Bliss," written at the same time and much more complex. There, the unreliable narrator first establishes an "innocent"

28. *Scrapbook,* 65–73.
29. *Ibid.,* 26–27.

couple, Bertha and Pearl, ecstatic in their enjoyment of beauty. But the "perfect pair" turns out illusory, and Bertha ends alone, watching the real grown-up couple made by her husband and Pearl. In "The Daughters of the Late Colonel," the theme has evolved, and it is two sisters, middle-aged and innocent, who are left aimless after the demise of the patriarch, in a house too big for them in every way.

More than biography comes out in these fictional couples. Mansfield is exploring as well, the Platonic theme of gemellity, of the two perfect halves. In the title "Sun and Moon," she also evokes the Egyptian royal incest, fully aware of its symbolic and emotional potential. Brother and sister in symmetry are, besides, an image of the divided self, related to the many dialogues between solitary heroines and their mirrors in her stories. As in Margaret Atwood's *Surfacing,* the brother represents one aspect of the self, that of tragic unconscious forces, the fear of death "submerged" but irrepressible. He wails in despair while the little girl, happy with the surface of things and the here and now, eats the key of the little house and compromises with their playful father.

The connection of that ideal twinhood with the little house of dreams is a very strong poetical theme. The story is about children, not for children, and skillfully blends portentous archetypes with the realistic clear-sighted representation of time and place. The adroit handling of the limited childish viewpoint in a Joycean manner helps establish both the pathos of innocent joy and despair and an irony as somber in its impact as that in "Her First Ball." "Je ne parle pas français" gives a comparably limited point of view to the corrupt adult watching the innocent couple. "Sun and Moon" fits in with the major works and with those that talk, as Dan Davin puts it, of the "dark places of childhood."

I have come a long way from my turn through the seaside village of Bandol. I have attempted to show how the creative vision of the artist reshapes personal griefs and joys and the actual components of time and place, and how the energy and the workmanship of the writing give to those elements a lasting and universal meaning. Knowledge of the place where Mansfield wrote arouses a wariness of facile connections between life and art. She stated clearly her aim: "Art is not an attempt of the artist to reconcile existence with his vision; it is an attempt to create his own world *in* this world."[30] Major fiction has its source in an inner creative

30. *Journal,* 273.

core and in dialogue with other texts. Who was the author who created as a character a woman who so grieved for her dead brother that her mourning seemed to supersede conjugal love? A husband can be found, children can be conceived, she says, "but it is impossible that another brother should ever be born for me." And she was told, "If you must love, go and love the dead." That was not a woman after the First World War, traumatized by love for a dead brother, like Mansfield or Virginia Woolf, but Antigone, created on the shores of the Mediterranean by Sophocles.

The finding and the losing of Leslie in 1915 helped Mansfield build the bridge to New Zealand. In 1918, her work was a bridge to her home and to her childhood self, in a Wordsworthian quest, but also to the great tradition. In a more intimate genre than Sophocles, she drew upon the universal themes of tragedy, love, time, and death. In the mythical figure of brother and sister, she explored an alternative to the dominating patriarchal system of the time, the "grown up world," under the cruel law of fathers who demand that women produce yet more sons but send young men to "feed the fields of France." In the fiction she wrote from 1915 onward, she not only painted with lucidity the loss of the "big house," a loss we must all face one day, but she set courageously to construct a little house that would be hers. It was to be not a solitary place, a "room of one's own," but a place for two, where two equal beings could love and work in peace, a refuge from the callousness described in "The Fly." Her private writings show her aware of the danger of such a dream construction. The little house could be regressive, connected only with the memory of the dead she loved—with her grandmother, the dead baby, and her brother, Leslie. Again and again in 1916, she recorded her memories and dreams: "Mrs. Heywood had just given us the doll's house. It was a beautiful one with a verandah and a balcony. . . . I felt frightened of Gwen, and I decided that even when she did play with the doll's house I would not let her go upstairs into the bedroom."[31] But the writing of fiction is itself an assertion of life.

The little house is like the almond tree: there is uncertainty about its fruitfulness and lasting fertility. Will there be any children apart from dolls? Is the husband real? Will there be almonds for the Christmas nougat? Yet Mansfield, in her knowledge of death, corruption, and solitude,

31. *Ibid.*, 101–102.

also celebrated life and its blossoms. The titles "Prelude," "Sun and Moon," even "Bliss," are not entirely ironical. In Bandol, in 1915, she mourned: *travail de deuil,* we call it there. Then, in 1918, when she faced her own mortality, she remembered and constructed a wishful dream future. But she also found intense joy in the here and now—"joy—real joy—the thing that made me write when we lived at Pauline [as] I could only do in just that state of being in some perfectly blissful way *at peace.*"[32] The strength of the consequent writing is that it expresses the lucidity of a tragic vision at the same time that it creates the beauty of lyrical poetry. I like to think that her joy in the almond tree of La Petite Pauline, the Bandol home she loved, exists in the last sentence of "Bliss." We hear grief, a "cry against corruption," and the tragic irony of life. Yet the serene rhythm is also an assertion: "But the pear tree was as lovely as ever and as full of flower and as still."

32. *Collected Letters,* II, 54.

"Finding the Treasure," Coming Home
Katherine Mansfield in 1921–1922

GILLIAN BODDY

Katherine Mansfield wrote a letter in 1922, in Paris, less than a year before her death, which was not included in the volumes edited by John Middleton Murry. That letter was to the South African writer Sarah Gertrude Millin, whose novel *The Dark River* Mansfield had reviewed in 1920.

Let me tell you my experience. I am a "Colonial." I was born in New Zealand, I came to Europe to "complete my education" and when my parents thought that tremendous task was over I went back to New Zealand. I hated it. It seemed to me a small petty world; I longed for "my" kind of people and larger interests and so on. And after a struggle I did get out of the nest finally and came to London, at eighteen, *never* to return, said my disgusted heart. Since then Ive lived in England, France, Italy, Bavaria. Ive known literary society in plenty. But for the last four-five years I have been ill and have lived either in the S[outh] of France or in a remote little chalet in Switzerland—always remote, always cut off, seeing hardly anybody, for months . . . Its only in those years Ive really been able to work and always my thoughts and feelings go back to New Zealand—rediscovering it, finding beauty in it, re-living it. Its about my Aunt Fan who lived up the road I really want to write, and the man who sold goldfinches, and about a wet night on the wharf, and Tarana Street in the Spring . . . I think the only way to live as a writer is to draw upon one's real *familiar* life—to find the treasure in that as Olive Schreiner did. Our secret life, the life we return to over and over again, the "do you remember" life is always the past. And the curious thing is that if we describe this which seems to us so intensely personal, other people take it to themselves and understand it as if it were their own.[1]

This paper considers some ways in which Mansfield "found treasure" during the last months of her life, in particular during her time in Switzerland that began in 1921 and finished at the Château Belle Vue, in Sierre, where she wrote her last story, "The Canary."

As so often happened in her restless life, the perfection she had first found in the little Villa Isola Bella, in Menton, faded. In May, 1921, wearied by difficulties in her relationship with Murry, irritated by L.M. (Ida Baker) yet inevitably dependent on her, and troubled by her rapidly deteriorating health, Mansfield left her beloved south of France for Switzerland, hoping desperately for a new cure: "All our flags are pinned on Switzerland. Meadows, trees, mountings, and kind air. I hope we shall get there in time."[2] Anxious not to repeat the humiliating experience of Italy, where her hotel room had been fumigated and her bed linen burned at her expense, she stayed in Swiss hotels posing "as a lady with a weak heart and lungs of Spanish leather."[3]

Her letters to Murry recorded her impressions: "The cleanliness of Switzerland! Darling, it is frightening. The chastity of my lily-white bed! . . . The very bird-droppings are dazzling."[4] A little later, in a more serious mood, she wrote, "Yes I *do* believe one ought to face facts. If you don't, they get behind you and they become terrors, nightmares, giants, horrors. As long as one faces them one is top-dog. . . . I think nearly all my falsity has come from *not* facing facts as I should have done, and it's only now that I am beginning to learn to face them."[5] That new honesty

1. To Sarah Gertrude Millin, March 22, 1922, in *Katherine Mansfield: Selected Letters*, ed. Vincent O'Sullivan (Oxford, 1989), 257–58.
2. To Dorothy Brett, April 20, 1921, in *Letters*, ed. Murry, II, 98.
3. To J. M. Murry, May 7, 1921, *ibid.*, 100.
4. *Ibid.*, 98.
5. May 19, 1921, in *Letters to Murry*, 634.

is the key to much of what followed in her remaining eighteen months. By mid-June, Mansfield had reached Sierre, in southwest Switzerland. Then, joined by Murry, she traveled, in perfect weather, by funicular up to the village of Montana-sur-Sierre, to rent the Chalet des Sapins from Colonel and Mrs. Maxwell. The intention was to stay for two years. It was a comfortable, three-story chalet. Balconies with beautiful views of the mountains opened off the bedrooms on the top floor; the living rooms were below. The household was managed by a gentle if rather erratic Swiss, Ernestine. Ernestine, like so many of the servants of the Beauchamp and Murry households, found her place in fiction, in "Father and the Girls," set in Sierre.

Although much of the ensuing period was spent in returning to the "'do you remember' life," it was also a time of new directions, including a new friendship. Mansfield's relationships with women were always important to her, as to so many of the central women characters in her fiction. In her abandoned novel *Juliet,* written in 1906–1907, she wrote of the advantages of such relationships in a conversation between two young women: "Our friendship is unique . . . All the comforts of matrimony with none of its encumbrances"; "We are both individuals. We both ask from the other personal privacy, and we can be silent for hours"; "Think of a man always with you. A woman cannot be wholly natural with a man—there is always a feeling that she must take care that she doesn't let him go."[6] Mansfield's relationships with women were always complex. Some of the early relationships, such as those with Edie Bendall and Maata Mahupuku, of whom there is no mention by name after 1916, seem almost to have been deliberately removed from her consciousness and subsequently replaced by others: the indispensable L.M., Anne Estelle Rice, Virginia Woolf, Lady Ottoline Morrell, Dorothy Brett. Some, like Woolf, felt that the relationship was "founded on quicksands."[7] But others provided a kind of intimacy and collusion that was so necessary in what was, in many ways, an alien society. Mansfield had a gift for friendship—what Frieda Lawrence called the "terrible gift of nearness."[8] She also had a deep need for the love, affection, support, and nurturing that such friendship provided.

6. "Juliet," in *Turnbull Library Record,* III (March, 1970).
7. Anne Oliver Bell, ed., *The Diary of Virginia Woolf,* 5 vols.; London, 1977–84), I, 243 (entry of February 18, 1919).
8. Frieda Lawrence to Gordon Campbell, in *Today We Will Only Gossip* [by Beatrice Lady Glenavy] (London, 1964), 95.

When, in 1908, Katherine Beauchamp had persuaded her father to allow her to return to London to write, she was able to provide him with a family precedent, May (Mary) Annette Beauchamp, or Countess Elizabeth Russell, as she had become. Born in Australia in 1866, May Beauchamp was the fifth child of Henry Herron Beauchamp, Harold Beauchamp's brother. In 1870, the family had returned to England. Her adult life was a dramatic one; married first to a Prussian Junker turned experimental farmer, she had published her first novel, *Elizabeth and Her German Garden,* anonymously in September, 1898. Although a small novel, it was immediately popular and went to eleven reprintings by the end of the year.

The two cousins apparently met only occasionally during Katherine Mansfield's early time in England, and not again until 1918. Then, in 1920, Elizabeth was invited to tea at Portland Villas. She was by that time a very successful novelist, one of several former lovers of H. G. Wells and the former wife of Francis, Earl Russell, Bertrand Russell's brother. (Whether Elizabeth ever knew of her younger cousin's close friendship with Bertrand Russell in late 1916 and early 1917 neither of the women's diaries reveals). Soon after their meeting, dismayed at Mansfield's departure for France, Elizabeth wrote, "I'm grievously disappointed that you should have had to go away again . . . Does it at all console you that your friends hate it on their account, quite apart from what they feel on yours. . . . It's splendid the way your work goes on and you snap your fingers at what your body is choosing to do."[9] Her next comment shows an early perception of what critics have since confirmed, and what Mansfield herself appears to have felt: "As you're not here I shall try to get to know Virginia Woolf, who is bracketed in my mind with you."

By 1921 Elizabeth was also in Switzerland, only a short distance away, staying at her Chalet Soleil, at Randogne. It is intriguing to imagine these two women, both from the other side of the world, living half an hour from each other on a mountainside in Switzerland. They were, as Mansfield noted with some satisfaction, "two women . . . and both Beauchamps."[10]

Although their writing was in many ways dissimilar, an early reviewer

9. Elizabeth Russell to Katherine Mansfield, October 27, 1920, in Elizabeth Countess Russell Papers, Huntington Library, Pasadena, Calif.

10. Katherine Mansfield Notebook, September 29, 1921, in Newberry.

of *In a German Pension* had compared it rather unfavorably to *Elizabeth and Her German Garden*. Both were naturally drawn to writing about children, though in different ways. They shared a love of music, especially Chopin, and of reading, flowers, sunshine, and family anecdotes and jokes. The lives of both had been personally chaotic and destructive. Most significant, perhaps, the death of Elizabeth's beloved brother in December, 1921, gave them a closer somber link as relatives. And although Murry was apparently widely disliked by his contemporaries, whose aversion was perpetuated in Aldous Huxley's *Point Counter Point*, Elizabeth was able to see what attracted her cousin to him. He visited her frequently to walk, talk, or play chess, and her diary gives us glimpses of him as "sensitive," "charming," and "delightful." There is, however, a note of wry envy in a remark Mansfield made to her friend Brett: "Elizabeth is happy. She has a perfect love, a man. They have loved each other for eight years and it is still so radiant, as exquisite as ever. I must say it is nice to gaze at people who are in love. Murry has taken up golf."[11]

Elizabeth's diary entries are generally very short and elliptical, compared with her cousin's, though sometimes equally illegible. They also reveal some similarities of style and humor. Mansfield, for example, first described James Joyce's *Ulysses* as "that great tome" with an atmosphere of "wet linoleum and unemptied pails," and Elizabeth commented, "Ulysses made me feel as if I were shut up with a lunatic who was doing what the courts call 'exposing himself.' I got as far as the detailed account of the man's visit to a lavatory and then boredom so profound fell upon me that I went to sleep."[12] Mansfield later revised her opinion, but I do not think Elizabeth ever finished the volume. On the other hand, both admired Jane Austen, and D. H. Lawrence's vitality when he was not obsessed by "sex in everything."[13]

As the relationship between the two women developed, there were some difficulties. It has been suggested, for example, that Elizabeth was in some ways the original for the character of Rosemary Fell, in "A Cup of Tea," written early in 1922, and later that year Mansfield advised her father not to read Elizabeth's latest book because it included too many

---

11. To Dorothy Brett, August, 1922, in Newberry.

12. To Violet and Sydney Schiff, January, 1922, in Katherine Mansfield Papers, British Library; Elizabeth Russell to J. M. Murry, May 23, 1922, in Russell Papers.

13. *Collected Letters,* I, 261.

jokes about husbands and God. Nevertheless, she described Elizabeth to Brett: "She appeared today behind a bouquet—never smaller woman carried bigger bouquets. She looks like a garden walking, of asters, late sweet peas, stocks and always petunias . . . I do hope we shall manage to keep her in our life. Its terrible how one's friends disappear . . . The point about her is that one loves her and is proud of her. Oh, thats so important." [14] Elizabeth, for her part, wrote with respect to *The Garden Party*, "I'm fearfully proud of her—just as if I had hatched her." [15]

Each obviously gave the other much-needed support at a difficult time. Yet the relationship was, like so many in Mansfield's life and fiction, never *quite* what it might have been. She wrote to Brett, "No doubt Elizabeth is far more important to me than I am to her." [16] And three and a half years after Mansfield's death, on reading her journal, published by Murry, Elizabeth confessed to him, "So strange . . . that she too felt our meetings unsatisfactory. I used to be so dreadfully *embarrassed,* afraid of . . . being stupid, slow." [17] Those are the same words that Brett used of her relationship with Mansfield. Elizabeth continued, sounding rather like L.M., "If only I hadn't been so much *afraid* of Katherine! . . . I felt so gross when I was with her, such a great clumsy thing, as if my hands were full of chilblains." Inasmuch as Elizabeth, unlike the "Rhodesian Mountain," L.M., was a tiny woman, that is a particularly revealing comment. What was it about Mansfield that had this effect on her friends?

Although the relationship between the two cousins was uncertain, they enjoyed each other's company for much of 1921 and 1922. During some periods, Elizabeth visited the Chalet des Sapins daily, or at least several times a week, laden with flowers, apricots, and books. Her letters and diaries reveal how very ill Mansfield was during the time she was drawing so much from her treasure house of memory. Often when Elizabeth visited her, taking one of her many houseguests with her—her lover or her old friend Hugh Walpole, for example—one of them would sit outside with Murry for half an hour while the other went in to talk to Mansfield. Elizabeth recognized her cousin's defiant vitality and humor:

14. To Dorothy Brett, October 1, 1921, in Newberry.
15. Elizabeth Russell, March 1, 1922, in Russell Papers.
16. To Dorothy Brett, October, 1921, in Newberry.
17. Elizabeth Russell to J. M. Murry, September 8, 1927, in Russell Papers.

July 14   Cooler, not so sunny . . . took Katherine some nasturtiums & talked a little. Thought she seemed less well than last time—she extraordinarily brilliant & alive.

Sept 26   Katherine & John, greatly adventurous drove down . . . to lunch.

Sept 28   Tea at Katherine's very amusing.

June 1922   She coughed a lot but her face looked rounder Talked vivaciously.[18]

Shortly after that entry, Mansfield left Murry and moved down the mountain to the Château Belle Vue, at Sierre. Murry visited Elizabeth daily for some weeks, and her diary gives some indication of the strain between him and his wife. In July, 1922, it was Elizabeth to whom Mansfield turned for a loan of a hundred pounds. "I will pay it back the moment my book is paid for. But that will not be before the late autumn. May I keep it as long? Of course, if in the meantime my Papa shakes a money bag at me—But it is far more likely to be a broomstick." Elizabeth's reply was immediate: "I'd love to. . . . Men do these things so simply and never give it another thought. Is it *really* impossible for us to be brothers?"[19]

Mansfield's letters to Elizabeth are among her most affectionate and amusing. One, from mid-1921, gives a key to much of her thinking and her writing at the time: "Perhaps the truth is some people live in cages and some are free. One had better accept ones cage and say no more about it. I *can*—I will."[20] That conjured a whole network of images: the image of the cage, with the physical and emotional restrictions this immediately suggests, and by implication images of flight, voyages, and home. Such images had become central, recurring in letters, diary entries,

18. Elizabeth Russell Diary, in Russell Papers.

19. To Elizabeth Russell, July 1922, in Turnbull; Elizabeth Russell to Katherine Mansfield, 1922, in Russell Papers.

20. To Elizabeth Russell, [June or July] 1921, in Mansfield Papers, British Library.

and fiction like "A Married Man's Story," "The Voyage," "Six Years After," and "The Canary."

On New Year's Eve, 1922, beside the fire at Gurdjieff's institute, at Fontainebleau, she wrote to Elizabeth, "When I came to London from Switzerland I did . . . go through what books and undergraduates call a spiritual crisis, I suppose. . . . If I had been well I should have rushed off to darkest Africa . . . or wherever. . . . But such grand flights being impossible I burned what boats I had and came here. . . . It is a fantastic existence. . . . I cannot tell you what a joy it is to me to be in contact with living people who are strange and quick and not afraid to be themselves." The letter concluded, "Goodbye, my dearest cousin. I shall never know anyone like you; I shall remember every little thing about you for ever." Elizabeth, not having received this, wrote on January 3, "Dearest cousin, I miss you so. . . . I like to imagine that you are suddenly going to walk in, radiant and well, and that . . . is why you haven't written. John too has disappeared into silence—but not for so long as you have, and I *miss* you so!"[21] Theirs had been a vital friendship.

Living "remote always cut off," as she was during that time in Switzerland apart from Elizabeth's visits and the presence of Murry and L.M., Mansfield continued to write. Her correspondence remained voluminous in spite of her illness and her commitment to her fiction. After her death, Murry confessed, "There were moments when I wanted to write to everybody and cry aloud: Can't you understand that she hasn't strength to write? For she gave so much of herself to her chosen friends . . . that a single letter sometimes would wear her out. And I used to do my utmost to stop her from writing letters."[22]

One of her correspondents was a young writer, Arnold Gibbons, who had requested her opinion of his work. Her letters to him may yield part of an answer to the questions of plagiarism of Chekhov that have concerned some critics. On June 24, 1922, she wrote, "I imagine your great admiration for Tchehov has liberated you but you have absorbed more of him than you are aware of and he's got in the way of your individual expression for the time being." In her next letter she continued, "Perhaps

21. To Elizabeth Russell, December 31, 1922, in *Letters*, ed. Murry, II, 267–68; Elizabeth Russell to Katherine Mansfield, January 3, 1923, in Russell Papers.

22. J. M. Murry to Sarah Gertrude Millin, March 22, 1923, in University of Witwatersrand Library, Johannesburg.

you will agree that we all, as writers, to a certain extent, absorb each other when we love. (I am presuming that you love Tchehov.) Anatole France would say we eat each other, but perhaps nourish is the better word. . . . All I felt about your stories was that you had not yet made the 'gift' you had received from Tchehov your own."[23]

But in her few remaining months, even the best-loved literature was not enough to nourish her, and she returned increasingly to her own life. In 1916, Frederick Goodyear, a friend of Murry's who was in love with Katherine Mansfield, had written from the trenches in France, "The game of 'Do you remember' should certainly be side-tracked somehow. You will always do plenty of that. It is a case of burning your boats, mentally, every morning when you get up."[24] That was his last letter to her before his horrible death in the Battle of the Somme. Luckily for literature, she ignored the advice. The words "Do you remember" became something of a touchstone, a password to the past. Sometimes it was deliberate, at others unconscious. She wrote to Violet Schiff from the Chalet des Sapins, "One lives in the Past—or I do. And here it is living."[25]

For the most part, she was referring to her earliest past, her Wellington childhood. Writing about New Zealand from the other side of the world and from a quarter-century later made it, of course, a "dream" country, as she herself admitted. Her memory was extraordinarily acute, her recall for small visual detail phenomenal. But Mansfield was writing fiction, not autobiography. Art always transcended reality, and real, remembered events or people were shaped and manipulated to fit the impression she wished to create. The New Zealand poet James K. Baxter explores this distinction between fact and fiction in his poem "The Doctrine":

> "Are they real?" you ask—"did these things happen?"
> My friend, I think of the soul as an amputee,
> Sitting in a wheel-chair, perhaps in a sun-room
> Reading letters, or in front of an open coal-range
> Remembering a shearing-gang—the bouts, the fights—

23. To Arnold Gibbons, June 24, 1922, July 13, 1922, in *Letters,* ed. Murry, II, 220–21, 228.

24. Frederick Goodyear to Katherine Mansfield, April 9, 1916, in Turnbull.

25. To Violet Schiff, September, 1921, in *Letters,* ed. Murry, II, 137.

What we remember is never the truth:
And as for the body, what did it ever give us
But pain and limit? Freedom belongs to the mind.[26]

"At the Bay" is a fascinating example of the process of turning fact into fiction. Much of the detail of the story is authentic, called back into existence in 1921, in Switzerland, on a chalet balcony overlooking a valley toward the snow-covered mountains. There, the writer revisited nineteenth-century Wellington Harbour in the very early morning, acknowledging to J. C. Squire that "to have been back to the Bay—after twenty one years no less—was a joy."[27]

Despite the opinion of Frank O'Connor that the characters of "At the Bay" exist in a vacuum, they belong in a social context that is very clear to those who share Mansfield's knowledge of Wellington. The trip to the Harbour Resorts as they were rather optimistically called in a brochure in 1907, took thirty-two minutes and cost one shilling. The popular ferry trip had also provided the setting for "The Education of Audrey," for "Daphne," and for the uncollected story "A Picnic." The series of bays across the harbor from the young city were often described together as Day's Bay. First a resort for day-trippers, about 250 "sections" of land had been sold by 1905. There were two stores, a school, and a horse-drawn "bus service" that met the boats. The first post office had been opened in 1898.

In "At the Bay," which like its predecessor "Prelude" encompasses the whole life-span of the women it is about, Mansfield drew particularly on her childhood memories of Muritai, the southernmost bay: "My precious children have sat in here, playing cards. . . . It is so strange to bring the dead to life again."[28] The biographical clues are there if we choose to pursue them. The anglicizing of Beauchamp produced Fairfield, and Burnell and Trout were actual family names. Pip and Rags were, of course, based on her cousins, and their father, Jonathan Trout, on her uncle, Valentine Waters. Like Jonathan, he was a highly regarded baritone singer, and office-bound in his position of second clerk at the General Post Office. In Jonathan, Mansfield created one of her more unusual char-

26. James K. Baxter, *Collected Poems*, ed. J. E. Weir (Wellington, 1979), 413–14.
27. To J. C. Squire, July 10, 1921, in Turnbull.
28. To Dorothy Brett, September, 1921, in *Letters*, ed. Murry, II, 134.

acters, in many ways an atypical male, articulate, imaginative, gentle, evolved. Through him she showed what men might be if only they, and society, allowed it. Beryl was based on Aunt Belle, whose full name was Isobel, and on the adolescent Katherine, whose fantasies she explores. Lottie and Isobel were drawn from two of Mansfield's sisters, Charlotte and Vera, and Kezia is in many ways a somewhat idealized self-portrait. Alice was yet another of the maids of the Beauchamp ménage. Mr and Mrs Harry Kember, the "fast" couple, were probably based on well-known townspeople of the same surname, the husband having had a colorful past in America. And Stanley Burnell—Harold Beauchamp—upset by his womenfolk's insensitivity, storms down to the gate where Dinny Kelly is waiting in his coach. An advertisement in 1907 in the Harbour Ferries brochure recommended the services of D. Kelly's Livery and Commission Stables.

What of the marvelously comic figure of Mrs Stubbs? Probably her store is a composite. Its physical description is that of the Muritai Park Store, opposite The Glen, the house the Beauchamps rented. The store had "two big windows for eyes, a broad veranda for a hat, and the sign on the roof . . . like a little card stuck rakishly in the hat crown" (458)—as it still does today. Its location, however, is that of Martin and Jones's store farther south, which forces Alice to walk nervously for some time along the empty road. And that stretch of road in the thinly populated resort would indeed have been empty. Mrs Stubbs herself was based on Nellie Jones, who owned that store; she was given the name of a bank clerk who had been the Beauchamps' neighbor in Tinakori Road.

As Mansfield turned from a concern with literature to the realities of her own life, she looked to the present as well as the past. Her relationship with her husband was also at the front of her mind. At the Chalet des Sapins, Mansfield asked, "What is happening to 'married pairs'? They are almost extinct. I confess, for my part, I believe in marriage. It seems to me the only relation that really is satisfying. And how else is one to have peace of mind to enjoy life and do one's work? . . . Does this sound hopelessly old-fashioned? I suppose it does. But there it is—to make jam with M., to look for the flowers . . . to talk, to grow things, even to watch M. darning his socks over a *lemon*."[29] But in a married pair, or any intimate relationship, it was clearly an equal partnership she

29. To Sylvia Lynd, September 24, 1921, *ibid.*, 138.

envisaged. She explained later to Murry from Fontainebleau, "You are you. I am I. We can only lead our own lives together."[30] The ideal of equality in relationships was a theme to which she had returned time and again. New Zealand had given women the franchise very early, in 1893, but that had done little to change the traditional attitudes of those like Henry Wright, a Wellington citizen, who issued a public notice advising "Epicene Women to go home, to look after their children, cook their husbands' dinners, empty the slops, and generally attend to the domestic affairs for which Nature designed them." An article in July, 1907, in a Wellington paper reported that the women's suffrage movement in the United States had been "bad for the women, bad for the men, bad for the little ones and bad for the nation." Another article, "Concerning Men and Women," in Wellington's *New Zealand Mail*, maintained that "the so called new woman is an utter failure. . . . The sort of woman that people call intelligent is the most awful nuisance in the world. . . . She combines the respectful dullness of a Church meeting with the mental fatigue of a mathematical problem. . . . *Moral:* bear in mind men like to be amused and *never* instructed."[31] Lawrence habitually described the relationship between men and women as the major contemporary problem. Mansfield constantly explored the problem in her writing, and in recent years this aspect of her work is belatedly receiving the critical attention it deserves. Little Frau Brechenmacher's sadly bitter comment on traditionally accepted roles in marriage, "Na, what is it all for?" (47), was echoed by the Woman at the Store: "Over and over I tells 'im— you've broken my spirit and spoiled my looks, and wot for?" (114). Their cry was repeated even more effectively by Linda Burnell in "Prelude" and then three years later in "At the Bay": "It was all very well to say it was the common lot of women to bear children. It wasn't true. . . . She was broken, made weak" (453). But as so often, in fiction as in life, the rebellion is silent: Linda Burnell escapes into her dreamworld.

In "At the Bay," Mansfield created a magical, nostalgic glimpse of her own past in the "dream" country—but for her the truth was never simple, never merely sentimental. "At the Bay" is a distant miniature and at the same time a vivid close-up. Its investigation of relationships— between child and adult, youth and old age, bourgeois and rebel, male

30. November 7, 1922, in *Letters to Murry*, 685.
31. *New Zealand Mail*, July 31, 1907, September 20, 1907.

and female—develops a subject that had long concerned Mansfield. On the balcony at Chalet des Sapins, populating her remote life from the treasure-house of memory, Mansfield also worked to come to terms with her own origins and perplexed identity, sharing an awareness with the narrator of "A Married Man's Story," written at the same time: "Who am I . . . but my own past? If I deny that, I am nothing" (484).

And how did her memories affect the language of that story? In a journal entry in 1916 she had recalled the elderly principal of Queen's College, in London: "I never came into contact with him but once, when he asked any young lady in the room to hold up her hand if she had been chased by a wild bull, and as nobody else did I held up mine (though of course I hadn't). 'Ah,' he said 'I am afraid you do not count. You are a little savage from New Zealand.'"[32] All her life she had had no choice but to see herself as an outsider, and in early-twentieth-century England she was also a colonial. Her English contemporaries, such as Lady Ottoline Morrell, certainly defined her as a New Zealander, with the many kinds of marginality that implied.

Not only did Katherine Mansfield write *about* New Zealand and, it seems, sound like a New Zealander, she also, increasingly openly, wrote like one. About 3 percent of the English spoken in New Zealand today is classified as New Zealand English. "At the Bay" unrepentantly includes colonial, and more specifically, New Zealand, language that would have made it alien to the English readers who bought it, evoking a different landscape and society: "The green blinds were drawn in the bungalows of the summer colony. Over the *verandas,* prone on the *paddock* . . . there were exhausted-looking bathing-dresses. . . . Each back window seemed to have a pair of *sand-shoes* on the sill . . . a collection of *pawa* shells. The *bush* quivered in a haze of heat" (455, my italics). In such stories it is a matter not simply of Maori words such as *whare, toi toi, manuka,* and *pawa* but of standard English words, such as *bush,* with new referents the colonists needed to describe their land. Mansfield used current colloquialisms too, as in "Cross my heart *straight dinkum*" (449), and others that came of compounding, as in Jonathan Trout's dream of getting "a job *up-country*" (465). (It is interesting to remember that she wrote a damning review of Jane Mander's *Story of a New Zealand River,* criticizing it for explaining too la-

32. *Journal,* 105.

boriously its frequent use of the names of New Zealand trees. The local usages she included came mostly from memory, though correspondence may have revived many. Her cousin Eric Waters, who appears as a child in the story, had written, for instance, from the front in 1918 to congratulate her on her admirable "possy" (position, place of hiding) in the south of France.[33]

Mansfield had been insistent with her agent about the deliberate misspellings *nemeral* and *inseck* in "At the Bay." Worried that her typist would think it "wanton ignorance on my part," she explained that "hand on my heart I mean every spelling mistake . . . it interferes with the naturalness of children's or servants' speech if one isolates words with commas or puts them in italics. Thats my reason for leaving them plain."[34] Again, as she wrote in the letter with which I opened this essay, she is seeking to re-create the "intensely personal" and so invite her readers to "understand it as if it were their own."

Nor was this story, with its thirteen sections, to be seen in isolation. In March, 1922, she wrote to her agent that she planned another series of twelve stories for the *Sphere:* "This sequence (according to my present plans) forms the principal long story in my new book and will be a third part of the 'story' which began with Prelude and was continued in At the Bay." She confirmed in a letter to her sister Chaddie, "I am going to write a kind of serial novel for The Sphere this summer."[35]

Writers like the Canadian Alice Munro, and like Zoe Wicomb, from South Africa, to whom students of postcolonial literature have paid considerable attention, have developed this idea of nonsequential narrative, of connected stories, a "kind of serial novel." Mansfield's plan was original and significant, though we can only wonder what she would have done with the Burnell family in the envisaged fictions. In the same letter to Chaddie in which she discussed her projected serial novel, she showed how aware she was of the autobiographical element in her writing, explaining why she had not sent her sister *The Garden Party and Other Stories:* "You may think it too 'personal.' . . . Thats so difficult to explain. You see the Daughters of the Late Col were a mixture of Miss Edith &

33. Eric Waters to Katherine Mansfield, January 3, 1918, in Turnbull.
34. To Mr. Pinker, 1921, in Turnbull.
35. To Mr. Pinker, March, 1922, in Turnbull; to Charlotte Perkins, March, 1922, in Newberry.

Miss Emily, Ida, Sylvia Payne, Lizzie Fleg and 'Cyril' is based on Chummie. To write stories one has to go back into the past. And it as though we took a flower from all kinds of gardens to make a new bouquet." She was also aware of the dangers of the autobiographical, of making fiction too specific. The first line of "The Doll's House," written in Switzerland the following month, was originally "When dear old Mrs Hay went back to Wellington." *Wellington* was then crossed out and replaced with the more anonymous *town*.

It was not all rediscovering the past, of course. Mansfield, during her time in Switzerland, habitually jotted down aspects of life around her in notebooks and letters, after which the descriptions were apt to reappear in her stories. Writing to S. S. Koteliansky from the Château Belle Vue, she described the sound reaching her from the garden below of the grasshoppers ringing their "tiny tambourines"; later, in "The Dove's Nest," she transposed them to the south of France: "Beyond the balcony, the garden, the palms and the sea lay bathed in quivering brightness. . . . There was the sound of grasshoppers ringing their tiny tambourines, and the hum of bees" (525).

The pains Mansfield was enduring also mixed inevitably with the treasure of the past. Often the fiction reveals far more of the writer's complex personality than she intended. Images of the cage and of birds, flight, voyages, and home recur. There is no doubt that, trapped by illness, physical isolation, and loneliness, she increasingly let her dream of escape and of a voyage home to New Zealand steer her thought. Illness is perhaps harder to bear when motion is in the blood. The Beauchamp family had always been great travelers. Arthur Beauchamp, grandfather of Elizabeth and Katherine, had been so well known for his peripatetic relocations that there was a family joke that when his hens saw him coming, they lay on their backs and stretched their legs, obligingly offering their feet to be tied in preparation for a move. In 1915, Annie Beauchamp, on hearing of another of her restive daughter's moves, had recalled the hens and had remarked to her son, Leslie, that Katherine was a "true Beauchamp," at least in her mobility. Mansfield's father surely smiled when he received her letter from Switzerland dated July 9, 1922: "I too wish that I were taking a trip home with you. It would be a marvellous experience. The very look of a 'steamer trunk' rouses the old war horse in me. I feel inclined to paw the ground and smell the briny. But perhaps in ten years time, if I manage to keep above ground. . . . I have just finished a story with a canary for the hero, and almost feel I have lived in a cage and pecked a piece of chickweed myself. What a bother!"[36]

That long journey was not possible for her. Instead, she traveled to Fontainebleau, explaining to Brett, "I am so glad to get your letter saying you would quite understand if I were to join the Institute. I have joined it for a time. I thought of writing about it. But its useless. Its too much to explain in any letter and I have so little time to write. So will you think of me as 'en voyage.' Thats much the best idea, and its the truest too."[37] From Fontainebleau, she wrote to her father on New Year's Eve, 1922, "The old year is at his last gasp and in the very act of turning up his toes! May the New Year be full of happiness for you. I wish I could imagine we might meet in it, but perhaps in the one after I shall be fortunate enough to turn towards home . . . It is a dream I would love to realise."[38]

I began with a letter from Mansfield to Sarah Gertrude Millin. After Mansfield's death, Murry continued the correspondence. In April, 1924, he wrote, "I envy you your feeling of coming home. I've had it so seldom, and so often longed for it, and now it's impossible. Katherine *longed* for it, I think beyond all other human happiness, and it was always denied her."[39] But in the months in Switzerland, she perhaps found in "At the Bay," "The Doll's House," "The Garden Party," "The Voyage," and other stories her home and the treasures it contained. At least, she had made it possible for her readers to find it.

36. To Sir Harold Beauchamp, July 9, 1922, in *Letters*, ed. Murry, II, 225.
37. To Dorothy Brett, 1922, in Newberry.
38. To Sir Harold Beauchamp, December 31, 1922, in Turnbull.
39. J. M. Murry to Sarah Gertrude Millin, April 3, 1924, in University of Witwatersrand Library.

Katherine Mansfield
and Gurdjieff's Sacred Dance

JAMES MOORE

The facts are singular enough: Katherine Mansfield, a young woman who could scarcely walk or breathe, absorbed in sacred dances that lie on the very cusp of human possibility.

Some ideal of inner conciliation—neighborly to the dancers' purpose there—seems to have visited Katherine almost precociously. At twenty, she had written, "To weave the intricate tapestry of one's own life, it is well to take a thread from many harmonious skeins—and to realise that there must be harmony."[1] The tapestry she had achieved in the ensuing years had been a brave one: on a warp of suffering she had imposed a woof of literary success. Slowly, implacably, her body but not her spirit of search had failed her, and in her final extremity she arrived at a resolution: "Risk! Risk anything!"[2] So determined, she entered the gates of the Château du Prieuré, at Fontainebleau-Avon, on Tuesday, October 17, 1922, and there, at George Ivanovitch Gurdjieff's Institute for the Harmonious Development of Man, she lived out her last, intense three months. There, on January 9, 1923, she died.

1. *Journal,* 37.
2. *Journal,* 333.

No one imagines that Mansfield's fundamental significance lies outside her oeuvre, her individuality, and her life's full spectrum of personal relationships; no one would claim some mystical apotheosis at Fontainebleau that overrode all that. But it is equally disproportionate and ignoble to strike the entire Gurdjieff entry from the Mansfield balance sheet, or to situate it within a beauty-and-the-beast fable, now so patently debilitated. To dismiss the consistently positive tone of all her letters from the institute, and not least her admission that "I've learnt more in a week than in years là-bas," would be as much a dereliction of scholarship as a failure of intuition.[3] Who was Gurdjieff? What did he teach, and how did his regime impinge on Mansfield?

Gurdjieff was fifty-six when he first met Katherine Mansfield. He had been born in 1866 in Alexandropol, on the Russian side of the Russo-Turkish frontier, his father a Cappadocian Greek carpenter and bardic poet, and his mother an illiterate Armenian. The experiences and special education to which he was exposed imbued him—transfixed him—with "an 'irrepressible striving' to understand clearly the precise significance, in general, of the life process on earth of all the outward forms of breathing creatures and, in particular, of the aim of human life in the light of this interpretation."[4] In unremitting pursuit of that question, he dedicated over twenty years, from 1887 to 1911, to a search for traditional knowledge, concentrated most heavily in Central Asia. His work as a teacher, begun in Moscow in 1912, was disrupted by the First World War and the Russian Revolution of 1917. Tirelessly ingenious, he succeeded in extricating his nucleus of Russian pupils by way of Yssentuki, Tbilisi, Constantinople, Sophia, Belgrade, Budapest, Berlin, Hellerau, and Paris. With a sense of new beginnings and high hopes, he settled at the Prieuré in October, 1922, and there upon the urgings of A. R. Orage, soon received the stricken Mansfield.

Although her motives were doubtless ambivalent, her spiritual aspiration seems transcendent. "I want to be all that I am capable of becoming," she had written, "so that I may be . . . *a child of the sun.*"[5] Considering the progressive course her pulmonary tuberculosis had taken from 1911,[6] her metaphor seems to link her ambitious hope of metempsychosis with a presentiment of death. Certainly, long before she met Gurdjieff

3. October 27, 1922, in *Letters to Murry*, 680.
4. G. I. Gurdjieff, *The Herald of Coming Good* (Angers, France, 1933), 13.
5. *Journal*, 334.
6. Alpers, *Life*, 27.

or even heard of him, she was steeped in the book *Cosmic Anatomy,* listed as being by "M. B. Oxon.," with its dangerously facile affirmation "To the Sun goes he who dying thinks upon the Sun."[7] Gurdjieff well knew that to receive an international celebrity in such a state was to lay himself and his institute open to denigration, but he felt compassion for Mansfield and responded to her wishes: "G. was very kind to her, he did not insist upon her going although it was clear that she could not live. For this in the course of time he received the due amount of lies and slanders."[8] None of Gurdjieff's four books had been written when Mansfield encountered him, and his awkwardness with English and French hindered him from presenting the vast canvas of his ideas through lectures. Mansfield, like others who joined him, was magnetized not by a system of self-supportive notional abstractions but by a human being of Rabelaisian stature, by the fine energies at his disposition, and by his empathy, his vision, his humor, and his sheer quality of "being."

The Prieuré was a school of attention and a sustained experiment in holistic living. Mansfield had not been there a day before she grasped that: "Here the philosophy of the 'system' takes second place. Practice is first."[9] And in that variegated practice, one thing especially and immediately interested her: Gurdjieff's "exercises," "Movements," or sacred dances. "I have never really cared for dancing before, but *this*—seems to be the key to the new world within me," she wrote.[10] In her focus, there is something touchingly apt, for it was as a "Teacher of Dancing," even as a "rather good teacher of temple dances," that Gurdjieff preferred to present himself.[11]

With the important caution that Gurdjieff did nothing to encourage choreographic analysis, we may suggest that the word *Movements,* which in 1928 replaced the term *exercises* in the Gurdjieffian vocabulary, embraces seven discrete categories: rhythms (harmonic, plastic, and occupational); preliminary exercises, or "Obligatories" (six of them); ritual exercises and medical gymnastics; women's dances; men's ethnic dances ("dervish" and Tibetan); sacred temple dances and tableaux; and the Movements of Gurdjieff's last series (thirty-nine of them, none of which

7. M.B. Oxon. [Lewis Alexander Richard Wallace], *Cosmic Anatomy and the Structure of the Ego* (London, 1921), 167.

8. P. D. Ouspensky, *In Search of the Miraculous* (London, 1950), 386.

9. October 18, 1922, in *Letters to Murry, 676.*

10. October 27, 1922, *ibid.,* 681.

11. G. I. Gurdjieff, *Beelzebub's Tales to His Grandson* (London, 1950), 9.

Katherine Mansfield saw). The provenience of the Movements is unre-
solved, though the geographical ambit of Gurdjieff's twenty-year search
in Central Asia is suggested in the programs of public demonstration
given under his direction in Paris and the United States in the winter of
1923–1924. In any case, though Gurdjieff clearly earned access to authentic material from many "inaccessible" places, the Movements bear
the stamp of his own genius as a master of dance.

Corroboration of Gurdjieff's mastery is implicit in Sergei Diaghilev's
visits to the Prieuré, and his wish, to which Gurdjieff did not accede, to
include the Movements as a novelty item in one of the Ballets Russes
seasons. Notable too is the explicit and generous acknowledgment by
Lincoln Kirstein, Gurdjieff's pupil at the Prieuré from 1926.[12]

Watching, Mansfield with all her force longed to take part. Did she recall, with some sense of waste, her use of former health? ("At B.'s this afternoon there arrived 'du monde' including a very lovely young woman—
married & *curious*—blonde—passionate—We danced together.")[13] She
could not dance when she was at the institute, yet she entertained a gal-
lant dream: "To think that later I shall do it is great happiness."[14] Seeing
her draw such nourishment from that impossible hope, did Gurdjieff have
the obligation to undeceive her? Mansfield never could and never would
dance at the Prieuré. It was a colorful invention when Vivien Eliot wrote
to Ezra Pound that Mary Lilian, viscountess Rothermere, was "in that
asylum for the insane called La [*sic*] Prieuré where she does religious
dances naked with Katherine Mansfield."[15] According to a more pasto-
rally adapted canard retailed by Miron Grindea, Mansfield "submitted
herself to the most farcical therapeutics imaginable, such as dancing
round the pig sties."[16] Gurdjieff, the "crazy Russian,"[17] has been treated
less than sympathetically for his kindness to the dying stranger.

But Mansfield was as integrated in the sacred dances as anyone not a

---

12. Lincoln Kirstein, "Gurdjieff," *Times Literary Supplement,* June 27, 1980. Kirstein's
authority derives from his work with George Balanchine, and his presidency of the School
of American Ballet.

13. *Collected Letters,* I, 164.

14. October 27, 1922, in *Letters to Murry,* 681.

15. Vivien Eliot to Ezra Pound, November 2, 1922, in *The Letters of T. S. Eliot,* ed.
Valerie Eliot (2 vols.; London, 1988), I, 588.

16. Miron Grindea, Editorial, *Adam International Review,* No. 300 (1963–65).

17. Ian A. Gordon, *Katherine Mansfield* (Rev. ed.; London, 1971), 29.

physical participant could be. Night after night—her face just sufficiently rouged to defy its pallor—she offered herself as a sensitive witness to the classes in the salon and study house: "She sat in a comfortable chair near the big fireplace. She always dressed beautifully, simply, with some little touch of colour. . . . She understood the beauty of symbolic movement. She watched so eagerly she seemed mentally to do the movements with all the rest." [18] Think what it cost her in terms of physical effort. When at midnight Gurdjieff taunted his pupils, "Whoever needs sleep, go and sleep," very few wavered. Nor did Mansfield: she was there at one, at two, at three—as long as that extraordinary drama developed before her eyes.

It is surely not by accident that Mansfield found her way to these dances: her quality, her aim, her question bore with them a predisposition to such a rare experience. She was not a mere aesthete or journalistic voyeur. She escaped Gurdjieff's indictment "You saw our movements and dances. But all you saw was the outer form—beauty, technique. But I do not like the external side you see. For me, art is a means for harmonious development." [19] She was of that rare company of witnesses who "are touched, because it is not a professional performance that they are watching, nor a demonstration of the results of schoolwork, but a living event that is taking place in front of them, with all its risks, its moments of rise and fall." [20] She had discovered, very late in her life, a spring of living water that corresponded to her special thirst.

Gurdjieff, in assigning helpers to Mansfield, seems deliberately to have fed her interest. Her roommate was the stately "front row" dancer Olgivanna, later the wife of Frank Lloyd Wright. Another of Mansfield's special friends was Jeanne de Salzmann, the "chief dancer here—a very beautiful woman with a marvellous intelligence." [21] Among her friends, too, was Gurdjieff's wife, Julia Ostrowska, the protagonist in Mansfield's favorite dance, "The Initiation of the Priestess," which was publicly

18 Olgivanna, "The Last Days of Katherine Mansfield," *Bookman,* LXXIII (March, 1931), 12. Olgivanna was the sobriquet of Olga Iovonovna Lazovich Milanoff Hinzenberg.

19. G. I. Gurdjieff, *Views from the Real World* (London, 1973), 183.

20. Pauline de Dampierre, "Sacred Dance: The Search for Conscious Harmony," *American Theosophist,* LXXIII (1985), 181. This is an interview by Jacques Le Valois. Dampierre is one of a number of senior teachers of Gurdjieff's Movements. The interview's placement in a theosophical journal is entirely coincidental.

21. November 12, 1922, in *Letters to Murry,* 686.

performed in its authentic form for the last time at Carnegie Hall, in New York, in April, 1924.[22] To this sacred tableau, a fragment of a mystery called "The Truth Seekers," Mansfield responded very strongly: "If only I could have just a little place in that group, if I could sit in front of Mrs O. with my arms crossed on my breast. I would listen to the beautiful music, I would feel Mrs O.'s marvellous arms raised above me in prayer. How grateful I could be for it."[23] Emotion indeed! Yet Mansfield, with her fine critical intelligence, was also keenly alert to decode the dance's thematic content: "There is one which takes about 7 minutes and it contains the whole life of woman—but everything! Nothing is left out. It taught me, it gave me more of woman's life than any book or poem. There was even room for Flaubert's *Coeur simple* in it, and for Princess Marya. . . . Mysterious."[24] She was beginning to approach Gurdjieff's ideas in that direct experiential way he so strongly preferred.

That men and women have always danced is a truism, but the roots of the Prieuré dances tapped deep into the subsoil of history, where they found a real culture that flows from one civilization to another. Mansfield gave credence to the antiquity of the material, and testimony to its effect, writing to Murry, "They are working at present at a tremendous ancient Assyrian group Dance. I have no words with which to describe it. To see it seems to change one's whole being."[25] In the most inaccessible monasteries of Central Asia, Gurdjieff as a young man had witnessed ceremonies and ritual movements that convinced him that millennia ago, at the time of the greatness of Babylon, sacred dances were created with the intention of preserving and transmitting a primordial science, even the memory of which rests in jeopardy and in fragments:

22. "The Initiation of the Priestess" has evidently not been included in the extensive film archive of the sacred dances produced by Jeanne de Salzman since Gurdjieff's death, and the unhappy inference is that it has been lost. No reliance can be placed on the description by Olgivanna Lloyd Wright in *Our House* (New York, 1959), 100: the choreography described there is ascribable not to Gurdjieff but to Olgivanna's second daughter, Iovanna. Somewhat nondescript photographs of the dance appear in Thomas de Hartmann's *Our Life with Mr. Gurdjieff* (New York, 1964), 71; and in C. S. Nott's *Teaching of Gurdjieff* (London, 1961), 51. Some recorded and sheet music for the piece remains extant.

23. Olgivanna, "The Last Days of Katherine Mansfield," 12.

24. November 12, 1922, in *Letters to Murry*, 685.

25. November 7, 1922, *ibid.*, 684.

The Dance had then a significance quite other than that which we of to-day are accustomed to give it. The ancient dance was a branch of art; and art in those early times served the purposes of higher knowledge and of religion. In those days, those who devoted themselves to the study of any special subject expressed their wisdom in works of art, and particularly in dances; just as we, to-day, give out our knowledge through books. Thus the ancient sacred dance is not only a medium for an aesthetic experience but also, as it were, a book containing definite knowledge. Yet it is a book which not everyone may read who wants—which not everyone can read who wishes.[26]

Gurdjieff believed that by experientially studying this nearly forgotten science for a long time, he had succeeded in divining its fundamental lines, and he took transmitting its essence to be one of the specific ends of his work.

Although he whimsically said of ancient dances that "in some of them one can even read a recipe for cooking a dish," their highest common ideological factor is undoubtedly a "metakinetic" one: "In man, as in the universe, everything is in motion. No movement, no energy, no vibration remains the same. Nothing continues forever nor ends completely. Within this universal movement each entity, each living being, must of necessity evolve or involve in obedience to lines of force that ascend or descend. The function of sacred dance is to reveal the play of these forces."[27] Despite the relativism that everywhere else pervades Gurdjieff's ideas, it is arguable that the revelation spoken of here—depending on the integrity of the manifestation—either succeeds absolutely or fails absolutely. Gurdjieff, in his autobiography, *Meetings with Remarkable Men*, described an apparatus "resembling a Vesanelnian tree" that was used to teach dancing to temple priestesses. Clearly conveyed here—without of course denying that popular devotional dancing is often expressionistic and even ecstatic—is the imperative purity of sacred dance at its highest level: "Everything must be rigorously exact. Each gesture, each attitude,

26. Program of *Movements, Sacred Dances, and Ritual Exercises of Gurdjieff*, Fortune Theatre, London, May 18, 19, 1950.
27. Gurdjieff, *Views from the Real World*, 183; Jeanne de Salzmann, *Sacred Dances* (1974), roller caption to film.

each sequence has its place, its duration, its proper density. The slightest error in the structure of the rhythm alters the sense, deforms the meaning, and the dance is no longer sacred."[28] How could this patrician demand, this quest for perfection, not resonate for Mansfield, who, in the placement of a comma or the cadence of a phrase, sought unremittingly for the truest form?

The idea is that the individual dancer, in striving second by second to understand and serve the Movement, aspires to touch a universal order where everything moves according to law, and that his painful sacrifice of habitual gestures and automatic attitudes orients him toward a deeper level of his own reality, far removed from the surface turbulence of his customary egoism. That would be a vindication in practice of Mansfield's earlier affirmation

> In the profoundest Ocean
> There is a rainbow shell,
> It is always there, shining most stilly
> Under the great storm waves.[29]

But the technical difficulty is prodigious. Gurdjieff so constructed his Movements that the participant cannot rely on repetitious practice, reflex functioning, or even, in the final analysis, Aristotelian logic. Characteristically he must allow each limb to conform to different contrapuntal rhythms, and he must vary his place in the ensemble at speeds that accord with mathematical criteria. Special counting exercises in canon may be added, and silent and spoken prayer.

The seemingly impossible demands upon the dancer can be reconciled only through totally mobilized attention. As intellect and body are sensitively calibrated, a certain feeling, supported by an indescribably fine energy, may enter and be given hospitality. Head, hand, and heart, in the name of an unknown I, are consecrated to the harmonious development of man—the institute's raison d'être. At this rare moment, the dancer is granted an entirely new sense of his awakened presence. To verbalize the noetic content of such a definite inner event is of course notoriously dif-

28. G. I. Gurdjieff, *Meetings with Remarkable Men* (London, 1963), 161–62; Salzmann, *Sacred Dances*, roller caption.
29. *Poems*, 34.

ficult, but it is perhaps nowhere more lyrically and successfully handled than in Mansfield's evocation of a "self which is continuous and permanent; which, untouched by all we acquire and all we shed, pushes a green spear through the dead leaves and through the mould, thrusts a scaled bud through years of darkness until, one day, the light discovers it and shakes the flower free and—we are alive—we are flowering for our moment upon the earth. This is the moment which, after all we live for, —the moment of direct feeling when we are most ourselves and least personal."[30]

After studying Gurdjieff's dances for three months, Mansfield died at the Prieuré. That is a simple and natural fact—a fact, however, that the European intelligentsia have granted a crepe-edged ascendancy over her entire experience at the institute—at the cost of contradicting every word she herself wrote there. Life—that is what she urgently sought, and found. Again and again she insisted on that:

> Mr Gurdjieff likes me to go into the kitchen in the late afternoon and "watch." I have a chair in a corner. It's a large kitchen with 6 helpers. Madame Ostrovsky, the head, walks about like a queen exactly. She is extremely beautiful. She wears an old raincoat. Nina, a big girl in a black apron—lovely, too—pounds things in mortars. The second cook chops at the table, bangs the saucepans, sings; another runs in and out with plates and pots, a man in the scullery cleans pots—the dog barks and lies on the floor, worrying a hearthbrush. A little girl comes in with a bouquet of leaves for Olga Ivanovna. Mr Gurdjieff strides in, takes up a handful of shredded cabbage and eats it. . . there are at least 20 pots on the stove. And it's so full of life and humour and ease that one wouldn't be anywhere else.[31]

Or, "What were all my teas and dinners and people, my writing—yes, my writing too— in comparison with the *real* life that I find here?" A sunlit zest and humor—caught in Fritz Peters' memoir, *Boyhood with Gurdjieff*[32]—permeated the institute by day; by night the sacred dances elevated the current of energy toward more subtle states of consciousness, in pursuit of a new perception of reality.

30. *Scrapbook,* 137.
31. October 27, 1922, in *Letters to Murry,* 680.
32. Fritz Peters, *Boyhood with Gurdjieff* (London, 1964), 175.

In the Bhaghavad-Gita, so cherished by Orage, Mansfield's friend and contemporary at the Prieuré, is a thrilling assurance of Krishna:

> The wise grieve neither for the living nor the dead.
>   Never at any time was I not, nor thou,
> Nor these princes of men, nor shall we ever cease to be.
>   The unreal has no being,
>   The real never ceases to be.[33]

That summons our attention from the mirage of past and future into the eternal now and demands a rightful self-nullification and a rightful self-regeneration. Mansfield, with her fine intelligence, grasped both: "One of the K.M.s is so sorry. But of course she is. She has to die. *Don't feed her.*" But there was also the other aspect: "Give it, the idea of *resurrection* the power that death would like to have. Be born again and born again faster than we die."[34] Mansfield had led, she felt, a very typically false life, but she had come to yearn for authenticity in all her being: "You see . . . if I were allowed one single cry to God, that cry would be: *I want to be REAL.*"[35] Her alignment with the institute's unique search for a conscious reality became her individual strength and augury of freedom: "More than ever I feel that I can build up a life within me which death will not destroy."[36] She made that affirmation defiantly in the very face of death.

"The Initiation of the Priestess" remained her favorite Movement, and poignantly enough, was the last she witnessed. Gurdjieff was present in the salon, and gathered there under his direction were all her newfound friends, her "living people who are strange and quick and not ashamed to be themselves":[37] Olgivanna, Jeanne de Salzmann, Olga de Hartmann, Elizabeth Galumnian—and beyond them, Julia Ostrowska. Then, shortly after ten o'clock on January 9, 1923, the light lit in Wellington in 1888

33. This inscription, in fact extracted from passages of the Bhagavad-Gita, is carved on the tombstone of A. R. Orage in Old Hampstead Churchyard, London.

34. *Journal,* 331; October 9, 1922, in *Letters,* ed. Murry, II, 253.

35. December 26, 1922, in *Letters to Murry,* 697–98.

36. Olgivanna, "The Last Days of Katherine Mansfield," 8.

37. December 31, 1922, in *Letters,* ed. Murry, II, 267.

simply went out. One could say, with forgivable poetic license, that Katherine Mansfield had died into the impressions of sacred dance.

Years passed. On Thursday, August 25, 1949, Gurdjieff, in his little apartment at 6 rue des Colonels Rénards, in Paris, spoke for the last time to his pupils about "my good friend" Katherine Mansfield.[38] On October 11, he gave his final Movement at the Salle Pleyel. On October 27, he called to his bedside his senior pupil, Katherine's friend Jeanne de Salzmann, and gave directions for the future. On October 29, aged eighty-three, he died of old age. He is buried near Mansfield at Avon.

The wise, we are assured, grieve for neither the living nor the dead. Katherine Mansfield commands a powerful constituency, and her writing will stand. As for Gurdjieff, the note he struck is slowly beginning to resonate in the domain of ideas. Only his most opinionated critics—not quite yet an endangered species—would today deny him a niche of significance in a variety of fields. Study groups and Movements classes are planted on five continents and have taken firm root in Paris, London, and New York. The nucleus of these groups will carry Gurdjieff's work into the future.[39]

What special initiation the young literary priestess Katherine Mansfield may have received at Fontainebleau we will never agree upon. Much depends on the estimate of Gurdjieff's stature. But already the belief that he was a "crazy Russian" is offset by Peter Brook's panegyric: "Gurdjieff is the most immediate, the most valid and the most totally representative figure of our times."[40] We understand enough to be unhappy with a stereotyping that assigns Mansfield the sheepish role of wronged woman to Gurdjieff's predatory male. Whatever else, it was not really like that.

Then what *was* it like? The colored glass windows of the study house at Fontainebleau lie shattered. Dispersed into private collections are all the vibrant paintings of Alexandre Salzmann and the "carpets [from] Persia and Samarkhand and the little rugs of Beluchistan."[41] One objective criterion remains, as alive today as in 1922: Gurdjieff's sacred dances. In October, 1988, on the hundredth anniversary of Mansfield's birth, Salz-

38. John G. Bennett and Elizabeth Bennett, *Idiots in Paris* (Sherborne, Eng., 1980), 44.

39. See Catherine Harrison, *George Ivanovitch Gurdjieff—the Man, His Work, and Its Influences: A Bibliography* (Wellington, 1976).

40. Interview of Peter Brook by James Moore, *Guardian* (U.K.), July 20, 1976.

41. [Ida Baker], *Katherine Mansfield: The Memories of LM*, 226.

mann—herself then in her hundredth year—sent Gurdjieff's dances in a carefully preserved film from Europe to Wellington as a testimony to her master's work and an affectionate tribute to her old friend. This cycle of return resembles a round or a canon that takes us by surprise. The dance goes on.[42]

42. The film *Gurdjieff's Sacred Dances* was shown to an audience of several hundred at the Katherine Mansfield Centennial Conference, at Victoria University of Wellington, in October, 1988. Jeanne de Salzmann continued to supervise classes in sacred dance up to a few months before her death. Almost certainly Mansfield's last surviving friend, she died in Paris on May 25, 1990, at the age of 101.

Contributors

JACQUELINE BARDOLPH teaches at the University of Nice. She has published books and articles on African novelists, and more generally on postcolonial literature, with a special interest in the short story.

GILLIAN BODDY is a senior administrator at Victoria University of Wellington. She is the author of *Katherine Mansfield: The Woman and the Writer* (1988) and is a coauthor and the coeditor of *Disputed Ground: Robin Hyde, Journalist* (1991). She wrote a documentary film on Mansfield's life and assembled and wrote text for the international Centennial exhibition in 1988. She is currently working on Mansfield's early notebooks.

ALEX CALDER teaches at the University of Auckland. He has a particular interest in New Zealand literature and is currently working on early European accounts of "tapu."

CHERRY HANKIN teaches at the University of Canterbury. She is the author of *Katherine Mansfield and Her Confessional Stories* (1983) and the editor of *The Letters of John Middleton Murry to Katherine Mansfield* (1983) and *Letters Between Katherine Mansfield and John Middleton Murry* (1991). Her main academic interests relate to twentieth-century New Zealand and British fiction.

GARDNER MCFALL teaches at the Cooper Union for the Advancement of Science and Art. Her Ph.D. dissertation for New York University was on Mansfield. A Newberry Library Fellow in 1987, she has lectured and published articles on Mansfield. She is a poet and a writer of children's books.

PERRY MEISEL is professor of English at New York University. His books include *The Absent Father: Virginia Woolf and Walter Pater* (1980) and *The Myth of the Modern: A Study in British Literature and Criticism After 1850* (1987).

He is coeditor of *Bloomsbury/Freud: The Letters of James and Alix Strachey, 1924–1925* (1985).

JAMES MOORE is the author of *Gurdjieff and Mansfield* (1980) and *Gurdjieff: The Anatomy of a Myth* (1992). Active in Gurdjieff studies and circles in London since 1956, he led the first seminar on Gurdjieff's ideas at Oxford University, in 1987, and is a member of the council of the Gurdjieff Foundation of New Zealand. He lives in London.

CHRISTIANE MORTELIER retired in 1993 from teaching nineteenth- and twentieth-century French poetry at Victoria University of Wellington. With a lifelong interest in Katherine Mansfield, she has recently worked on French accounts of New Zealand, publishing articles on the Maori in French writings, and translations of French whaling narratives.

W. H. NEW teaches at the University of British Columbia. He is the editor of *Canadian Literature* and a specialist in the literatures of the Commonwealth. His books include *Among Worlds* (1975), *Dreams of Speech and Violence* (1987), and *A History of Canadian Literature* (1989). He is currently writing a book about Mansfield's fiction.

VINCENT O'SULLIVAN teaches at Victoria University of Wellington. He is the editor of Katherine Mansfield's poems and a coeditor of *The Collected Letters of Katherine Mansfield* (3 vols. to date; 1984–). He also wrote *Jones and Jones* (1988), a musical play based on Mansfield's relationship with Ida Baker. He is a playwright, poet, short-story writer, novelist, and critic.

RUTH PARKIN-GOUNELAS teaches at the Aristotle University, in Thessaloníki. She grew up in New Zealand, and her book *Fictions of the Female Self* was published in 1991.

ROGER ROBINSON teaches at Victoria University of Wellington. He initiated and convened the Katherine Mansfield Centennial conferences held in Chicago and Wellington in 1988. A Newberry Library Fellow in 1988, he specializes in nineteenth-century and New Zealand fiction and is an internationally published essayist and sportswriter.

SARAH SANDLEY completed a Ph.D. dissertation entitled "Epiphany in the Short Stories of Katherine Mansfield" for Victoria University of Wellington. A speaker at the Katherine Mansfield Centennial Conference, in Wellington, she has also published articles on Mansfield and on New Zealand fiction. She lives in Auckland.

Index

Alpers, Anthony, 3, 4, 14, 36, 91, 93, 147, 155, 157
Andersen, Hans Christian, 163, 165
Apollinaire, Guillaume, 139, 155
Aristotle, 13
Armstrong, Martin, 92n
Artaud, Antonin, 136
Athenaeum, 46, 71, 91
Atwood, Margaret, 170
Austen, Jane, 177
Ayer, A. J., 22

Baker, Ida, 2, 41, 45, 158, 174, 175, 178
Bandol, 158–72
Banks, Joseph, 10
Bardolph, Jacqueline, 7
Barrès, Maurice, 42
Barrie, J. M., and *Peter Pan*, 28–29, 30, 33, 35
Barthes, Roland, 69
Bashkirtseff, Marie, 45
Baxter, James K., 181–82
Beardsley, Aubrey, 44

Beauchamp, Leslie, 2, 14, 16, 31, 159, 161, 163, 168–69, 171, 187
Beauchamp, May (Mary) Annette. *See* Russell, Countess Elizabeth
Bell, Clive, 54, 59
Bell, Vanessa, 54
Bendall, Edith, 77, 175
Berger, John, 16
Bergson, Henri, 22
Berkman, Sylvia, 26, 90n, 92n, 103–104
Bibesco, Princess Elizabeth, 63
Bloom, Harold, 117
Blue Review, 4, 26
Boddy, Gillian, 8, 92n
Bogan, Louise, 26
Bowen, Elizabeth, 5
Brett, Dorothy: friendship of, with Mansfield, 7, 53–69, 175; and films, 15; childhood of, 53; as exile, 53–54; as painter, 53–56, 59, 66, 68; deafness of, 55, 57; affair of, with Murry, 56, 57, 61–63; first meeting of, with Mansfield,

58–59; Mansfield's criticisms of, 60–61, 64; Mansfield's need for distance from, 60–62, 64; at Mansfield's wedding, 60; at Mansfield's funeral, 65; and Mansfield on art, 153; and Countess Elizabeth Russell on Murry, 177; and Mansfield on Countess Elizabeth Russell, 178; and Mansfield on Gurdjieff's Institute, 188
Brontë, Charlotte, 37
Brontë, Emily, 37, 42–43
Brooks, Peter, 121, 123, 199
Brophy, Brigid, 40
Brother-sister theme, 166, 168–71
Bryher, W., 46

Calder, Alex, 7
Carco, Francis: and Mansfield, 7, 18, 40, 138–39, 141–42, 145–54; bohemian life of, in Paris, 139–40; childhood and family of, 139; poetry of, 142–45, 147, 148, 154–55; first meeting of, with Mansfield, 145–46; and Murry, 145–47; and music, 147; as influence on Mansfield, 156–57
—works: *Les Innocents,* 141*n,* 149–56; *Jésus-la-Caille,* 140–41, 146, 153–54, 155
Carrington, Dora, 59, 60
Cézanne, Paul, 72*n*, 73
Chaplin, Charlie, 74
Chekhov, Anton, 1, 36, 180–81
Childhood, cult of, 25–35
Childra, Jean de, 141*n*
Chodorow, Nancy, 51
Cixous, Hélène, 51–52, 108*n*
Clouard, Henri, 137*n*
Coleridge, Samuel Taylor, 73, 77

Colette, 7, 37–41, 49, 51–52, 138, 141, 147, 156, 157
Conrad, Joseph, 4, 12
Curnow, Allen, 12

Dance, 189, 191–200
Dante Alighieri, 9, 10, 17
Davin, Dan, 170
Dawson-Scott, C. A., 79*n*
Derème, Tristan, 142, 143–44
Derrida, Jacques, 10–11
Dickens, Charles, 27–28
Dorgelès, Roland, 139
Dowson, Ernest, 12
Duhamel, Georges, 138

Eliot, George, 52, 102–106
Eliot, T. S., 18, 43, 54, 77–78
Eliot, Vivien, 192
Euripides, 10, 11
Existentialism, 21–24

Fabre, Jean Henri, 162
Fergusson, J. D., 60, 164
Film, 15, 17, 74–77
Flax, Jane, 51
Forster, E. M., 18, 114, 137
France, Anatole, 81
Freud, Sigmund, 16–18, 119, 121, 124–25, 128, 133
Fry, Roger, 72

Gadamer, Hans-Georg, 13
Galumnian, Elizabeth, 198
Gauguin, Paul, 72*n*
Gibbons, Arnold, 180–81
Gilbert, Sandra, 101–102, 104–106
Godard, Jean Luc, 116
Goodyear, Frederick, 181
Grimm brothers, 163, 165

Grindea, Miron, 192
Gubar, Susan, 101–102, 104–106
Gurdjieff, George, 1, 2, 22, 64, 65,
    180, 188, 189–200
Gurr, Andrew, 92

Halter, Peter, 92*n*, 93*n*
Hankin, Cherry, 7, 36
Hanson, Clare, 92
Hardy, Thomas, 6, 19, 77, 157
Harper, George, 26, 27
Hartmann, Olga de, 198
Hawthorne, Nathaniel, 12
Heidegger, Martin, 21–22, 23
Heraclitus, 16
House motif, 164–71
Hutchinson, Mary, 41, 138
Huxley, Aldous, 59; *Point Counter
    Point*, 3, 25–29, 34, 177
Hysteric, 45–47, 52

Impressionism, 73–74, 144
Institute for the Harmonious Develop-
    ment of Man, 2, 8, 65, 180,
    189–200
Irigaray, Luce, 98*n*

Jacob, Max, 139
Jarry, Alfred, 141*n*
Johnson, Lionel, 44
Jones and Jones, 3
Joyce, James, 5, 7, 43, 89, 177

Kafka, Franz, 20–21
Kazantzakis, Nikos, 23
Keats, John, 163
Keynes, Maynard, 59
Kid, The, 74
Kirstein, Lincoln, 192

Koteliansky, S. S., 64, 187
Kristeva, Julia, 45, 131–32, 135

Lakoff, Robin, 48
Laurencin, Marie, 139
Lawrence, D. H., 1, 3, 43, 58, 118,
    147, 177, 184
Lawrence, Frieda, 3, 58, 147, 175
Lewes, George Henry, 103
Lewis, Wyndham, 7, 118
Lilian, Mary, 192
Lloyd George, David, 18
L.M. *See* Baker, Ida
Lodge, David, 80

McFall, Gardner, 7
McNeill, Brian, 3
MacOrlan, Pierre, 139
Magalener, Marvin, 90*n*
Mahupuku, Maata, 175
Mander, Jane, 46
Manet, Edouard, 4, 66, 72
Mansfield, Katherine: death of, 1, 2,
    8, 21–23, 189; friendships of, 1,
    41, 54, 175, 178; general view of,
    1; marriage of, 1, 2, 60; relation-
    ship of, with Virginia Woolf, 1, 41
    55, 103, 175; biographical informa-
    tion on, 2, 173–74; and brother's
    death, 2, 14, 16–17, 31, 159,
    163, 168–69, 171; childhood and
    family of, 2, 27–29, 38, 176, 187–
    88; early relationship of, with
    Murry, 2, 31–32, 47–48, 163;
    and First World War, 2, 14, 16,
    18–21, 138–39, 148, 171; illness
    of, 2, 18, 20, 32, 55, 92, 133–34,
    173–74, 187, 190; literary output
    of, 2–3; significance of, 2, 5–6,
    30, 44, 89, 118; as character in

novels, 3, 25–28, 34, 40, 149–56; childlike qualities of, 3, 25–27, 30–32, 35, 163–64; dramas and films on, 3; themes in works of, 3–7, 70–72, 166; friendship of, with Brett, 7, 53–69, 175; dying weeks of, at Gurdjieff's institute, 8, 22, 64–65, 180, 188, 189–200; writing style of, 14–15, 17, 44, 45, 71–72, 75–89, 95–97; and film, 15, 17, 74–76; poetry of, 16–17, 19, 20, 23, 29, 77–78, 196; reviews by, 16, 46, 71, 78n, 79n, 83–84, 173; and Carco, 18, 40, 138–39, 141–42, 145–54; reading of, 21, 27–28, 29, 37–44, 77, 141, 147, 177, 191; and cult of childhood, 25–35; juvenilia of, 27, 29; child verse of, 29, 77; children in works of, 33–35, 168–70; withering of romantic love of, toward Murry, 33, 34, 174, 179, 183–84; on personal versus self, 34–35, 41–42, 44, 92n; and suffragette movement, 36, 37; on women writers, 37–44; journals and letters of, 44–45, 47–48, 53, 56–58, 65–69, 71, 82–83, 87, 91–92, 168, 180; Woolf on, 46, 47, 100, 103, 115; feminine qualities in writings of, 47–49, 52; women characters in works of, 49–52, 175; as exile, 53–54; contradictions in life of, 57–58; first meeting of, with Brett, 58–59; physical appearance of, 58–59; homes of, 59–60, 164, 165; and painting, 66–68, 72–74; pictorial detail of, 66–69, 82–83, 91n, 137–38; on "glimpses," 71–72, 74; and light effects, 75–76, 161;

poetry's influence on prose of short story of, 77–82; punctuation of, 79; musicality, voice, and tone in works of, 80–82; external atmosphere and state of soul in, 82–84; time and tense in writing of, 85–89; imagery of, 92, 97–101, 108, 161–72, 179–80; syntactic structures in works of, 95–97; and importance of reader's activity, 117–18; tribute to, 120; birthplace of, 135; trial signatures of, 135–36; French influences on, 137–38, 156–57; at Bandol, 158–72; in Switzerland, 174–88; friendship of, with Countess Elizabeth Russell, 176–80; New Zealand language of, 185–86

—works: *The Aloe*, 17, 28, 49, 70, 74, 148; "The Apple Tree," 161, 166, 169; "At the Bay,"5, 34, 44, 49–50, 63, 67–68 74, 75, 78, 86–88, 108–109, 134–35, 167, 182–86, 188; "The Baron," 5; "Being a Truthful Adventure," 45; "A Birthday," 50; "Bliss," 6, 7, 33, 49, 71n, 76, 84, 88, 92, 108, 112–18, 157, 159, 161, 162–63, 165, 169–70, 172; *Bliss and Other Stories*, 89, 155; "Brave Love," 30; "The Canary," 4, 20, 64, 68–69, 180; "Carnation," 71n, 78–79; "A Cup of Tea," 177; "Daphne," 182; "The Daughters of the Late Colonel," 4, 33, 49, 71n, 76, 88, 166, 170; "A Dill Pickle," 70n, 85–86; "The Doll's House," 4, 6, 14, 34, 63, 68, 71n, 83, 165, 169, 187, 188; "The Dove's Nest," 187; "The Education of Aubrey," 182; "Epilogue II: Violet," 45; "The Escape," 4, 7, 49, 71, 77, 89, 90–111; "A Fairy Story," 29; "Father and the Girls," 48*n*, 175; "The Fly," 5, 6, 19–20, 21, 168, 171; "The Garden Party," 4, 6, 63, 71*n*, 75, 89, 165, 188; *The Garden Party and Other Stories*, 178, 186–87; *German Pension* stories, 45; "Her First Ball," 6, 71*n*, 170; "Honeymoon," 71*n*, 88; "An Indiscreet Journey," 4, 7, 139, 148–49, 156; "Je ne parle pas français," 7, 33, 49, 70*n*, 81, 84, 88, 92, 112–18, 146, 149, 155–57, 163, 165, 166, 170; *The Journal of Katherine Mansfield*, 71; *Juliet*, 175; "Kezia and Tui," 166, 167; "The Life of Ma Parker," 4; "Little Fern Fronds," 29; "The Little Girl," 34; "The Little Governess," 4, 33, 40, 82; "Love-Lies-Bleeding," 169; "The Man Without a Temperament," 49, 79, 92; "Marriage à la Mode," 33, 84, 92; "A Married Man's Story," 7, 63, 71, 77, 81, 125–33, 134, 135, 180, 185; "Miss Brill," 4, 71*n*, 81, 88; "Mr and Mrs Dove," 49, 84, 92; "New Dresses," 34; "Night Scented Stock," 77–78; "Ole Underwood," 5; "Pearl Button," 4; "Pic-Nic," 56; "A Picnic," 182; "Pictures," 4; "Poison," 4, 84, 122–24; "Prelude," 4, 15, 17, 18, 27, 30, 34, 39, 49–51, 66, 70*n*, 74, 78, 86–88, 165, 166, 167, 172, 182, 184; "Psychology," 4, 71*n*; "Revelations," 71*n*, 88, 93; *The Scrapbook of Katherine Mansfield*, 71; "Six Years After," 4, 14, 15–17, 180; "Something Childish but

Very Natural," 33; "The Stranger," 4, 5, 19, 75, 79; "Strife," 13–14; "Sun and Moon," 8, 159, 163, 165–70, 172; "This Flower," 71*n*; "To L.H.B., 1894–1915," 16–17; "The Voyage," 4, 6, 34, 63, 71*n*, 134, 135, 167, 180, 188; "The Weak Heart," 85; "The Wind Blows," 75, 82, 161, 166, 168, 169

Maupassant, Guy de, 138, 156

Meisel, Perry, 7

Melville, Herman, 10, 12–13

Le Mercure de France, 140–41

Meryon, Charles, 12

Meyers, Jeffrey, 165

Millin, Gertrude, 173, 188

Mirbeau, Octave, 138

Modernism, 3, 7, 34, 43, 52, 80, 89, 118

Modigliani, Amedeo, 139

Moers, Ellen, 49

Moi, Toril, 98*n*, 108*n*

Monet, Claude, 16

Moore, James, 8

Morrell, Julian, 59

Morrell, Lady Ottoline, 2, 15, 28, 31, 53, 54, 59–61, 66, 162, 175, 185

Mortelier, Christiane, 7

Munro, Alice, 186

Murger, Henri, 140

Murry, John Middleton: as editor of Mansfield's unpublished works, 1, 3, 173, 178; marriage of, 1, 2, 60; as character in fiction, 3, 25, 103, 177; and Mansfield on First World War, 16; and Mansfield's illness, 20, 180; as editor of *Rhythm*, 22, 29, 80, 138*n*; Mansfield's last letters to, 22–23, 194; and Mansfield's interest in Dickens, 28; early relationship of, with Mansfield,

31–32, 41, 47–48, 163; withering of romantic love of, toward Mansfield, 33, 34, 174, 179, 183–84; on Colette, 40–41; in Garsington crowd, 54; and Brett, 56, 57, 59, 61–63; and Ottoline Morrell, 60; and Princess Elizabeth Bibesco, 63; reading of dramatic sketches by, 81; in France, 138, 145–46; and French literature, 138*n;* and Carco, 145–46; *Between Two Worlds* by, 146–47; in Switzerland, 174, 175; Countess Elizabeth Russell on, 177; correspondence of, with Millin, 188
Music, 17, 80–82, 147

New, W. H., 7
New Age, 46, 156

Object-relations theory, 51
O'Connor, Frank, 41, 182
Orage, A. R., 36, 44, 190, 198
Orton, William, 30, 31
Ostrowska, Julia, 193–94, 198
O'Sullivan, Vincent, 3, 6, 7, 8, 54, 73, 74, 92*n*

Painting, 66–68, 72–74, 139
Parasol imagery, 97–101
Parkin-Gounelas, Ruth, 7, 138
Pascin, Jules, 139
Pater, Walter, 15, 16, 80, 114
Peters, Fritz, 197
Picasso, Pablo, 139
Plato, 10–11
Pound, Ezra, 43, 192
Praz, Mario, 104
Proust, Marcel, 36, 138
Puccini, Giacomo, 140
Pudovkin, V. I., 17

Rachilde, 7, 40, 42, 140–41, 153–54, 156, 157
Rawlinson, R. E., 120*n*
Renard, Jules, 141*n*
Renoir, Pierre Auguste, 66, 73
Rhythm, 4, 22, 26, 29, 80, 138*n*, 142, 143
Rice, Anne Estelle, 56, 175
Ridge, W. Pett, 83–84
Rousseau, Jean Jacques, 10, 36
Russell, Bertrand, 54, 55, 60, 70, 176
Russell, Countess Elizabeth, 48, 52, 176–80
Russell, Francis, Earl, 176

Sackville-West, Vita, 103
Salmon, André, 139
Salzmann, Alexandre, 199
Salzmann, Jeanne de, 193, 194*n*, 198, 199–200
Sand, George, 37
Sandley, Sarah, 7, 91*n*, 93*n*
Sargeson, Frank, 47
Schiff, Violet, 181
Schreiner, Olive, 157, 174
Scott, Margaret, 3
Shakespeare, William, 21, 41, 77, 81*n*, 158–59
Shelley, Percy Bysshe, 162
Sophocles, 171
Squire, J. C., 182
Stanley, C. W., 26, 27
Stead, C. K., 126
Steiner, George, 19
Stephen, Leslie, 46
Stevenson, Robert Louis, 29, 77
Strachey, Lytton, 41, 54, 59
Suffragette movement, 36, 37
Swinnerton, Frank, 26–27, 29, 30
Symonds, Margaret, 46

Theocritus, 36
Thoreau, Henry David, 12
Tomalin, Claire, 36, 45, 103, 110,
    165
Transference, 121–22, 133–34
Tree imagery, 92, 108, 161–63, 169,
    171–72, 186
Trowell, Garnet, 80
Twinhood theme, 166, 168–70
Two Tigers, The, 3

Utrillo, Maurice, 139

Vallette, Marguerite. *See* Rachilde
van Gogh, Vincent, 66, 72*n*, 73
van Gunsteren, Julia, 73
Veil imagery, 98, 101–107
Verlaine, Paul, 138, 144, 145*n*, 155
von Arnim, Elizabeth. *See* Russell,
    Countess Elizabeth

Walpole, Hugh, 178
Waters, Eric, 186
Wedde, Ian, 122
Wells, H. G., 157, 176
Whaley, Arthur, 77
White, Patrick, 12
Wicomb, Zoe, 186

Wilde, Oscar, 43
Williams, Mr. and Mrs. Hannibal, 80
Wilson, Woodrow, 18
Wind imagery, 161
Woolf, Virginia: relationship of, with
    Mansfield, 1, 41, 55, 103, 175;
    and writing, 5, 7, 17, 30, 46, 117;
    and Mansfield on Dante, 17; and
    women's movement, 36; Mansfield
    on, 42, 47*n;* "moments of being"
    in, 71; and Mansfield on T. S. El-
    iot, 78; on Mansfield, 46, 47, 100,
    103, 115; and Countess Elizabeth
    Russell, 176
—works: *The Common Reader,* 103;
    Mrs. Dalloway, 71, 89; *Night and
    Day,* 16; *To the Lighthouse,* 71
Wordsworth, William, 73, 77, 114
World War I, 2, 14, 16, 18–21, 22,
    138–39, 148, 171, 181
Wright, Frank Lloyd, 193
Wright, Henry, 184
Wright, Olgivanna, 193, 194*n*, 198
Wyspiansky, Stanislaw, 23

Yeats, William Butler, 43
Young, F. Brett, 78*n*